GROUP PROCESSES

An Introduction to Group Dynamics

THIRD EDITION

Joseph Luft

San Francisco State University

Mayfield Publishing Company

HM
133
.L8
1984

Library of Congress Catalog Card Number: 83-062828
International Standard Book Number: 0-87484-542-4

Manufactured in the United States of America

Mayfield Publishing Company
1240 Villa Street
Mountain View, CA 94041

Sponsoring editor: Franklin C. Graham
Development editors: Liz Currie and Rita Howe
Copy editor: Marie Enders
Managing editor: Pat Herbst
Art director: Nancy Sears
Designer: Brenn Lea Pearson
Illustrator: Dale Smith
Layout: Matrix
Production manager: Cathy Willkie
Compositor: Acme Type Co., Inc.

Credits

P. 28:   Figure 1.1 is from *Textbook of Psychology*, 3rd ed., by D. O. Hebb.
Copyright ©1972 by W. B. Saunders Company. Reprinted by permission of
Holt, Rinehart and Winston, CBS College Publishing.
Pp. 62–63:   Quotation reprinted from Adolf Portmann, "The Special Problem
of Man in the Realm of the Living," *Commentary*, November 1965 (p. 40), by
permission; all rights reserved.
P. 68:   "Revelation" is from *The Poetry of Robert Frost*, edited by Edward Connery
Lathem. Copyright 1934 by Holt, Rinehart and Winston. Copyright ©1962 by
Robert Frost. Reprinted by permission of Holt, Rinehart and Winston.
P. 105:   Figure 7.4 is reprinted by permission of Timothy Leary.
P. 106:   Figure 7.5 is from *Personality and Interpersonal Behavior* by Robert Freed
Bales. Copyright ©1970 by Holt, Rinehart and Winston, Inc. Reprinted by
permission of Holt, Rinehart and Winston, CBS College Publishing.
P. 120:   Figure 9.2 is from *Human Behavior at Work: Organizational Behavior*, 6th
ed. (p. 103), by Keith Davis, 1981, New York: McGraw-Hill. Reprinted by
permission of McGraw-Hill Book Company.
P. 136:   Figure 11.1 is from "On the Conflicts Between Biological and Social
Evolution and Between Psychology and Moral Tradition" by Donald T.
Campbell, 1975, American Psychologist, 30 (p. 1118). Copyright ©1975 by the
American Psychological Association. Adapted by permission of the author.
P. 146:   Table 11.1 is from *Theories of Personality*, 2nd ed. (p. 92, Table 17-1), by
C. S. Hall and Gardner Lindzey, 1978, New York: Wiley. Reprinted by per-
mission of John Wiley & Sons, Inc.

To Rachel and Joshua

Contents

Preface to the Third Edition

The purpose of this edition of *Group Processes* is twofold: first, to take stock of the latest developments in the theory and practice of group dynamics; and second, to organize the knowledge so that it makes sense as an introduction to the study of group behavior.

Since the publication of the second edition, more than a dozen years ago, the field of group processes has expanded significantly. In his *Handbook of Small Group Research* (1976), A. Paul Hare notes over 6,000 references compared to some 1,300 only fourteen years earlier. The Human Interaction Research Institute (1976), in collaboration with the National Institute of Mental Health, reports that the number of citations in this knowledge utilization field has increased fiftyfold, from 400 to 20,000 references. At the same time there is growing controversy about basic theory underlying the study of group interaction. Although a unifying paradigm is yet to emerge, one cannot but feel the vitality and interest in this field.

In the 1970s, serious questions were raised that often polarized social scientists around issues such as investigator influence on group members, the study of natural groups versus research with convenient laboratory subjects, and concern about levels of group life versus superficial variables. Researchers and practitioners alike were sometimes criticized for studying individual behavior rather than group dynamics in a group setting. While the behavioral scientists debated, however, the number of persons using groups increased. In industry, team building, quality circles, and participative management are widely employed in the United States, Japan, and Western Europe, and each of these practices is based on group processes. Peters and Waterman (1982) in their book *In Search of Excellence: Lessons from America's Best-run Companies* rediscover the fact that effective organizations thrive on small group processes. They report that the best companies tended to decentralize authority and decision making to small groups of from six to ten individuals, built support and trust, affected an action bias (for example, "management by wandering about" and talking with employees informally), kept written communication direct and brief, paid careful attention to listening, developed a tolerance for risk taking and for mistakes, frequently gave recognition and rewards to employees, and encouraged entre-preneurship. In brief, Peters and Waterman found excellence where group processes were well developed.

In 1982, *U.S. News and World Report* in its May 2 issue noted that according to the U.S. Public Health Service 15 million citizens were working together in 500,000 groups designed to help members cope more effectively. Just as Alcoholics Anonymous was helping drinkers with their problems, other groups were forming to help deal with gambling, child abuse, drugs, over-eating, divorce, the care of aged parents, and cancer; and new groups keep forming.

Laboratory training or experience-based learning, which was well established in the 1960s and 1970s, continues to flourish. Research on the effectiveness of these groups has proven to be more complex and difficult than originally thought. Neverthe-less, as the number of studies has increased, the evidence sup-porting their value has grown considerably. In the best studies available, P. B. Smith's *Psychological Bulletin* article (1975) notes that in 78 out of 100 studies the results supported laboratory training over control groups. Other research found these groups no more hazardous than what would normally occur in the exigencies of everyday life (Cooper, 1977). And the Lubins (1971) showed empirically that human interaction groups generated less anxiety than college examinations.

While the field of group dynamics continues to evolve, there is value in assessing the most promising of current developments. This is what the third edition of *Group Processes* attempts to do. At the same time, the best of the older ideas and practices are included because they are fundamental to an introduction to group processes.

The time has come, perhaps, for the behavioral scientists and the behavioral artists (the practitioners who work with groups on a more intuitive, human basis) to talk together. There are signs that this dialogue is beginning, and that's a very exciting prospect.

I am grateful to the many colleagues and friends from whom I learned, with whom I've shared, and from whom I borrowed for this book. Special thanks to Professor Helen Wheatley Schrader of Stanford University, and to Pat Herbst and Franklin Graham and Boyce Nute of Mayfield Publishing Company for their skill, helpfulness, and patient cooperation.

And to the people with whom I worked in small face-to-face groups, thank you, not just for what you taught me, but for the privilege of being with you on the journey toward becoming a group.

Preface to the Second Edition

The field of group processes, or group dynamics, is a roughly defined area in the social sciences. It overlaps disciplines such as social psychology, sociology, psychiatry, industrial psychology, social work, and clinical psychology. Contributions come from a range of applied and theoretical sources: from practical problems of everyday life to highly specialized theoretical issues; from the intuitions of researchers and psychoanalysts to the practical experiences of industrial managers; from work with families to conceptions of mathematical models of communication; from the observations of children at play to the reports of councils of nations:

The subject matter of group processes is nowhere clearly organized. It continues to grow and sprout in all directions. Much of the knowledge is tentative and many of the theories are spotty and inadequate. Indeed, the field itself is so controversial that some legitimate investigators are wary of associating themselves with the name for fear questions be raised about their reputations as scholars. But then, the history of science informs us of similar fears and problems in astronomy, physics, medicine, psychoanalysis, and many other disciplines which are today well established. Philosophers of science tell us that knowledge begins with problems. If that is so, then the study of people in face-to-face groups is pre-eminently qualified as a field for scientific inquiry. Perhaps it has always been a principal concern of thoughtful men in every era. But today the need to learn about human behavior in groups is greater and more urgent than at any other time since the beginning of human society.

GROUP PROCESSES

INTRODUCTION

Where does one start in the study of group behavior? A philosopher of science, Charles Peirce, comments:

> Nowhere in science do we start from scratch. There is only one place from which we can ever start . . . and that is from where we are. The task is not to move from wholesale ignorance to knowledge, but from less knowledge to more, from knowledge of some things to knowledge of others, from vague and uncertain to what is clear and warranted. . . . We draw our suppositions from earlier inquiries, from other sciences, from everyday knowledge, from the experiences of conflict and frustration which motivated our inquiry, from habit and tradition, from who knows where? (in Kaplan, 1964, p. 86)

Cartwright and Zander (1968, p. 7) express a related idea: "Viewed in historical perspective, group dynamics can be seen as the convergence of certain trends within the social sciences and, more broadly, as the product of the particular society in which it rose."

If it is true that a discipline is defined by the questions that it asks, then this approach provides a direct and sensible beginning, for even at first glance, the field is rich in questions. The term *group dynamics* usually refers to the study of individuals interacting in small groups, and this thumbnail definition gives rise to a number of questions related to groups. What is a group? Is the concept "group" needed? Is group behavior the precise sum of the behavior of individuals? Are groups real, or are they imaginary or mystical notions? If groups exist, how do they function? Are there principles or laws governing group behavior? If not, does there seem to be sufficient regularity or order to suggest predictability and pattern?

Why do people form groups? How are groups controlled? What

happens to individuals within groups? Why do groups have such difficulty making decisions? Can groups run themselves? Do groups develop like plants or animals? Do groups have illnesses or pathologies? Are there such things as sick groups? Healthy groups? Productive groups? If so, what makes for differences in groups? Can groups help people with psychological problems? If so, how? Can groups be harmful or dangerous to people? If so, how and when? Are groups accountable and responsible? Who is in charge of groups? Are group leaders born, or are they made? Do people behave differently in a group than when they are alone? Why are group activities often so clumsy and complicated?

Can people learn to function better in groups? Do groups brainwash individuals who join them? Are groups instruments for conformity? With respect to the quality and quantity of work produced, are organized groups superior to the same number of persons working individually?

These questions represent just a sampling of the many raised by people interested in the field of group dynamics. In my opinion, such questions help to define the field, but they do something else as well. They point to the scatter and diffusion within the broadly defined area.

As a point of reference, I would like to suggest that a *group* is a living system, self-regulating through shared perception and interaction, sensing, and feedback, and through interchange with its environment. Each group has unique wholeness qualities that become patterned, by way of members' thinking, feeling, and communicating, into structured subsystems. The group finds some way to maintain balance while moving through progressive changes, creating its own guidelines and rules and seeking its own goals through recurring cycles of interdependent behavior.

Then there is the word *dynamics*, which implies forces that are complex and interdependent in a common field or setting; but again, there is as yet no more precise definition. The word has actually fallen into some disrepute because it is sometimes used to convey rather unclear or mystical entities. It is necessary to determine any special meaning by examining the particular sense in which it is used, and because of its vagueness, it is probably best to avoid using it except in a general way to indicate the broad field of group dynamics.

Three more questions serve as a guide to the field of group dynamics. What is group dynamics? What are the basic issues in group dynamics? Why is the laboratory method used to teach group dynamics?

The field is growing so rapidly that any attempt to summarize the work must necessarily be selective and reflect the point of view and the biases of the author. Further, this book focuses primarily on the learning and teaching of group dynamics — group processes — rather than on the industrial, educational, or experimental aspects of the field. I attempt to describe and to define group processes from many perspectives and then to draw together the pieces, keeping in mind the interests of both the theorist and the group practitioner.

One would expect that a double-pronged attack on group problems would be welcome and rewarding, but thus far there has been very little harmony between theorists and practitioners. The theorists or researchers are skeptical about knowledge based on subjective and intuitive approaches (see the counterintuitive studies of Ross, 1977; Tversky & Kahneman, 1974). They warn that "naive realism" is treacherous, that we are trained by our cultural upbringing to see only certain things and to be blind to others. Practitioners who work with groups tend, in contrast, to concern themselves mainly with the dynamics of persons and do few controlled group studies. They charge that researchers gather huge amounts of data that mean very little, that they misapply a narrowly conceived scientific methodology, and above all, that they lack an appreciation and understanding of the subject matter — people and groups.

There are, however, other scholars of group behavior who are less involved in strident controversy and who express appreciation for both the practitioner and the researcher. They recognize that, after a century of scientific psychology, the subject matter in all areas has become more, not less, complex and that progress seems to ebb and flow contingent upon many factors, especially the limited supply of good ideas. This is one of the few things upon which scholars in the field agree. There is a dearth of theory, a lack of coherent, integrated assumptions, postulates, and propositions that constitute sound theory. Even more serious is the fact that the many investigators and practitioners prefer to use their own assumptions, constructs, and theories rather than integrating them into a comprehensive discipline. It is ironic that specialists in the field of group behavior would prefer such an individualistic approach. Maybe this fact, too, has helped to define the field.

The closely related fields of personality theory and social psychology also suffer from a lack of theory, according to authorities in those disciplines (see Hall & Lindzey, 1978; Mills, 1979). In a similar vein, Piaget decries the "poor" relations between psychology and sociology: "This poverty is certainly due to the sterile disputes aimed at determining to what extent the action and thought of people are based on social factors and to what extent they are due to individual initiative" (1979, p. 6). Piaget also points out, as many others have done, that in the history of science an upsurge of real progress in a field occurs suddenly in a number of places at the same time. The Zeitgeist, or the spirit of a time, seems to determine what will be salient and where productive effort will thrive. It is interesting that these productive efforts are always a combination of collaborative work and individual enterprise. In short, I predict with confidence that advances in the theory and practice of group processes will come about through the concerted efforts of rugged groups and organized individuals, practitioners who value the objective as well as the subjective, and researchers whose love of crisp behavioral data is matched by an appreciation of raw instinct.

PART ONE

GROUP PROCESSES IN PERSPECTIVE

Group processes are introduced in Chapter 1, first, by showing where such processes fit into the larger picture of the behavioral and the social sciences and, then, by examining early efforts in the study of collective behavior, particularly the contribution of Kurt Lewin. This is followed by a look at the group as an emergent whole, with an examination of group structure and of role patterns as they relate to the group and to individuals within the group. Finally, Chapter 1 introduces the reader to selected group processes, including conflict, morale, trust, tension and motivation, the importance of listening, and a discussion of rumor and humor as related to group unknowns.

Chapter 2 approaches stages of group development through a look at group behavior and emotional states in transition. The preferred method for learning about group processes would appear to be the laboratory method, and the reasons for this, as well as goals for group learning, form the basis for Chapter 3. Chapter 4, which concludes this part of the book, looks at the outcomes of learning in self-analytic groups.

CHAPTER 1

Basic Issues

> The self-analytic group is indeed a micro-
> cosm of societies and cultures. A given group
> is very limited, and like a jewel, reflects only
> tiny flashes, but the poetic observer will not
> miss the true and penetrating reflections that
> it gives. Not only the unusual situations
> studied in anthropology, but also certain
> aspects of our classical and literary past are
> sometimes astonishingly illuminated by
> experiences in self-analytic groups.
>
> — *Robert F. Bales*

At the very beginning of a course or a laboratory on group psychology, students quickly grasp the fact that a mere collection of people does not constitute a group. Even a newcomer to the field recognizes from personal experience that a group must meet certain criteria:

1. Some interaction must take place.
2. Some purpose or goal must be shared.
3. Some differentiation of behavior or function must begin to emerge.
4. There must be more worth or value in being within the group than in being outside of it.

Each of these criteria is enormously complex, and the fact that researchers are struggling to understand how they work is not troubling, at least in the beginning.

The beginner does not realize that these criteria require a shift in thinking, for the concept of group is separate from the concept of individual, and many persons studying group processes for the first time never master this leap in thinking. One reason for the difficulty is that "the person" in the culture of our time is explicitly recognized as the basic, if not the ultimate, unit of life, and anything that draws attention away from the sacredness or specialness of the individual is somehow suspect. The self is alive. It is something you can feel, touch, see. It has a personality. The self is identified, specified, classified, and verified from the moment of birth and for a good number of months before that (see the discussion of bias toward individualism from a historical perspective in Chapter 11).

Groups, in contrast, come and go; they are created and disappear swiftly without great labor pains. Who remembers groups? Who cares? One hears such reactions many times, especially among beginners in psychology and in other social sciences. I mention them here not to set up straw men or to derive simplistic notions but to bring out attitudes that seriously concern many people—those just starting out and those who have had more experience trying to come to terms with a difficult and challenging subject.

There are, of course, groups that are temporary, groups that deal with superficial concerns, and groups that are eminently forgettable. And there are troubled, angry, and aggressive groups, irrational and destructive groups. But there are other groups that are unrivaled in importance and in worth for the individual and for society, groups that not only sustain life but also make it possible to live in civilized, peaceful, and creative ways. A family as a group, for instance, may endure beyond the life span of any one of its members. There are groups to which individuals devote time, skill, energy—even their lives (see Greenbaum, 1979, for a discussion of relationships in combat). In short, whatever the human imagination can conceive can be carried out and experienced in groups.

Early Efforts to Understand Group Behavior

One of the earliest social psychologists in the modern tradition, Gustav Le Bon, in 1895, raised troubling questions about collective behavior based on his observations. How is it possible, he asked, that responsible and cultivated individuals sometimes behave like savage animals when caught up in a group? Does some spell, some powerful hypnotic, overtake and transform people's minds when a group takes control? Are some persons more vulnerable? Should group behavior be kept under surveillance, perhaps outlawed, or taxed? (See Le Bon, 1960.)

Group dynamics is most closely associated with field theory in contemporary psychology because of the work of Kurt Lewin, who is generally considered to be the founder of the study of modern group dynamics. (See accompanying biography.) *Field theory*, as defined by Lewin (1951), is not a theory in the usual sense but "a method of analyzing causal relations and of building scientific constructs." It is closely related to Gestalt theory, especially regarding the interdependence of part-whole relationships in behavior and experience. Some basic field theoretical constructs are (1) life space is all the facts that have existence for the individual or group at a particular time; (2) tension, energy, need, valence, and vector are dynamic concepts essential to the analysis of behavior; (3) processes such as perceiving, thinking, feeling, acting, and remembering are the means by which tensions in a system become equalized; (4) learning refers to a variety of processes involving change, such as a change in cognitive structure (new knowledge), change in motivation (learning new likes or dislikes), or change in group affiliation (growing into a new culture).

Kurt Lewin
(September 9, 1890–February 12, 1947)

Kurt Lewin was born in a small town of Prussia called Mogilno, which is now part of Poland. He was the second of four children. His parents ran a general store and were active in Jewish community affairs. In 1905 the family moved to Berlin, where Kurt attended the Kaiserin Augusta Gymnasium (high school). He was not outstanding as a student until he began to study Greek philosophy, a subject he loved throughout his life.

Lewin planned to study medicine; he later shifted to biology. He transferred to the University of Berlin and worked in the field of philosophy for his doctorate. He was especially interested in the philosophy of science. His talks with fellow students were often concerned with democratizing pre–World War I Germany and with liberating women from strong cultural restrictions.

Lewin worked under Carl Stumpf, director of the psychological laboratory. At the same time, Gestalt psychology was founded at the University of Berlin by Max Wertheimer, Kurt Koffka, and Wolfgang Köhler. Another strong influence in Lewin's intellectual development was Ernst Cassirer, with whom Lewin studied philosophy of science in 1910.

War broke out just as Lewin completed his doctoral work. He served through the war as an infantryman and was wounded and hospitalized in 1918. He was awarded the Iron Cross and had been promoted to lieutenant by the time the war ended.

Lewin returned to the University of Berlin as an instructor and as research assistant at the Psychological Institute. He and his associates published a series of original experimental and theoretical papers, and in 1926 Lewin was promoted to the rank of professor. A few years later, while he was a visiting professor at Stanford University, profound political changes were occurring in Germany. Hitler came to power. Lewin returned to Germany for the last time to settle his affairs. He accepted a professorship at Cornell University from 1933 to 1935, then moved to the Child Welfare Station at the University of Iowa. Lewin's work in community relations and his unique attack on social problems earned for him a professorship at the Massachusetts Institute of Technology in 1945. A growing number of students and colleagues were stimulated by the originality and cogency of his work.

Lewin established the Research Center for Group Dynamics at MIT in 1946 and soon launched a wide variety of "action research" projects. He died of a heart attack on February 12, 1947. (The Research Center for Group Dynamics was moved to its present site, the University of Michigan, after Lewin's death.)

In their critical review of contemporary theory, C. S. Hall and Gardner Lindzey conclude, "It is evident that in both social psychology and personality psychology Lewin's theory ranks with the most influential in the quantity and quality of research that it has generated" (1978, p. 695).

Lewin's work opened exciting new vistas for psychologists, sociologists, educators, and other social scientists, and his articles and books (1935, 1947, 1948, 1951) paved the way for the flood of investigation and publication that followed World War II. A decade after Lewin, Crutchfield (1954), reviewing research in social psychology and group processes, found that the "frontier field of group dynamics shows perhaps the greatest upsurge of all, with its convincing demonstrations of how crucial psychological variables can be dealt with experimentally in a genuine group setting" (p. 171).

One important finding by Lewin and his associates has a direct bearing on why the laboratory method is used to teach group dynamics. Lewin reported on experiments aimed at teaching people how to change eating patterns because of food shortages or increased work production during World War II. He found that certain methods of group discussion and decision were superior to lecturing and individual instruction for changing ideas and social conduct. Eventually, the application of group methods to the learning of group dynamics became a field of knowledge and skill.

Simply providing information about food does not result in changes in food preferences because personal attitudes remain unaffected by the mere presentation of facts. Similarly, very little seems to be learned through telling people about interpersonal behavior in groups because personal attitudes and behavior are not affected. Given an opportunity to work in a laboratory group, however, most people become sufficiently involved so that they can feel and observe the processes while learning to conceptualize them. Participants learn something about their own behavior in groups and develop insights into group dynamics in general.

The Group Mind

Group behavior is guided by a group mind (Le Bon, 1960) or a herd instinct (Trotter, 1916), according to some writers at the turn of the century

(McDougal, 1920). But *group mind* as an explanatory construct was rejected as being too vague and mystical. Still, years later theorists found it necessary to invoke concepts about collective mental phenomena that were not much different from group mind.

Lewin (1948), for instance, talked about group atmosphere. He claimed, for example, that a teacher's success in the classroom depended not only on the teacher's skill but also on the atmosphere created. "This atmosphere is something intangible; it is a property of the social situation as a whole, and may be measured scientifically if approached from this angle" (p. 4). Cattell (1956) used the term *syntality* to describe the personality of a group; Cartwright and Zander (1968) referred to the emotional dimensions of a group, the emotional tone of a group, and groups as healthy or pathological; Festinger, Schacter, and Back (1950), Libo (1953), and Back (1954) wrote about group cohesiveness; Asch (1952) and Crutchfield (1955) examined group pressures and group conformity. These productive inquiries showed the need for group-relevant terms to serve as intervening variables in the building of adequate theories. Today there is less resistance to the use of a construct pertaining to the group as a whole, provided that there are the same efforts at operational definition as there are for other constructs such as intelligence and personality.

Combining elements to produce a qualitatively new entity occurs throughout both the organic and the inorganic worlds. Understanding the isolated parts of a new phenomenon may not be sufficient to understand the whole. The principles of behavior of a group are best understood at the level of group activity rather than at the level of individual personality. Otherwise we risk falling into errors of reductionism. Each of the sciences — among them, biology, physics, chemistry, astronomy — consists of levels of understanding. A human being is more than and other than a combination of chemicals. A nation is more than and other than a collection of states, or cities, or individuals. All sciences are based on assumptions regarding the area under inquiry, and the same is true with respect to the study of group behavior.

There is nothing mystical about assuming that a group (as well as a certain number of individuals) is present. The group perspective is but another way of approaching a familiar phenomenon. Thus far a number of ideas and insights have been generated from this point of view, and these will be added to observations drawn from other perspectives as well.

Focal Conflict

The idea that the group as a whole is involved in a central conflict or concern at any given time was first proposed by Freud (1922) and later by Bion (1961) and by Ezriel (1950) at the Tavistock Clinic in London. If one accepts the theoretical position of Klein (1948), the conflict is seen as growing out of the wishes and fears of members at a particular stage in a group's development. The focal issue usually centers on questions surrounding authority, the leader, and intermember relationships. Although conflict is active in the immediate present, it is a conflict of which members are not conscious. The leader's job is to help the members understand the conflict, particularly as it relates to regressive behavior going on at the same time. One group, for example, began with unusual hilarity to share anecdotes of children who have to put up with inconsiderate or insensitive adults. Later the leader drew a parallel between what was going on and complaints about the leader for leaving the group floundering, as well as veiled hostility toward him as the leader.

Ezriel and his associates at Tavistock concern themselves almost exclusively with group-level themes. It is assumed that each member is involved in the common group tension and that only by proper interpretation of the group dilemma and its unconscious nature can progress by individual members be advanced. This common group tension approach can also direct attention away from one or two members who, because of their assertiveness or narcissism, may consume too much of the group's time. Ezriel (1950) calls the common group theme the "common group tension"; Bion (1961) calls it "the common assumption"; Whitaker and Lieberman (1964) use the term "group focal conflict."

Besides their focal conflict theory, Whitaker and Lieberman also take a more flexible approach to the way in which the issues are interpreted. They advocate looking at interaction between the leader and individual members as well as between the leader and the group as a whole. Also, their theory invokes group process ideas as well as psychodynamic concepts. This thumbnail sketch of focal conflict theory merely introduces the idea. Practitioners who use it are psychoanalytically oriented therapists, but an important kernel of the theory is applicable to all groups. It is, therefore, essential at least to be aware of the existence of the theory if one has an interest in groups. In addition to the work of Whitaker and Lieberman and of Yalom (1975), Horowitz (1977) and Bridger (1980) provide more comprehensive discussions of these core group forces.

Interconnection

One of the most important assumptions underlying contemporary group psychology states that all of the various aspects of group behavior are interconnected. Exactly how they are related is only beginning to be understood, but the idea that they are appears promising. As some of the basic issues are discussed in this chapter, look for clues to interconnectedness, because the series of topics selected and discussed in this chapter is particularly germane to a laboratory approach to group study. Comments on one topic invariably bring in other issues, and the division of group behavior into different segments and processes is an arbitrary dissection of an integrated whole for purposes of simplification and discussion.

Process and Content

When a group assembles to do a particular job, such as working out a new budget or learning about history, the members concern themselves primarily with *content*, that is, the literal task or the subject matter. Difficulties that have no direct relation to the budget or to history may, however, emerge in the group. Problems in communication may develop even though the language is clear. Harsh feelings between the history instructor and the students may develop, or the budget committee may bog down in fruitless squabbles between factions. These indirect problems involve *processes* and require recognition and special attention if the group is to get on with its work. In a group dynamics laboratory, the distinction between the two levels of functioning is clarified, and various approaches are presented to show how processes can be constructively identified. The participant-observer learns to consider these processes in a nonjudgmental manner so that they may be understood without threatening the members.

Because many of the processes are subtle and difficult to identify, it is necessary to learn them by experience and by practice. Any aspect of group activity may involve processes, and each of the basic issues discussed in this section concerns itself in one way or another with these underlying phenomena. *Process* refers to the real meaning of ongoing activity in a group, in a relationship, or in an individual. For example, a group attempts to plan an agenda for a meeting. Several proposals are made, but all attempts to resolve differences are blocked. Later, participants realize that the real issue was not the agenda but a struggle for control between two factions.

Many different levels of processes may be going on simultaneously in the group as a whole, in subgroups, and in individuals. A developing group tries to tap these unfolding processes so that the purpose for which the group was organized can be served. In a laboratory group, but not necessarily in other kinds of groups, it is possible to find ways to learn about these processes.

In everyday life we are usually not particularly explicit or candid about underlying processes. We deal, instead, rather directly with the business at hand (*content*). It takes special conditions of cooperativeness and trust to acknowledge the hidden phenomena, and that is the main concern of a laboratory on group processes.

Bion's Processes

A well-known system of processes was developed by the British psychiatrist W. R. Bion (1961), who found his ideas useful beyond their original application in group therapy. He refers to the underlying emotional patterns of group life as *modalities*. These may or may not interfere with the work of a group, but they should be thought of as characterizing essential psychological processes. The fight-flight modality describes ways in which group members fight as a concomitant of work. Sometimes fighting occurs instead of group work because of inevitable differences in emotional needs. Fighting may be subtle and covert or open and aggressive. Flight identifies the many different ways in which a group runs away from or avoids the task for which it is organized. Pairing is a modality in which members join one another, often without being aware of it, in order to cope with problems or to increase personal satisfaction. Dependency is a modality that typifies a group seeking support from a person or thing that the members see as stronger than themselves.

Many other ways of systematizing group processes exist. For research purposes, investigators may develop their own system or select one or a few processes for special attention.

Dependence, Independence, and Interdependence

Many studies demonstrate how important the dependence-independence-interdependence variables are in group life. French (as described in Lewin, 1948) shows experimentally that organized (interdependent) groups in fear situations are superior to unorganized groups in that they demonstrate greater social freedom and equality of participation under stress. Lewin, Lippitt, and White (1939) find that experimental "democratic" groups of children are more independent and interdependent than "autocratic" groups. Seeman (1950) notes that teachers oriented toward high status favor superintendents who provide more direction and tell them what to do. Dependency and need for status seem to go together.

If independence means relying on one's own feelings, impressions, and judgments as a guide to action and dependence means relying on others, then it would seem that interdependence can be postulated as being a significant process in a maturing group. Interdependence develops as a collection of individuals works out new procedures, standards, and values appropriate to the goals and membership resources of the group. In addition to a division of labor within the group, interdependence means learning to accept dependence when it is realistically needed, as in a work crew or in team sports.

Sherif (1936) and later Asch (1952) showed experimentally how people tend to yield their own judgment and depend on others, particularly when the situation is ambiguous. Asch's study is especially important because he shows that, even when the stimulus situation is not ambiguous, a significant number of people will yield independent judgments. Asch finds that individual estimates of line lengths against a standard line are accurate. Conflicts arise for a significant number of subjects, however, when others present deliberately give erroneous judgments. About one third of the subjects yielded to pressure exerted by confederates of the experimenter and gave incorrect responses.

Crutchfield (1954) extended Asch's experiments using abstract as well as physical stimuli as a basis of judgment. He agrees that independence in thinking about ideas is also readily abandoned by significant proportions of individuals when exposed to the misleading opinions of others. As in Asch's experiment, the single individual in Crutchfield's experiment had no opportunity to check his or her impressions with others; there was no communication with dissenters.

The dependence shown in the experiments of Asch and Crutchfield was inappropriate to the problems confronted. In field theoretical terms, a group changes by restructuring part-whole relationships into a new configuration. Changes in standards, roles, and patterns of communication influence the motivation of individuals as well as the group atmosphere. Lewin (1948) calls this an unfreezing, a change of level or standards, with refreezing at a new level. Groups achieve interdependence through resolution of differences, so that cooperation and collaboration are optimal while independence of judgment and of action is maximized.

In the dependence phase of encounter-group development, participants are likely to show counterdependent behavior as a reaction to the ambiguous role of the leader, who seems to violate their expectations. They quickly become dissatisfied with the leadership. Members tend to see the leader as ineffectual or obstructive. As Bennis and Shepard (1956, p. 256) state, the leader is "ignored and bullied almost simultaneously," and his or her silences are "regarded by the dependents as desertion; by the counterdependents, as manipulation. Much of the group activity is to be understood as punishment of the trainer, for his or her failure to meet needs and expectations, for getting the group into an unpleasant situation, for being the worst kind of authority figure—a weak incompetent one, or a manipulative, insincere one."

Hare (1976) and Lundgren (1979) find that people tolerate more leader-centered behavior in larger groups than in smaller, more personal ones. Bavelas (1948) also shows how the conditions under which a group functions influence factors such as independence. He experimented with group communication network systems and found that dependency and leadership vary with the network structure.

Group Structure and Norms

Emerging Group Structure

Structure in groups is invisible; it must be inferred. There is something about the notion of group structure that makes it awkward to explain and clumsy to grasp. Perhaps it is difficult to visualize because it is so different from the structure found in biology, architecture, or engineering.

Researchers, especially psychologists, tend to ignore group structure in their studies or to take it for granted (Zander, 1979), while students find it uninteresting and prefer to focus on personalities. A work group, however, which requires some division of labor and coordination of effort, depends on structure, and as the group moves through stages of development, its structure changes.

There have been many attempts to understand group behavior through the study of individual members, but the value of such studies is limited. Predicting behavior from individual assessment has not proved to be effective (Steiner, 1972) because there are so many other important influences on and constraints in a group. The more important things to look for are pattern and relationship. According to Katz and Kahn (1978, p. 7), "the structure is to be found in an interrelated set of events that return upon themselves to complete and renew a cycle of activities. It is *events* rather than *things* that are structured" (italics added). Hierarchy, too, is a part of structure, as are influence processes reflecting control. "To create structure, the responses of A would have to elicit B's reactions in such a manner that the responses of the latter would stimulate A to further responses." But then these subunits are tied together in a group as a whole. This is the basis for the idea of a system made up of subsystems governed by task requirements and relationships.

In brief, structure grows out of a need for effective *group* work. It is necessary to take into account the motivation of participants and their skills and resources, as well as the surrounding physical and social environment.

The structure of a group refers to the arrangement of its parts and how those parts relate to one another and to the group as a whole. The parts consist of persons, units, roles or positions, and offices (Zander, 1979). Status (value, prestige, power) and hierarchy of group subunits are aspects of structure, and these may be established formally and informally.

Group norms, rules, and procedures give some degree of order and predictability to the functioning of the parts of a group. They consist of guidelines to behavior, that is, value judgments about what should and should not be done and how to maintain social relations (Shaw, 1981).

The ability of a group to make norms and rules appropriate to its own needs and purposes is important for group effectiveness and the well-being of members.

Personalities of the Members

The effectiveness of a group depends on matching the type of group structure with the particular qualities of members' personalities (Wilson et al., in Zander, 1979). Individuals searching for safety or security are likely to feel better in a more authoritarian group, and their performance seems to improve. The person for whom self-esteem is important, however, seems to prefer groups in which the structure and leadership are more egalitarian.

Within the group, the structure and organization that emerge from the *resolution* of discrepancies between position and role yield greater learning and productivity, according to Shepherd and Weschler (1955) and Bales and Slater (1957). At times a member may take on the role of a leader, or a member might become a leader in a subgroup that, under the self-styled leadership of one of its members, may resist or oppose the designated leader (see Chapter 2). And members work in relationship to other members within a variety of dimensions such as dominance, support, cooperation, competition, symbiosis, and attraction. These are just a few of the factors that underlie the development of relationships among members, and members are frequently unaware of the psychological bases behind these interpersonal ties.

One of the purposes of a laboratory on group dynamics is to learn about group structure as it emerges and as it changes. An important aspect of group structure consists of the growing relationships among members and between members and leaders. Thus laboratories on group processes (sometimes called human interaction laboratories) provide ample opportunities for these relationships to develop.

Setting or Environment

It is easy to lose sight of the fact that the physical and social environment influences the life of the group and its developing structure. There is a universal tendency to bring into a group ground rules, guidelines, roles, and status from outside the group. The physical and social environment can have a powerful influence on a group. Consider settings as diverse as a factory, a hospital, a school, an army base, a corporate penthouse, a Pacific island, a ghetto slum. Through the social surroundings, the group obtains emotional and cognitive resources, or supplies, and energy. In addition, the human environment is itself organized according to its own structure, norms, and values. There is a tendency for functionally related and contiguous groups to influence as well as to accommodate one another.

The real challenge to a collection of people who have a job to do or needs to be met is to develop custom-made structure. Like a good suit of clothes, the custom-made structure fits only one group. The structure will enable the group to function well, to achieve its purpose, and to derive satisfaction from its efforts. It is not easy for a group struggling to develop its own culture (that is, its own structure, norms, and values) appropriate to its needs and purposes. In dealing with conflict, sometimes group members will suggest that a vote be taken to resolve differences. Voting may be a good procedure for populations of certain size, purpose, and setting and for certain issues. But a small group trying to work and learn together needs to understand the basis of conflicts and attempt to resolve differences toward a true consensus. Even though consensus may not always be possible, participants must at least try to recognize the group's limits as well as its capabilities. Thus learning to learn becomes more important than majority-minority rule as an operating guideline for decision making.

Change of Structure

When the group succeeds in establishing its own structure, there is cause for rejoicing, for this is an important and useful achievement. But it does not take long to recognize that some parts of the structure function better than others, that certain structural factors are in need of repair, and that some aspects are already obsolete. Change can also be required because of a transition to a new stage of development or a significant change of membership, in spite of the evidence (Jacobs & Campbell, 1961) that group structure can outlive new generations of members. It is interesting to note how frequently a group or organization finds itself in the position of having to change its structure rather than to invent or create a completely new one.

A laboratory course on group processes provides a unique opportunity to create new structure because there is no accumulation of structure to deal with except that brought in by members. In a workshop or a laboratory the leader tries to keep the setting as unstructured as possible, but there are always some limits or some elements of structural constraint imposed because of the environment or by the person in charge. Nevertheless, the amount of ambiguity remains large. The experience of working in an unstructured group can arouse anxiety, but it can also be evocative, challenging, and useful.

√ Cohesiveness

The term *cohesiveness* has been defined as "the resultant of forces which are acting on the members to stay in the group" (Back, 1951; Zander, 1979).

Researchers have identified a number of group characteristics associated with cohesiveness: Members are motivated to work toward the group's objectives. The group is well organized or becomes well organized. Members are attracted to members. The group achieves its goals (Hare, 1976). In industry, where group cohesiveness is high, absenteeism, labor turnover, and anxiety are lower than where cohesiveness is weak. Cohesiveness and feelings of prestige attributed to one's own job are also positively correlated (Seashore, 1954).

Ritual and Tradition
As structure develops, rules and procedures can become rituals, for groups have the capacity for generating purposes that have little if anything to do with the ostensible reasons for coming together. According to some theorists, the need to protect oneself against strong and deep-seated anxiety frequently causes individuals to behave in ways that appear to make no sense (Bion, 1961; Jacques, 1974). Groups also behave collectively in ways that seem illogical, unproductive, and even irrational at times. Certain procedures and structure appear to grow out of a need for the group to defend itself against real and imaginary dangers from the environment surrounding the group, from within the individual, or from the group itself.

Simple rituals such as seating arrangements, the way meetings begin, and inside jokes may offer group members a feeling of control and predictability. Rituals and traditions may also be more irrational, bizarre, and self-destructive. News media often recount stories of group behavior and rituals that appear senseless to an outsider, and they are not just referring to cultists and political zealots. According to police reports, the largest single setting for crimes of violence may well be the ordinary family; often the precipitating agent is a violation of ritual or tradition. There may be value in reflecting on a wide spectrum of behavior, from everyday events to more unusual incidents, from the tranquil to the tragic, in our effort to understand the underlying structure of group processes.

Collective behavior is, therefore, influenced by both rational and irrational processes, as in myth, fantasy, tradition, and ritual. These group processes may be as difficult to perceive as they are to control (Dunphy, 1974, p. 297), and investigators coming from the same culture may be unaware of these influences (a principle that anthropologists understand very well).

Established groups also impose their norms on individuals, even strong dominant individuals. In an important study on the power of group qualities, Ferenc Merei (1949) formed 12 homogeneous groups of children over a period of days. The groups soon developed their own rules, structure, rituals, and traditions regarding play activities, seating, order, and arrangement of various events. Each group had its own special language. Then a new member was placed in the group after its "culture" had emerged. The new child was carefully selected as a leader because of his or her ability to initiate action, give orders, and direct others rather than be directed by them. Nevertheless, the new child was forced to follow the rules, norms, and traditions of the group in 25 out of 26 cases because the child was either ignored or rebuffed for violating the group's way of doing things. The only way the child could again become influential was to learn the rules and traditions and then take some initiative in giving orders and carrying them out. Having observed that other new leaders managed to acquire leadership in the established groups by joining in games played their way, the new child in time suggested small changes in the games, and the changes were accepted. Not until later, when the newcomer with leadership qualities was absorbed into the group and was able to influence others *in line with the group's tradition*, could the child initiate major changes in the way games were played.

Social Structure and the Self

For Gestalt psychologists Wertheimer, Köhler, and Koffka, behavior is determined by the psychophysical field or organized system of forces in which the individual is embedded. And Lewin's field theory was strongly influenced by Gestalt (configurational) ideas. The term *field* is defined by Lewin as "the totality of coexisting [psychological] facts which are conceived of as mutually interdependent" (Lewin, 1951, p. 240). The term *psychological* is added parenthetically to indicate that Lewin emphasized psychological as against physical facts.

It is useful to think of nonphysical facts as being organized in terms of social structure and of the self in relation to others (Strauss, 1977, pp. 278–279). Social positions and roles exist on the job, in the family, and everywhere people interact. Student, boss, colleague, wife, manager, parent, sales clerk, coach—all are ways of identifying roles, positions, statuses, or offices, and certain patterns of behavior go with particular positions or roles. There may be wide variation in how an individual carries out a role, but those patterns provide guidelines and rules for behavior. Each person within a culture learns how the patterns work.

How many selves are there? Each individual may have many different roles and statuses (for example, spouse, mechanic, student, parent, friend, manager, neighbor). In answer to the question of how many selves there are, William James indicated in 1890 that, for him, there were "as many different social selves as there are distinct groups of persons about whose opinion he cares." We can expect problems to arise out of conflict among roles. Similarly, because personal jobs, roles, and statuses often change over time, problems can arise in subjective careers, in multiple careers, and in *passage through various stages within a career* (Strauss, 1977). An engineer promoted to supervisor, for example, may deal more with people (for which he or she may have little talent) than with things and facts and symbols. Or a psychotherapist who enjoys people and works well with them may become involved in empirical research and writing. Or a physician may take on administrative responsibilities in a hospital and find himself or herself dealing with organized labor instead of treating a disorganized liver for which he or she was well trained.

Group Roles

Group behavior is not random behavior. Studies of group development quickly reveal pattern and order amid varying degrees of surface confusion. As mentioned earlier, one of the ways groups distinguish themselves from collections of individuals is through the development of patterns of behavior.

Natural groups such as those found at work in shops or offices, as compared to laboratory or experimental groups, will show greater role differentiation, especially if they have been in existence for some time (Hare, 1976). A role refers to a set of expectations shared by group members concerning the behavior of a person who occupies a given position in the group, according to Gross, Mason, and McEachern (1958), Levinson (1959), and Hare (1962). Role is not to be confused with personality. Role is imposed by the context, by the person, and by others; personality expresses itself from within. These two patterns may match perfectly, partially, or not at all.

Role conflict arises out of discrepancies between how one is expected to behave and one's natural inclinations. Expectations about a group leader, for example, may not match that person's personality or way of being a leader. Expectations concerning how a particular member should work on a group task may cause tension, irritation, withdrawal, or anger, among other possible reactions, if the member's own style of working is significantly different (Sarbin & Jones, 1955).

Every group faces the problem of matching or fitting role with person. The work consists of enabling individuals to express themselves so that feelings and thoughts can be disclosed. Self-imposed constraints may interfere with the disclosure of role-based problems. A person who fears criticism may displace a complaint. Another may simply withdraw. A third may express boredom. Still another may do a poor job of carrying out the role assigned.

Assignment by Covert Collusion

Consider the plight of a group member who is assigned an unwanted role by group members acting in covert collusion. Sometimes the group will make a member a scapegoat. Or consider the group that presses a particular member to assume leadership functions. Roles can vary greatly.

It may be difficult to deal with misfit role problems because they are often not recognized or discussed. There may be complex underlying reasons for the group's unawareness of its own actions, just as there might be for individuals. And a group's low level of trust, which limits open communication, may be related to this unawareness and compound the problem.

If the individual were to acknowledge the difficulty, it would surely help, but this may not be easy in an unfriendly climate. Acknowledgment by the group that it may have a problem could be an important step. As mentioned elsewhere (see Chaper 10 regarding metacommunication), to be able to talk about the difficulty of communicating can be useful in broadening a shared base with other members so that resources within the membership may be tapped, opening the way for further exploration.

Functional roles of group members are described as a way of cataloging task-oriented activities. Terms such as *initiators*, *opinion or information givers and seekers*, *evaluators*, and *recorders* are used to describe the behavior of group members concerned with the work of the group. Group building and group maintenance (social-emotional) activities are described by another set of roles. Bales (1970, p. 92) describes 12 broad categories of group behavior that are sufficiently descriptive to be used, with some practice and training, to observe a member's role activity (see Chapter 7).

One of the interesting problems regarding roles is to identify the principles underlying changes in the role of a group member. Sociometric questionnaires may be used to learn how each member sees the other members and himself or herself at different stages in the life of the group. Also the Zucchini Connection (see Chapter 6) may suggest ways of mapping interpersonal perception.

Group Membership: A Process in Motion

A major difficulty facing every group results from the fact that problems affecting individuals, such as inappropriate role assignment, may be interlocked with problems at a group level. The problems of the group appear to depend upon actions taken by individuals. As one awaits movement by the other, deadlock sets in and the group appears immobilized.

Fortunately, however, not all subparts of a group are equally immobilized. Sometimes a moderator or facilitator (or a member who can take that stance) can gain enough distance or perspective to introduce new information. It may be useful to hold the troublesome task aside and to explore feelings for a while as a way of making new information available.

The point here is that a number of problems, seemingly unrelated, may exist simultaneously. A good illustration of this is the relationship between role and goal. Initial goals may be too vague or general to be of much use. Emergent goals depend upon the development of the group toward a further stage of maturity. Hence the early assignment of roles may be inadequate or inappropriate for the group's ultimate objectives. Clearly the roles themselves must change as the group's needs become clearer. Thus we can see the shaping of goals affecting the nature of roles, and the composition of group membership will also influence the extent to which the group's resources will be available. It is a process in motion—trying, fitting, adapting, correcting, and rematching in recurring cycles.

Group Size

The influence of the sheer number of persons contained in a group is entangled with other variables such as the purpose of the group and the composition of the membership. A few generalizations can be made on the basis of specific studies. Cohesion tends to be weaker and morale tends to be lower in larger groups than in comparable smaller ones. How often groups meet varies inversely with size and duration and directly with closeness of feelings (Coleman & James, 1961; Fischer, 1953; Tannenbaum, 1962).

Two-person and three-person groups have unique characteristics with reference to closeness of feeling and power as interaction factors (see especially Theodore Caplow's *Two Against One*. Thomas and Fink (1961) also report that, for most kinds of tasks or problems where group discussion is desirable, a five-person group appears to be an optimal size. Hare (1976) presents a summary of research bearing on group size. Referring to work by Bales and Borgatta (1965), Hare notes, "as size increases, there is a tendency toward a more mechanical method of introducing information (by round robin procedure, for example), a less sensitive exploration of the point of view of the other, and a more direct attempt to control others and reach solution whether or not all group members indicate agreement" (p. 226). Consistent with these findings is Simmel's (1955) observation, "a group upon reaching a certain size must develop forms and organs which serve its maintenance and promotion, but which a smaller group does not need. On the other hand . . . smaller groups have qualities, including types of interaction among their members, which inevitably disappear when the groups grow larger" (in Nixon, 1979).

Role Playing as a Tool

Role playing is a method for studying the attitudes and feelings of individuals in simulated situations. A supervisor may, for example, have traced some of her difficulties on the job to the problem of employee evaluation. Under the direction of an experienced group leader, the supervisor is asked to reconstruct a concrete problem situation. Group members are asked to take different roles, with the supervisor participating or observing others after she has participated. Then the members improvise dialogue and action to fit, roughly, the problem situation. In this spontaneous interaction, group members may learn more about their own attitudes and behavior and try to find new ways of dealing with their problems. Role playing is usually followed by a free discussion of what went on and how the actors and observers felt about the interactions. Thus productive new insights and ideas may be gained.

Role playing as a form of psychodrama (described by Moreno, 1946) is more complex than it seems, and it would be unwise to apply it without the supervision of an experienced person. It can be particularly valuable as a diagnostic device in controlled research situations. Carried out by inexperienced people, however, it can be misused and do more to arouse anxiety and to confuse than to help people learn.

Conflict

> The utter doubt and confusion characteristic of reality shock may merely be the result of finding oneself at variance with the perceptions of others.
>
> — *Burkart Holzner*

Conflict is defined by Brown and Keller (1979, p. 243) as "differences involving real or perceived incompatible positions." Conflict within groups is inevitable, according to writers possessing a wide spectrum of views (Coser, 1956; Deutsch, 1973). Mills (1967, p. 14) expresses it most emphatically when he says: "Group experience *is* conflict. It is a response to the reality that there is a shortage of what people need and want." Who gets restricted or ignored, what part of the group is approved of or rewarded — these are typical psychological sources of conflict. The quality of group progress depends upon constructive resolution of conflict, which in turn is based on the development of implicit rules and values regarding the expression of differences and dissent.

According to one writer in this field, the five ways in which groups typically deal with conflict are (1) by eliminating the opposition, (2) by subjugating the opposition, (3) by forming an alliance to overpower the opposition, (4) by reaching a compromise with the other side, and (5) by integrating opposing ideas toward new solutions (Ewbank, in Hearn, 1967).

The crucial issue in dealing with conflict concerns the feelings of participants. To attack the person instead of the problem is to risk a declaration of psychological war. In most conflicts the attacker will deny any intent to criticize or demean others. In destructive conflict there is disagreement in which the relationship is damaged. If festering, unresolved group or interpersonal issues remain below the surface, then simple disagreement can be transformed into interpersonal criticism or attack, and displaced feelings may convert a workable problem into destructive conflict. Unless there is ample opportunity to work on these neglected or unrecognized matters, it will be difficult to resolve even the simpler problems.

In constructive conflict, participants place the highest value on sustaining their relationship and on awareness of one's own feelings as well as the feelings of others. And further, while real differences are aired and developed, in constructive conflict an effort is made to let all parties know that their views are acknowledged and understood. Also involved is recognition of the hazards for all when interaction threatens to become a win-or-lose situation. If participants suffer loss of self-esteem, the conflict was not constructively managed.

Morale

The term *morale* is sometimes used interchangeably with *cohesiveness* (Hare, 1976), but the definition "an average feeling of contentment or satisfaction about the major aspects of the work situation" (Campbell & Tyler, 1957) is preferred. Good and Nelson (1973) have also worked in this area, and Frank (1961) sees demoralization as a universal condition among candidates for group therapy. Current research in organizational psychology centers on job satisfaction and productivity (Landy & Trumbo, 1980), and morale is considered a quality of organizational climate.

Confidence, zeal, and spirit are also related to morale (Dunnette, 1976; Herzberg, 1966). *Burnout* is currently in vogue as a term implying fatigue and diffuse feelings of malaise and demoralization. Although such terms usually refer to persons individually, they can also tell a lot about groups. Informal surveys show, for example, that a significant number of people are dissatisfied with the group meetings they attend at work, at school, or even for recreation. Unsatisfactory meetings (dull, frustrating, stormy, and unproductive) are symptomatic of poor morale elsewhere in the organization.

Of the many definitions of group morale, the most common refers to the level of effectiveness of the group and how the members feel about belonging to it. Morale may be described in terms of feelings of belonging together or esprit de corps. A high-morale group can endure greater conflicts and stress without serious damage, without falling apart.

There are two interrelated aspects to a group's morale: the extent to which an individual's personal needs are met and the effectiveness with which the goals of the group are realized. But these two aspects do not always coincide (Dunnette, 1976).

In a laboratory on small groups, participants are exposed to the complexity of social and personal forces that have a bearing on morale, and participants can actually experience the fluctuation of morale in themselves and within the group. In describing the emergence of group feeling from conflict, Hearn (1955) focused on group work at the University of California at Berkeley and found two issues over which the groups struggled:

> The first was the problem of *authority*. Expressed in terms of ideological differences concerning the role of the instructor, it had to do with the issue of dependence versus independence. Each member struggled with this problem in his own way based, undoubtedly, upon his various experiences and reactions to authority in other settings. The other issue was expressed in questions concerning how much and what kind of *structure* was desirable in a group of this kind.

Hearn found that his groups worked on these two issues throughout the entire course, as evidenced by the process records that he wrote at the conclusion of each class session. By tracing the genesis of these issues, Hearn showed "how groupness emerges out of intermember conflict." Fluctuation in morale served as a barometer measuring the effect of conflict resolution.

The meaning of morale is not yet adequately understood, even though at times it seems perfectly obvious. Attempts to raise morale must take into account interaction among members as well as overt and covert motivational forces of both the members themselves and the *group as a whole*. And, lastly, when we recognize that a group may be part of a larger social organization that exercises direct and indirect influence over the smaller group, we may appreciate better the range of problems involved.

Trust and Implicit Confidentiality

> I go to my friend steeped in the turbid dirty
> water of my self-ignorance and he/she will give
> me back to myself crystal-clear as spring.
> — *Francine Du Plessix Gray*

Trust makes relationship possible. Uncertainty and risk are reduced; vigilance and the need to control others also decrease. Trust makes it possible to give of oneself to another, to give attention, time, consideration, information, energy, and—above all—to invest feelings. In return, one experiences tangible and intangible satisfactions as the other person reciprocates.

There is always some uncertainty, however small, that may be dispelled for brief periods by waves of warm, shared feelings. Hence trust is given and accepted, shared repeatedly, and confirmed. Conflict and disagreement may be expressed, worked over, and lived with, often deepening and strengthening trust. Relationships are celebrated again and again by special activities, by festive meals, by music, by laughter, by the pleasure of being together as a dyad or as a group. Something significant is achieved and mutually celebrated.

People ordinarily have more than one relationship at a time, with other friends, colleagues, or relatives. To what extent are relationships shared? Or are they contained within a code of privileged communication? Precisely what can be taken from one relationship and told or given to another? Are there rules to guide the exchanges? Openness goes with forming interpersonal ties, but once established, selective closedness is essential to protect the inherent privacy of that relationship.

All relationships are confidential, unless explicitly modified. That must be clearly understood by all parties involved before any exclusive information is released to others outside the relationship. This is a remarkable state of affairs, and yet the conditions of confidentiality are rarely, if ever, spelled out. Somehow, we all learn that relationships are fragile and what the rules of confidential involvement consist of. Everyone must have experienced the distress caused by the violation of confidentiality, even unintentional violation. Perhaps, too, everyone who has broken confidentiality has learned from the pain and hostility caused in others.

Rotter (1980), writing on trust, states: "People who trust more are more likely to give others a second chance and *to respect the rights of others* [italics added]. The high truster is less likely to be unhappy, conflicted or maladjusted, and is liked more and sought out as a friend more often, both by low-trusting and high-trusting others" (p. 6). Although this study on trust is useful and relevant, it still does not bear directly on the ties between trust, relationship, and confidentiality. While we await more empirical investigations, explorations within a group-process laboratory could provide valuable and enlightening insight into the way special relationships are formed and how the implicit rules of confidentiality, both in interpersonal relationships within the group and in relationships with the group itself, are recognized and respected.

Self-Regard and Group Evaluation

In experiments intended to determine relationships between group achievement and feelings of self-worth, it is reported that people with low self-esteem are inclined to see the group's performance as being the same as their own, regardless of the group's effectiveness, and that people who regard themselves highly are likely to take credit for their group's successes but not for its failures. In the latter case, they tend to blame others.

How well groups perform is often at variance with how well they think they are doing. In one study, members tended to overestimate their performance when working in groups but not when working alone (Janssens & Nuttin, 1976). Original work in this area was done by Ferguson and Kelley (1964), who took estimates from group members about how well they did compared to other groups before scores were known. Participants typically overestimated their group's scores.

Tension, Motivation, and Learning

Hebb's work (1966) on the relationship between arousal (or emotional stimulation) and cue function (or learning) is relevant (see Figure 1.1). His experiments with higher mammals and human subjects show that as tension increases (along the horizontal axis), so does motivation to learn (on the vertical axis), up to a certain point. Then motivation declines. Motivation is defined as the tendency to produce organized, effective behavior. The shape of the curve would be different for different habits, according to Hebb.

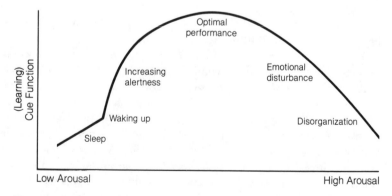

Figure 1.1
Relationship of the effectiveness with which stimuli guide behavior (cue function) to the level of arousal. *From* Textbook of Psychology *(p. 235) by D. O. Hebb, 1966, Philadelphia: W. B. Saunders.*

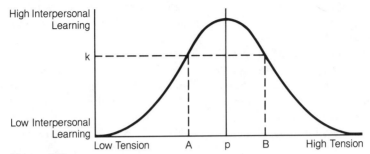

Figure 1.2
Relationship of interpersonal learning to tension.

Because group experience inevitably generates tension in members, it is reasonable to question the relationship between level of tension and learning. Figure 1.2 presents a hypothetical relationship as a basis for further speculation. As the tension level rises, motivation increases to stimulate learning up to a point, p. With rise in tension beyond p, there is a decline in learning achievement. The optimal range of tension is in the A to B range. Below the A level, learning may go on, but at a slower rate. At very low tension levels, learning drops toward zero. In other words, boredom sets in. When tension is too high, learning drops also, but for different reasons: Individuals may have difficulty organizing their experiences because they are too busy trying to survive psychologically.

Groups have the capacity to raise or lower tension as needed (Hartman, 1979; Lakin, 1979; Smith, 1975). Typical tension raisers are behaviors such as attack, judgmental feedback, confrontation, and humor. (Humor may discharge tension as well as raise the level, depending upon who jokes and how.) Other tension reducers are supportive behavior, certain kinds of intellectualizing, flight (see Bion [1961]), and expressing friendliness.

It should be noted that individuals, like groups, vary as to the curve characteristics suitable for them. Certain emotionally blocked individuals and perhaps some highly creative persons need high tension levels, but for different reasons. Some clue to the presence or absence of this quality may be observed in the way individuals typically induce mild or intense behavior in others as a function of their interaction style.

Listening
In a letter to Jung, Freud once wrote, "One cannot explain things to unfriendly people." With animosity or disinterest, there can be little if any

understanding. Freud's "unfriendly people" could hardly be expected to empathize and, hence, would not be able to hear or be receptive to new ideas. To listen is to experience some degree of empathy as well as to acquire information.

Because attention is brief and fleeting, effective listening is an active process, moving out to the other, returning to one's own thoughts, and then going back out to the other—in continuing cycles of attention, empathy, reflection, and expression. There is activity and an effort to appreciate. "Without appreciation, good listening can be exploitive. Listening with appreciation is probably the most sophisticated and the most imaginative act a person performs" (Brown & Keller, 1979, p. 70). Many people would agree with this statement, for it takes just this quality of listening to give another a feeling of being understood. To experience this kind of feeling, of being really understood, is apparently all too rare, according to a study by Van Kaam (1959). Most of us can recall instances over time when it has happened, and Van Kaam reports that people treasure the experience as extraordinarily warm and enriching.

To enhance relationships, to acquire information, to learn and to get work done require active listening. Whatever talent an individual may have for appreciative listening, small-group interaction provides an area for practice. It is important to let others know that they are understood. Small-group interaction seems to dramatize the idea that "no one can speak more intelligently than he or she can listen" (Brown & Keller, 1979, p. 72).

Rumor, Humor, and the Unknown in Group Life

Rumor and humor are special manifestations of communication. Social psychologists have studied rumor formation and the spread of rumors, particularly during wartime. Rumors tend to develop when there is a strong need to know what is going on but, for various reasons, information and communication are limited. Crises in one's organization or community provide fertile soil for the growth of rumors that reflect the anxiety and the hopes of individuals as they attempt to piece together what is unknown from the little that is known. Tolerance for ambiguity and for unknowns is a personality characteristic as well as a function of group behavior. Because we can never know everything or even a major part of the feelings and thoughts of interacting group members and because most groups continually undergo change as they work on new problems, the group situation continually generates rumors. Rumors may be viewed as a way of structuring the group. Unexpressed feelings, in general, and silent members, in particular, tend to stimulate rumors, as do regions of high potential, that is, people or subgroups that exert strong influence.

Humor may be related to group tension and the unknown. Group-relevant feelings, when brought into the open suddenly and in a manner that is not too threatening, may precipitate a discharge of feeling with an accompanying sense of relief. Groups often generate themes or processes that are particularly important to the life of the group, and it is around these themes that indigenous humor may arise. Jokes may be made, for instance, about taking the initiative or about the degree of structure, and these humorous events may then become a part of the group culture. Because humor touches on vital matters, albeit in a special and limited way, it facilitates communication and decision making. Humor may, of course, serve as a means of expressing hostility in the group and may be exercised at the expense of some person or subgroup. Or humor may be a means of temporary flight from the situation at hand. There is probably no limit to the kinds of processes to which humor may be related.

Both rumor and humor among subgroups may occur outside the physical setting of the group. During a break, one often hears laughter and quick exchanges as group members huddle in twos or threes. The constraining influence of the group is lifted temporarily, and now tensions can be discharged. Personal reactions can be shared and compared, rumors exchanged. When the group meeting resumes, one can sometimes sense a change of mood and a new flow of events reflecting the group processes that have occurred in the interlude.

Each of the basic issues just described calls attention to some aspect of group processes. The issues are actually complexly interwoven, with one another, with ongoing interpersonal relations, and with the group as a whole. The basis for selection of topics was the potential usefulness of the ideas, as well as suitability for an introduction to the dynamics of groups.

CHAPTER 2

Stages of Group Development

It is curious that members of a group are often at a loss to appraise the group's progress, whether the group is a work committee, a class in school, a business organization, or an encounter group. The two principal indicators, subjective state and productivity, often seem insufficient. Yet group members are quite certain at other times that they know precisely where the group stands.

According to some theorists, the answer to the question "How are we doing?" depends on an appreciation of group processes, in general, and of stages of development, in particular. Group behavior itself may be misleading. Polite, peaceful meetings could indicate a sterile group, while stormy, contentious sessions might yield progress and growth. That is why some idea or theory of development is needed in order to appraise group progress.

Do groups develop through recognizable stages toward maturity and effectiveness? From the time a group is formed until the time it is terminated, it passes through a number of stages of development. Initially, the members may be strangers or only slightly acquainted. Communication may be difficult; the members may be somewhat uncomfortable with one another. Investigators have noted certain regularities, as well as puzzling and paradoxical developments, in the growth and maturation of groups.

At times there is excitement, communication flows easily, and satisfaction is marked. Then, for no obvious reasons, tension suddenly mounts, bickering breaks out, the purpose for which the group came together seems blocked, and stalemate sets in. At other times groups go through the motions of working but little gets done, and what is worse, no one may even want to talk about what is happening. Sometimes talking about what is going on only seems to stir up more confusion, annoyance, and tension. Examining how collections of individuals grow into groups might help us understand some of the reasons for these problems.

Several patterns of development are summarized here. Most of the studies are of natural groups, that is, groups undergoing neither therapy nor training.

Empirical Studies of Stages of Group Development

Zurcher (1969) based his sequences on observations of 174 meetings of various neighborhood action committees over a 19-month period. A team of participant-observers collected data. The phases through which the groups moved were (1) orientation; (2) catharsis; (3) focus; (4) action; (5) limbo, relatively unproductive; (6) testing; and (7) purposive.

LaCoursiere (1974) based his stages on observations of student nurses who were being trained to work in a psychiatric setting in a state mental hospital. The nurses met for an hour and a half each week for 10 weeks. At stage 1, an orientation period, there were anxieties as well as positive feelings and expectations. By stage 2, called dissatisfaction, frustration had mounted, and feelings of discontent and anger were expressed toward the staff, the hospital, and psychiatry in general. Stage 3, called production, was accompanied by a more realistic assessment of what the nurses could actually learn and accomplish. Stage 4, the final stage, was called termination, and it was reflective, with some sadness.

Another study dealing with nurses in training was carried out by Spitz and Sadock (1973). They found three stages: (1) guardedness, anxiety, dependency, mixed with curiosity and confusion; (2) group interaction, beginning to yield trust, cohesiveness, and interdependence; and (3) disengagement, separation anxiety, and positive feelings toward the leader. Spitz and Sadock also observed third-year medical students, and although the same general stages were noted, the observers found more guardedness and overt hostility.

Yalom (1975) offers a four-phase model based mainly on psychotherapy groups: Phase 1 is marked by orientation and hesitant participation; phase 2, by conflict, dominance, and rebellion; phase 3, by closeness, warm feelings, and cohesiveness; and phase 4, by termination concerns.

Braaten (1974) surveyed some 14 different studies of developmental stages and offered his own composite. In stage 1, lack of structure is most prevalent. In stage 2, when subgroups begin to emerge, they precipitate conflicts and hostility. In stage 3, norms develop, and there is a mature work phase, with interdependency and trust formation. Finally, in stage 4, at termination, there is concern with disengagement.

Using a computerized content analysis, Dunphy (1974) based his model on observations of two sections of a social relations course at Harvard. The results suggested that in phase 1 external norms and patterns of behavior are maintained; in phase 2 individual rivalry predominates; in phase 3 conflict and aggression occur frequently; in phase 4 negative moods prevail; in phase 5 concern with feelings increases; and in the final phase high affection is experienced.

Mann (1975) also used factor analysis and, after several revisions, offered a five-stage model of group development: (1) dependency upon leader or trainer; (2) initial anxiety or resistance; (3) increase in frustration and hostility; (4) intimacy, integration, and mutual synthesis in the work phase; and, again, (5) a separation phase.

Tuckman and Jensen (1977) developed their own model, with five similar phases: forming, storming, norming, performing, and adjourning.

These stages of development in natural groups are presented here in skeletal form for purposes of comparison. Although certain trends and commonalities are present, researchers warn that variations occur when group populations, purposes, and contexts differ. According to some investigators, many group events are not seen by observers because they lack familiarity with group theories and concepts. Another common failing is the inability to see phenomena that are embedded in the observer's own cultural background. (In this connection, see Chapter 11 on problems of observation and influence on those observed and pages 206–207 on the search for a paradigm for group psychology.)

The Bennis and Shepard Model of Group Development

A theory of group develment based on Freudian principles of personality (especially those found in Freud's *Group Psychology and the Analysis of the Ego*) and on the dynamics of family and tribe is presented by Bennis and Shepard (1956). The authors suggest two basic phases. The first centers on dependence, that is, power relations. In this phase, group processes are concerned with how members attempt to cope with the unequal distribution of power in the group. Will members act submissively, dependently? Will some members become annoyed with the leader but fight with other members instead of confronting the leader directly? Will members find seemingly rational ways to act against the leader and against any possible progress by resorting to counterdependent actions? (The counterdependent person is still dependent on another; such a person goes against the one he or she is dependent on no matter what position is taken.)

As Bion (1961) has found, members often find temporary relief from unequal distribution of power by joining forces (pairing) with certain other members during the first phase. Pairing, or subgrouping, occurs when two or more members develop ties with each other on the basis of some common understanding, feeling, or mutual need. Each individual then takes the other(s) in the subgroup into account in special ways. Two people, for example, may see each other as allies, or three members may feel they share the same goals. The basis of the relationship of the pair, the triad, the foursome, or other subgrouping may be real or illusory, and it is subject to change over time. The rise and breakup of subgroups is an important process to watch for in the group's development (see Barrett-Leonard in Cooper, 1975).

Another way in which members deal with the unequal distribution of power in a group is by flight. This tactic manifests itself in interactions and discussions in which the content has little or nothing to do with the issue at hand. It is fascinating to watch the skill with which members will engage in irrelevance, happily supported by their peers. Eventually someone, driven to distraction by the triviality or irrelevance, is likely to call attention to the general evasion.

In the first phase described by Bennis and Shepard, there is frequently concern with building *structure*, but efforts at making explicit guidelines may be frustrated by members who are tangled in their relationship with authority. Implicit structure does begin to take shape, however, as ground rules and minimal limits are defined by an imperfect consensus and by the nature of emerging relationships. From a psychodynamic position, particular qualities of group members hold the key to progress. Members least troubled by their experiences with power and love can help the group work on communication processes. Clarification, listening, reflecting, and supportive behavior are typical of the valuable assistance one member can provide another. Should the nominal leader help in this manner, his or her authority and fantasied expertise are enhanced, and many members gladly allow the leader to take over once again.

Patterns of withdrawal on the one hand and overassertiveness on the other hand become less apparent as the group begins to realize that it can improve its communication processes by using its own competencies among the membership. Attacks on the leader may continue; charges of incompetence, rigidity, manipulation, and authoritarianism, among others, may still be heard; but the group has begun to change. Members are beginning to assume responsibility for work.

The second phase described by Bennis and Shepard (1956) usually follows some highly charged group event, when the group undergoes emotional release, or *catharsis*. There may be strong exchanges between group members and the leader or between subgroups. Whatever the motivating force, some tentative resolution is achieved through improved and validated communication and the expression of feelings. The group, in effect, congratulates itself, heals the split, at least for the time, and revels in *harmony*.

Personal relations among members, according to Bennis and Shepard, dominate the processes of this phase. Interaction among members takes place on a more direct, personal basis rather than in the less personal manner associated with roles. In the first phase, the individual is seen as representing a role, a job, a class, or an ethnic group. By the second phase, members are more likely to interact as people with unique qualities and feelings.

As relationships become restructured, members are freer to work out ways of achieving *consensus* and of moving more realistically toward group goals. There may be a letdown here, too — disenchantment because what is being achieved does not meet members' fantasied expectations. Again subgroups may form to deal with anxieties and to increase the degree of involvement with others.

Finally, the ending itself may stir feelings of anxiety or sadness. Characteristic coping defenses — intellectualization, denial, and displacement, among others — may again distinguish the different personalities.

In a later version of their two-phase model, Bennis and Shepard (in Gibbard, Hartman, & Mann, 1974) observe that in phase 1 the group emerges out of a collection of disparate individuals; in phase 2 the individuals emerge out of a working group. Further, they emphasize that group progress depends ultimately on the membership and that not every group achieves all substages of development. The ability of some members to function realistically while others are under significant stress and constraint is a crucial resource to the whole group. Progess is made as validated communication grows. It is not unusual for groups to regress temporarily after having made significant progress.

Criteria for Group Growth

One sociologist (Mills, 1967) summarizes criteria for growth and development for a wide variety of groups in our society:

> *Adaptation:* "An increase in openness, that is, an increase in the range, diversity, and effectiveness of [a group's] channels of intake of information from the world outside" (Deutsch, 1973, as quoted by Mills, p. 21). Capacity to extend the scope of the group's contracts and obligations beyond current boundaries. Capacity to alter the group's customs, rules, techniques, and so on to accommodate new information and new contracts.

Goal attainment: Capacity to hold goal-seeking efforts in abeyance while alternative goals are being considered. Capacity to shift to, or add, new goals.

Integration: Capacity to differentiate into subparts while maintaining collective unity. Capacity to export resources without becoming impoverished and to send emissaries without losing their loyalty.

Pattern maintenance and extension: Capacity to receive new members and to transmit to them the group's culture and capabilities. Capacity to formulate in permanent form the group's experience and learning and to convey them to other groups and to posterity.

Every Group Is Also Unique

How much time is spent in each stage of development varies greatly. Some groups move relatively swiftly through the early stages, only to level off at a more advanced stage. Some groups regress or fall back frequently to earlier stages. Serious difficulties in establishing goals will also prevent progress. The composition of group membership may affect development, particularly if certain member skills, knowledge, or other resources are limited. However, the temptation to pin the blame for group failures on individual group members should be resisted. Look for causes of slow progress or reasons for group inefficiency at the group level, not at the level of individual personalities. The most practical approach to the diagnosis of problems relies on an understanding of the group's processes in general and on its stages of development in particular.

CHAPTER 3

The Laboratory Method in the Study of Group Processes

> The mark of a civilized man is his
> willingness to re-examine his most cherished
> beliefs.
>
> — *Oliver Wendell Holmes*

Among the more conventional approaches to learning are the lecture method, the use of case studies, and the textbook approach. In the study of group processes, the laboratory method has come to be preferred because it is experience-based. In the words of Mills (1967, p.7):

> One means of becoming a student of group dynamics is to set up a special type of group which examines itself. At Harvard University, Semrad conducted seminars wherein medical students and young social scientists met together, observed their own interaction, and interpreted to each other what the group was doing. Although a simple enough arrangement, it is becoming increasingly apparent that such groups are a *revolutionary departure* [italics added], in the sense that they are a new order of social system. The collective purpose of their members is to learn about their collective experience. Goals preoccupying other groups are set aside so the group is free to develop an awareness of itself, to discover what its "self" is, where "self" means the group. Such groups have a built-in potential for becoming self-aware, self-knowing social systems, and consequently, of being a new order among social systems.

Experience-based learning is essentially inductive. It allows what is learned about specific group experience to be generalized into ideas about group processes. Participants come together in an informal, relatively unstructured way. By drawing on their own resources, the members attempt to come to terms with the task of becoming a group and increasing their understanding of group processes. The more conventional methods — lectures, assigned readings, textbooks — may also be used, but only as they are needed to supplement the interaction experience. Other names for the laboratory approach to group learning are human interaction, human relations training, and T-group (T stands for training).

Characteristics of the
Laboratory Method Relevant to Group Study

The physical arrangement of the class is similar to that of a seminar or workshop. There is no head of the class; there are no assigned seats. Such an arrangement facilitates free interaction and discussion within the group. In addition, it encourages independent members to take the initiative instead of relying on the teacher as head of the class.

Removing the study group from usual surroundings and usual social pressures is advocated in some laboratories. A "cultural island" has many advantages. By freeing the individual from the customary work setting, the "island" tends to encourage a fresh look at familiar problems. It offers more time to feel and to think over these problems and to discuss them in pleasant surroundings with others who are equally interested. Although such a setting is preferred, it is not always possible for practical reasons.

The newly formed group in the laboratory is encouraged to leave behind the usual symbols and trappings of status. Dress is usually quite informal. Titles are often omitted, and people are addressed simply as "Mister" or "Ms." instead of "Doctor" or "Professor." Sometimes members choose to use first names, but this remains a matter of individual preference.

The instructor has some special functions and responsibilities but participates as a member of the group and encourages other members to participate freely. The instructor assumes a more passive role than is usually the case in college classes. There are many important reasons for this. Because the group is new and has never before worked together, the instructor avoids imposing a pattern of work that may not spring from the unique characteristics of this particular collection of people. Also, the members are immediately faced with the problem of finding their own way of proceeding in the group. Thus important issues — such as the setting of short-range and long-range goals, the establishment of ways and means of working on problems, the nature of the group's own communication system and decision-making processes—must somehow be faced and resolved. The basis for learning about group and individual behavior is grounded in the struggle with these issues.

The content of group discussions and the processes underlying group behavior are distinguished and clarified. The word *process* here refers to an inference about the meaning of behavior in the group. Behavior may be verbal, as in discussion, or nonverbal, as in keeping silent or facing a particular person while addressing the group. There is an unlimited variety of group processes, some of which are commonly used and easily understood. For example, some group members may become involved in matters that take the group away from its immediate work. Most of the group will go along with the detour, but it is only later that the members will recognize the real need for temporary escape from the task at hand. Such detours or flights from the necessary work of the group are important processes, and they probably constitute one of the properties of all groups. Lewin makes a useful distinction. He uses the term *phenotype* to refer to observable behavior, that which is actually said or done. The term *genotype* refers to an idea or construct about the underlying meaning of behavior.

The laboratory method relies on a permissive atmosphere. Participants recognize, after a while, that they are free to probe, to ask, to challenge, to question, to contribute, to listen, and to explore. Members discover that they can be themselves, say what they really think, and express attitudes that they would ordinarily disguise or ignore. After a cautious beginning and after testing the "temperature of the atmosphere," members find it increasingly valuable to be able to check their impressions with others, to admit that they do not understand something when they really do not, or to participate in new ways that they may never have permitted themselves. An atmosphere free of the usual psychological threat is most conducive to learning about one's own behavior and the behavior of others in a group.

One of the reasons for relying on informal discussion and interaction methods for learning about groups is that the learner, in his or her experience within the group, discovers how closely and complexly related are the various processes of group life. It is one thing to talk or read about how groups make decisions, but it is quite another matter to participate with peers and struggle through to a decision. In the laboratory setting, the learner can see, for instance, that decisions of the group may be influenced by overt as well as by covert conflicts in the group, by communication problems, by the status acquired by members while in the group, by sensitive conciliators as well as by assertive leaders and by passive supporters.

The laboratory method makes it possible to discover certain phases in the development of the group. During the initial phase, a laboratory group usually concerns itself with orientation and security operations. Efforts tend to be directed toward finding out what the purpose or goal is and what needs to be done. At the same time, there may be some tension, particularly if members are strangers, about how to deal with one another and what the level of trust is. Because all groups try to come to terms with issues of power and influence, feelings, and structure, they move through stages of development (see Chapter 2 for a description of the major stages). Participants thus have an opportunity to work through these stages while attempting at the same time to become aware of what the experience of each phase is. As the group matures through the utilization of its own resources, particularly its communication skills, it becomes possible to recognize the qualitative changes of the different phases within the group as a developing system.

Learning Goals and the Laboratory Method for Studying Group Processes

A small group can be an informal laboratory to supplement learning-through-experience in everyday life. The task of the assembled persons is to become a group, to make note of the processes involved in becoming a group, and to learn about group and human interaction in face-to-face settings. Bringing together for this task persons who may not know one another in an arrangement that is unstructured offers a unique challenge. In a sense, it is a fresh start, a new way to learn what we are really like. To look upon ourselves, as anthropologists do, as participant-observers in an alien or unfamiliar culture may not be easy. Because we take for granted the way we typically interact, we no longer even consider habitual ways of thinking and feeling and behaving. "The commonplace tends to go unnoticed by those who are thoroughly indoctrinated" (Steiner, 1974, p. 106).

A growing body of evidence indicates that exploring interaction in a small group can be productive and enlightening (Dies, 1979; Lakin, 1979; Lieberman, 1976; Smith, 1975). A key value is a sense of inquiry in a permissive climate. People feel encouraged to interact with one another and to think out loud about what is happening. Because it is a shared task, collaboration and cooperation grow in importance.

In addition to being useful, cooperation feels good. There is a little less need for being guarded and defensive. Outside the group many people behave with caution, as well they might, depending on the situation. Within the group, in contrast, a different norm develops. It is based on the unique purpose of the group and emphasizes a degree of openness and of trust appropriate to the task.

Because there are no specific instructions about what to do and how to do it, each group member is faced with the problem of how to proceed.

Assumptions are made about what is relevant, appropriate, and effective. Usually these assumptions are imported from previous group experience, and before long they are often found unsuitable in the new setting. Rules and constraints about what to do or say, how to deal with the designated authority, what limits to apply, and so forth are also brought in.

Because this situation is basically different, however, participants begin to realize that procedures, guidelines, and rules of conduct may have to be invented to fit the particular setting or people.

In effect, the work of the group requires that each participant be himself or herself as much as possible. The idea is that, by sharing one's thinking and feeling, members can make sense about what is happening and about how to proceed.

Some of the coping strategies one uses outside the group may not be useful in the laboratory setting. It is not easy to set aside one's usual way of behaving, but it helps to be able to talk about one's reactions and observations for purposes of learning. To be a bit more open about what is going on may make one feel less guarded, and a little more uneasy or anxious at first. Ordinarily this is just not done. In itself, this is instructive, for what is being disclosed is generally innocuous or else already known to other group members. Hence one piece of learning, a bonus, so to speak, may be the realization that what you thought you were covering up so successfully over the years was obvious to all. For example, a group member had a way of smiling whenever he had something to say that made him feel anxious. Later he was surprised to learn that the rest of the group understood how he felt, but they had silently and unanimously agreed not to tell him that they knew. Because this revelation came at a time when he had more confidence in the group and in himself, he felt relieved that he did not have to try to mask his face when he felt anxious. Instead, acknowledging how he felt left him freer to say what he wanted to.

The group's own development (see Chapter 2) powerfully affects how individual members behave. And how each member thinks and feels and acts will affect the group's development. Because the group and the individual are part of a common system, the objectives of the laboratory include learning about both.

Groups, like other living things, quickly begin to differentiate into parts or subgroups. Subgrouping may happen so swiftly that no one may recognize it. A subgroup can be an individual, a pair of individuals, a threesome, a quartet, or any number of persons who function together with respect to other members or toward the group. Some behavioral tie or bond, however tenuous, holds them together. For example, in the beginning three members may speak more than the others and seek to guide or lead the group in different directions. Other members may remain silent but ally themselves with one or another of the more vocal members. Opposing camps may vie for influence over the whole group without necessarily being aware of or admitting their intentions. Another subgroup may challenge the designated leader or staff member for structure, guidelines, and agenda. This subgroup takes an adversary stance against the designated authority who seems to have abdicated responsibility. Members of the subgroup thereby speak for others in the group in an effort to reduce anxiety by generating structure or by offering leadership.

Because different individuals have different needs, goals, and abilities, they tend to perceive situations differently. Conflict may arise because people and subgroups may want to move in different directions and to work on different tasks using different norms. A major job of the group is to enable members and subgroups to express differences and try to resolve or to integrate them. But first an effort must be made to understand that legitimate differences do exist. Some differences are matters of information and ideas. Others involve attitudes, feelings, and values. Alliances may be formed as individuals and subgroups present their positions and listen to opposing points of view. Misunderstandings are inevitable because often these positions are based on deep-seated attitudes that are not easy to express. Feelings may be hurt and communication may become distorted or blocked. As tensions grow, defensiveness may also increase. Stalemate may settle in.

It is fortunate that in each group there are people with skills to match the group's needs. Some people may be skilled in reducing interpersonal tensions. Others may be sensitive to the emotional needs of participants and be able to offer close attention and support. Sometimes quiet members, through active listening skills, open useful opportunities to express feelings. They might demonstrate by their actions that they do care for others and that they trust the group by being a little more open themselves. Thus the climate of the group can be changed by the members so that resolving differences and conflicts can proceed.

Trying to resolve differences is real work, and when some progress is made in recognition of commonalities as well as differences, a feeling of power and wholeness based on achievement sweeps over the group. Often a happy and playful mood sets in as if to celebrate the good work and the more cohesive group feeling.

The group may then move on to additional cycles of progress and frustration, to new learning and the awareness that new questions and dilemmas lie ahead.

A by-product of these cycles of work is that participants often learn about their own ways of learning. For example, one may learn that every statement made in the group consists of two parts, content and feeling.

But the two parts may not fit together. When someone says, "I was not uncomfortable during this last silence," the emotional part of the message, conveyed by voice and physical manner, may actually be conveying that "I was uncomfortable."

A participant also may discover that his or her ability to attend to and think about what is going on is a function of the climate of the group. Thus one learns how feelings (interpersonal variables) can affect how one thinks (cognitive functioning).

Learning and Change

The laboratory method encourages new awareness about one's coping style. Ordinarily one's way of doing things is in the service of some objective (for example, your way of doing your job, your style of social interaction). One may discover that the impact of one's characteristic way of doing things is different from what had been thought. One's style of asking questions, for example, may be seen by others as intrusive; another's way of being quiet and going easy may be seen as being defensive and afraid.

Becoming aware of one's way of interacting makes change possible. This is not to imply that change is easy or that it follows increased awareness in some logical order. Actually, real change is always complicated because one's personality is a closely intermeshed whole, and changing one thing invariably means changing other things, including how one interacts with others.

In the supportive atmosphere of a learning lab, however, one may discover that certain alternatives are open and available. It may actually be possible to try somewhat different ways of interacting, different ways of being with others. The realization that alternatives are available if one is interested may be as important a learning experience as one can have. Such awareness may be the beginning of change itself.

Wholeness

The work involved in enhancing individual differences by facing and resolving conflict strengthens the group as a whole. It may seem ironic that the synthesis and integration of a group can be based on the recognition of the real individual differences of its members. Action and movement in a group may shift from one subgroup to another or from person to person, depending on implied consensus of where the group is going and who has the particular knowledge or skill to contribute. The whole serves the parts, and the parts serve the whole—just as in any living system.

One can sense wholeness qualities in a maturing group, a group that meets the needs of individual members and at the same time meets the group's needs. Communication flows easily, and correction takes place because of greater openness and awareness. When new problems or crises emerge, when unfamiliar tasks are faced, when communication breaks down, a well-developed group can mobilize itself to learn about what is going on. At the growing edge of a group's progression, it is always murky and unclear.

The group as a system interlinks its subparts so that everyone feels in touch with what is going on. Almost without words one knows what is happening and can feel the surge of tension or satisfaction anywhere in the group. A group's problem may be invisible to the members, but it can show itself indirectly in the kinds of topics under discussion, in a rise in anxiety, or in unexplained lapses in the group's effectiveness. A sudden drop in competence in dealing with tasks or with social-emotional needs can be a dramatic indicator of hidden problems.

Regression in the service of the group, when seemingly immature behavior and feelings explode momentarily, may be but another step along the way of group progress. From a distance it may seem like a group temper tantrum, and things appear to be out of control, even chaotic. New thoughts, unblocked feelings, different behavior may pour into the group as it breaks the usual configuration while struggling with a difficult problem. Soon the cathartic wave subsides and the mood changes. There is more to work with now, and the group life flows once again, perhaps in a slightly different direction.

There can be great variability in group behavior even though some general patterns are predictable. Like tropical storms, most of the power and dynamic and structural variables of a group are invisible to the eye, but one can sense changes in atmosphere and climate before turbulence strikes or the high winds subside.

The laboratory group came together originally to learn about group processes and about human interaction. The mission or purpose is achieved, to some extent, depending on all concerned. Because the work was accomplished through group and interpersonal relationships, there may be understandable sadness to see it all end. Members realize that they may never see one another again, at least not in this group's context. Some may try to hold on to an experience that has become meaningful in their lives.

Others may have mixed feelings not unlike those experienced at the end of a symphony, a drama, or a journey into unfamiliar territory. Perhaps here, too, one learns something significant not only about groups and relationships but about people in their diversity and about oneself. Facing terminations calls forth other human qualities, including a sense of loss that is perhaps better acknowledged and accepted than avoided or denied. Making way for new beginnings is not a bad way to end a learning experience.

CHAPTER 4

Outcomes of Group Training and Learning

Current research on the effectiveness of small-group work to produce behavior and attitude changes in individuals was surveyed by Hartman (1979, p. 453), who found a "staggering variety of group techniques to deal with an ever-widening array of problems and populations." He went on to add: "Yet there is probably no area in psychology where such research is more difficult and controversial, more fraught with philosophical and methodological conundrums."

As in other areas of applied psychology, there are major dichotomies between investigators emphasizing the individual and those interested in the group, between use of a clinical approach and use of a statistical methodology, between research with a process orientation as opposed to focus on outcome. The goals, methods, instruments, and other procedures are varied and difficult to compare or combine.

Rohrbaugh and Bartels (1975, p. 471), in their study of validity constructs used in pretest and posttest research, further cautioned that "members' perceptions of curative events [in groups] do not necessarily conform to what actually happened or what was causative in the change process."

Despite schisms and methodological shortcomings, however, many researchers would concur with Hartman on the need for improved validity and reliability measures of outcome, on inclusion of both clinical and statistical approaches, and on support for the study of both group process *and* individual orientations. The importance of a group-centered approach to the undestanding of change is actually highlighted by a number of research findings about individuals. For one thing, efforts to relate self-disclosure and feedback to change in individuals have not been confirmed directly. "Their importance may rest instead on the role they [self-disclosure and feedback] play in the maintenance and development of any *person-changing group*. Their absence would suggest an environment that is inimical to change, but their presence has not been directly tied to learning" (Lieberman, 1976, p. 24).

47

More studies of naturalistic groups and of groups that combine outcome with process variables and better studies of intervention techniques
and adequate follow-up are needed. This is a large, complicated, expen-
sive order, but Hartman feels that "small, tight, replicable studies" are
now feasible.

With these cautions in mind, let us turn to the study of encounter
groups undertaken by Lieberman, Yalom, and Miles (1973), which Hartman considers to be "the most extensive and sophisticated in the group
field to date." The study became better known as the Stanford Group
Experience Research, or simply the Stanford study.

Research on Experience-Based Learning Groups

The huge increase in the number of encounter groups (also called
training groups, T-groups, human relations training, and human interaction groups) throughout the country and in many parts of the world,
especially during the 1960s and 1970s, generated a variety of excesses and
absurdities. Instant insight and overnight changes, joy and fulfillment,
panaceas of all kinds were offered. Many practitioners had little training
and limited background; some professionals exhibited a marked anti-
intellectualism. A wave of protest soon followed, including expressions of
concern from the American Psychiatric Association.

Morton Lieberman, Irvin Yalom, and Matthew Miles formed a research group at Stanford University and set out to study encounter
groups, to identify their effectiveness in working with people to produce
positive learning and change, and to identify negative effects. They
found, among other things, that "the most important and stable areas of
change were in values and attitudes and in self. Participants were more
likely to shift their value structure in the direction of being more change
oriented and more growth oriented" (Lieberman, Yalom, & Miles, 1973,
p. 129). Self-image and ideal image moved closer together, and improvement in interpersonal relations was noted.

The research group did discover incidences of casualties (members
upset or sufficiently distressed to require psychotherapy) and found that
this was related to certain leadership styles that emphasized aggressive,
intrusive interventions and charismatic authoritarian personalities. According to the researchers, these leaders seemed to be forceful and im-
patient, "they paid little heed to the concept of 'working through' and
demanded that their members change and change now." They acted as
though all participants needed the same thing, failing to recognize individual differences among members. Investigators found, in contrast,
that leader behavior that emphasized caring and meaning attribution

appeared to be effective. Emotional stimulation and executive function were also found to be related to desirable outcome in a curvilinear manner, which means that behavior reflecting too much or too little of either of these dimensions was not effective leader behavior (p. 240). Other researchers have failed to confirm the incidence of disturbances noted by Lieberman, Yalom, and Miles.

The Stanford study had one outcome that was totally unexpected. When results of negative effects were first published, thousands of requests for copies, mainly from people in the field of mental health, were received. Another part of the same study that later reported the favorable effects of encounter groups was ignored. Not a single request for reprints was received (p. 482). Apparently, readers of psychiatric journals wanted to know what if anything was wrong or harmful about the groups, but no one seemed to be particularly interested in significant gains, favorable changes, and worthwhile findings (Yalom, 1975).

Lieberman, Yalom, and Miles made the following observations concerning activity in encounter groups:

1. Expression of feelings is important when it is accompanied by thought and reflection: "Self-disclosure and the expression of positive feeling led to personal gain when accompanied by cognitive insight" (p. 422).
2. Feedback appears to contribute significantly to learning, but the process must take account of the *group* conditions and what is going on with persons.
3. The expresson of strong negative feelings, especially anger, needs to be tempered by group support and ample indications of caring.
4. Restriction to the present, the here and now, can be overdone. Freedom to move into the past and future can be useful, particularly when expressing personal experience.
5. As mentioned in earlier sections, neglect of group processes in favor of exclusive individual attention can result in poor timing, missed opportunities, and ineffective learning.
6. Although encounter groups can be productive of learning and change, they are not without risk, especially when charismatic and aggressive leaders encourage high emotional stimulation.
7. Prospects for delayed appearance of learning effects many months after termination are not good unless there are indications that some learning has already begun while with the group.
8. What the individual learns through group experience tends to be retained long after the close of the group (pp. 422–428); there is limited fadeout after one year.

In conclusion, Lieberman, Yalom, and Miles acknowledge other values offered by encounter groups besides opportunities for learning and change. They agree with Back (1979) and with Sarason (1981) that encounter groups provide a temporary sense of community and engage in rituals of social value. They satisfy a need for "momentary relief from alienation, which some have called the most prevalent illness of our time" (p. 452).

Further Research on Training (or Learning) Groups

Taking note of criticism directed at methodological weakness in many published investigations, Peter Smith (1975) undertook a survey of studies on the validity of T-groups. He selected studies that met demanding standards of research by insisting that measures for the studies be obtained from controls as well as from group participants; that the design include repeated measures; and that the groups meet for at least a designated minimum period of 20 hours.

All available studies of the effectiveness of T-groups that were documented and published were surveyed, and the methods used were critically evaluated. No single study was flawless with regard to research design, size of samples, follow-up procedures, measurement instruments, conditions of settings in which training took place, or statistical techniques applied. There was, nevertheless, a substantial body of research on the usefulness of T-groups.

Because of the care in selection of studies used by Smith, it was possible to compare directly psychological disturbances of members of control groups with those of participants in training groups. Again, the methodological difficulties that face all studies, including the Stanford group experience, were noted and taken into account. Smith concluded that "there is at present no dependable evidence as to whether adverse effects occur more or less frequently than among equivalent untrained controls" (1975, p. 618). Control groups, after all, suffered the stresses of everyday life, coping with problems, making a living, attending college, getting along with people.

Overall, Smith found that, in 78 of the 100 studies, positive effects greater than those found in control groups were documented. The kinds of gains depended on the nature of measuring instruments used, group composition, leader style, and time distribution, but participants typically showed more favorable self-concept, reduction in prejudice, and improved interpersonal relations. Gains in organizational effectiveness were achieved for participants in general and for groups composed of persons from the same organization in particular.

Cooper and Mangham (1971) had earlier reported that "significantly more changes are noted for T-group trained participants than either matched-pair control group subjects or participants of other training programs comparable in length and in objectives" (p. 10). More specifically, they found that participants improved in ability to diagnose individual and group behavior and showed "clearer communication, greater tolerance and consideration" toward others. Improved action skill and flexibility were also noted. In general, Cooper and Mangham's studies showed that changes did last, although evidence about fadeout over one year is still inconclusive.

Similarly, Cooper (in Golembiewski & Blumberg, 1977) refers to a number of studies in his inquiry into the psychological danger of T-groups and encounter groups. He finds clear evidence of benefits to participants and summarizes his survey with a quote from the authors of one of the studies: "Thus in the present study at least the encounter group experience does not provide more psychological distress than what would normally occur in people coping with the exigencies of life" (p. 253). In fact, Lubin and Lubin (1971) showed that encounter groups generated less anxiety than college examinations. They studied seven college classes and seven T-groups. Comparing the most stressful sessions of each T-group to the anxiety levels students experienced just prior to taking examinations, they "found that in approximately 80 percent of the cases the average college examination stress scores were significantly higher than the T-group means" (Cooper, in Golembiewski & Blumberg, 1977, p. 251).

Unencountered Facts

Lieberman, Yalom, and Miles (1973) studied the effect of group experience on participants, especially regarding personal change and emotional well-being. As a task force representing the American Psychiatric Association's concern with psychological casualties, the research group worked out an elaborate system of measurement, observation, and follow-up of participants, paying close attention to leaders' plans and theories and stressing, above all, leadership in action. Because the groups were set up for students at a university for three units of academic credit, it seems reasonable to assume that the purpose was learning and the gaining of knowledge or skill, in addition to personal awareness and personal change. The students were given a brief orientation, a demonstration of small-group interaction, and told that "they would be free to pursue any personal learning goals" (p. 10).

As far as I could tell, the research did not include learning about groups, per se. Although a number of important group and interpersonal processes were identified on the scales and questionnaires, the items addressed the individual's experience and reaction in the group — not the ideas or meaning of the process in the group's development. Some of the leader orientations were, frankly, therapeutic (psychoanalytic or Rogerian). But even in these groups learning must have taken place not only about self and others but about group processes as well (see Hill, 1974, for a similar suggestion based on his study of some 50 groups).

It could be argued that cognitive learning about groups is not relevant to personal growth and change. As far as I know, this hypothesis has not been explored or tested.

It could be argued that knowledge about group processes could augment understanding about self and others, that the individual who has problems often has problems in settings other than monadic or dyadic, and that insight into group contexts is at least as important as understanding of persons in the abstract. Furthermore, the individual's ability to cope with real life outside the encounter group would include coping with groups in various social situations. It is reasonable to assume that knowledge about groups could be useful for social as well as for emotional purposes.

Having assembled vast arrays of data, it would have been possible to relate knowledge of group phenomena to other indexes of change. A number of questions suggest themselves:

1. What if anything is learned about group behavior that is generalizable to other groups?
2. Is there any relationship between emotional change and cognitive change, that is, learning about groups?
3. To what extent do participants learn about groups without explicit instruction as compared to those groups whose leaders include information about groups?
4. The authors suggest that the more seriously disturbed participants frequently turned inward more than others did. Does this suggest that the emotionally distressed are less aware of or less interested in knowledge of the group as a whole? One of the surprises turned up by this study is the fact that "meaning attribution," together with "caring," contributed more to change than the other categories of leader intervention.
5. The study as a whole is skewed toward the individualism side of a continuum running from the intrapsychic to the personal, the interpersonal, and the intragroup. Because each participant is currently an active member of several groups — for example, classes, housing, work, family, social groups — would not an explicit review of the participant's role in the various settings, the group structure

and its effects, as well as the different forms of influence and leadership to which he or she is currently exposed have relevance to personal transfer of learning?

As a matter of fact, Smith (1975, p. 617) found that the most successful effects of the group-training experience occurred for participants who returned to settings similar to the training setting. For those who met with people in their own organizations or with professional peers, there was more gain and less fade. For those who met with strangers markedly different from the participant, there was more fade of positive gains. Explicit knowledge of group process and structure taken together with experiential learning may well be the significant link for the transfer of training to old and new settings.

MODELS AND METAPHORS

Part One dealt with the background of and basic issues in the study of group processes. In this part several models and metaphors of interpersonal perception and human interaction are presented. The models are intended to encourage speculation and the play of ideas regarding collective behavior, and each model goes beyond the individual personality, the *monad*, in an attempt to show relationship and interdependence. A brief discussion of multiple group membership brings Part Two to a conclusion.

CHAPTER 5

The Johari Window: A Graphic Model of Awareness in Interpersonal Relations

> In our culture, human beings tend to
> develop from a lack of awareness of the self
> as an infant to an awareness of and control
> over one's self as an adult. The adult who
> tends to experience adequate and successful
> control over his own behavior tends to
> develop a sense of integrity and feelings of
> self-worth.
>
> — *Chris Argyris*

The Johari* window is described in terms of awareness of behavior and feelings in a relationship. Ideas and assumptions underlying the model are presented. Interaction between two or more people depends on the

---

*The word *Johari* does not refer to the southern end of the Malay Peninsula. That is Johore. *Johari* is pronounced as if it were *Joe* and *Harry*, and that is just what the word means. Harrington V. Ingham, M.D., of the University of California at Los Angeles should not, however, be held responsible for releasing this neologism. Dr. Ingham and I developed the model during a summer laboratory session in the 1950s. It first appeared in notes I prepared for the *Proceedings of the Western Training Laboratory in Group Development* issued by the Unviersity of California at Los Angeles, extension division. In 1961 and 1963 I published enlarged versions of the original article (Luft, 1961, 1963). Little did I know of the hidden meanings in the word *Johari*. Many years later I discovered that *Johari* is rooted in ancient languages such as Sanskrit, Swahili, Arabic, and Hindi. In Hindi, the word means "a person who knows the value of gems or jewels." In Sanskrit, I am told, it refers to the "god who sees within." A student from Africa, who noted the word in a book while at my desk, also seemed to recognize it. I asked her what it meant in her native language. She smiled and said, "In Swahili, it means someone who is brave and strong." Recently I learned that *Johari* means "gold" or "golden" in Arabic.

extent of openness as well as the context in which the interaction occurs. Blindness to one's own behavior and feelings, as well as to what is hidden and unknown, is also part of the relationship model. In this sense, the Johari model is a matrix within which the psychology of interpersonal transaction occurs. The model is then used to depict principles of change in relationships, the objectives of a laboratory on group processes, and to illustrate intergroup relations. Problems and dilemmas of deliberate and unintended disclosure are noted.

The Johari window is a graphic model of interpersonal behavior that rests on a number of basic assumptions. These assumptions are derived from selected theories of personality and social psychology. The assumptions reflect the biases of certain theorists and, of course, my own bias. Because the assumptions, or paradigms, are not shared by all or even most psychologists, there may be value in making them explicit. They are expressed here rather dogmatically, but only for the sake of brevity and clarity.

Holistic versus elemental units: Human behavior is best understood in terms of wholes or large units of behavior. Analyses of small units of behavior, such as what the muscles or sense organs are doing, are of value only as they relate to the total person and context.

Subjectivism versus objectivism: The key to what is happening in a group or between people is subjective, that is, related to feelings. It is subjective factors such as attitudes and values that tell how individuals see themselves and others and order their world.

Irrationalism versus rationalism: Although some of the events in groups and between persons can be viewed as being orderly and making good sense, behavior is influenced more by emotional, largely nonrational strivings; logic and reason play relatively minor roles in human interaction.

Behaving without awareness versus behaving with awareness: Individuals, like the group of which they are a part, have limited awareness of the sources of their own behavior and of the effects of their behavior on others. Crucial aspects of behavior are best understood by taking into account sources and determinants of behavior that are hidden or about which the person has limited understanding.

Qualities versus quantities: It is desirable to be able to measure and weigh the forces governing behavior. The best understanding comes, however, with an appreciation of the qualitative differences of the processes of interaction between people and within groups. Qualities such as acceptance, collusion, influence, conflict, and trust, for example, are important, even though they cannot be defined or measured with great precision.

Change states versus structural properties: Attention should be directed toward ongoing processes and the changes that are taking place. Structure helps to identify underlying order; structure may also lie outside of awareness.

Fluid versus restrictive approaches: The fluid approach is favored, that is, "a basic predisposition to experience people and life in all their complexity in a rather relaxed fashion" (Coan, 1968, p. 719). The restrictive approach suggests "a tendency to deal with reality in a more controlling and compartmental fashion, through restriction of attention and through isolation of entities and events" (Coan, 1968, p. 719).

The Johari Awareness Model

The Johari window concerns awareness in human behavior. Implicit in the model is a recognition that awareness and consciousness are uniquely human attributes. *Consciousness* usually refers to what is felt within oneself; *awareness*, to what is felt outside oneself. The terms are used interchangeably here. These states of knowing are supremely human and central to any consideration of human interaction. The model starts with both states simultaneously.

Then there is an acknowledgment that intrapersonal and interpersonal affairs are inextricably united. Regardless of one's preferred orientation in personality theory, identity and relationships are so intertwined that it makes sense to consider them together. This can be done in the Johari framework without committing the theorist to an untenable position.

The model is essentially content free. This means that no assumptions need be made about the sources of human behavior, such as growth, psychosexual or security needs, or other social and psychological needs and drives. Yet the model is sufficiently broad and open so that any of these assumptions could be applied. Owing to the model's structure, however, the theorist can never lose sight of the various states of awareness and consciousness.

In terms of the model itself (see Figure 5.1), the constructs implicit in each of the quadrants lend themselves to verification. The open quadrant (Q1), the blind quadrant (Q2), and the hidden quadrant (Q3) are known to at least one person and are thus potentially confirmable. Even the unknown quadrant (Q4), which is known neither to the person nor to others, is eventually confirmable.

The model can also be applied to any human interaction. There is no inherent subject limitation. Gangs fighting, friends talking, executives

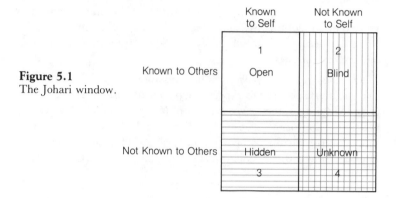

Figure 5.1
The Johari window.

leading, lovers loving—any can be viewed and conceptualized within the model's framework. In this sense, at least, the model is universally applicable.

In addition, the model is so uncomplicated that it can be readily used. A wide range of people, lay as well as professional, are able to grasp the model and use it to think about interaction. It does not require extensive background in the behavioral disciplines.

Finally, the processes inherent in the model guide the reader to important characteristics of human interaction. Considerations of change in the first quadrant, for example, call attention to processes involved in moving to greater or lesser openness. Similarly, the processes involved in reducing or increasing blindness in the second quadrant focus on crucial developments in a relationship. The significance of any interpersonal event is sharpened when it is seen in the context of all four quadrants.

The four quadrants of the "window" (Figure 5.1) represent the total person in relation to other persons. The basis for the division into quadrants is awareness of behavior, feeling, and motivation. Sometimes awareness is shared; sometimes it is not. An act, a feeling, or a motive is assigned to a particular quadrant on the basis of who knows about it. As awareness changes, the quadrant to which the psychological state is assigned changes. The following definitions and principles are substantially the same as those that have appeared in an earlier edition of this book (Luft, 1970, pp. 10–11):

Quadrant 1, the open quadrant, refers to behavior, feelings, and motivation known to self and to others.

Quadrant 2, the blind quadrant, refers to behavior, feelings, and motivation known to others but not to self.

Quadrant 3, the hidden quadrant, refers to behavior, feelings, and motivation known to self but not to others.

Quadrant 4, the unknown quadrant, refers to behavior, feelings, and motivation known neither to self nor to others.

Quadrant 1: Openness to the World

The open quadrant (Q1), the area of free activity, is a window raised on the world, including the self. Behavior, feelings, and motivation known to self and known to others constitute the basis for interaction and exchange as these are commonly understood. The simplest way to represent such interaction is to use two figures, with arrows indicating the direction of the exchange (Figure 5.2).

Note, however, that the dynamics of the exchange differ for the two different individuals involved. This is represented in Figure 5.3 by the arrow from Q3 to Q1 for Person *A*.

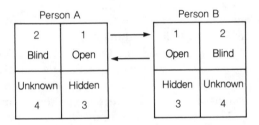

Figure 5.2
Interaction between two people.

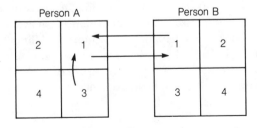

Figure 5.3
Direction of exchange between two people.

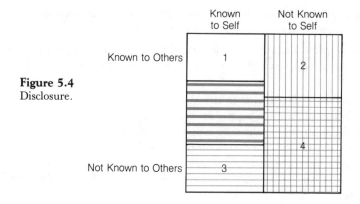

Figure 5.4
Disclosure.

If Person *B* points to *A*'s car and asks, "What happened to the fender?" the pointing and the spoken words, as well as the tone and manner, express a readily shared focus of exchange. *A*, however, can recall the parking accident that caused the dent; something known to him and not known to *B* (in Q3) is then disclosed to Q1.

For each person, the open quadrant, Q1, varies in size within a definite range and around a modal area. In most instances the modal area characterizes how open one is in general, even though one may behave differently with a different person or with the same person at different times. Compare early and later stages of friendship. Or note the great difference between early and later stages in the development of a group. In Figure 5.4, each bold horizontal bar between Q1 and Q3 represents a different degree of openness. Because Q3 is known to self and not to others, the individual has control of this area and may deliberately open or cover parts of the third quadrant.

Although the awareness model itself is simple, any exchange can quickly complicate it. It is important, therefore, to apply the model in the simplest way so that the essentials of interaction are shown. It is tempting to play in the same manner with the interaction possibilities of each of the four quadrants. Before yielding, it might be well to consider what this open, or known, quadrant means for human beings.

Adolf Portmann, a Swiss biologist, calls attention to the unique human capacity for openness:

> The relative openness of an animal to the world is always circum-
> scribed by a very narrow circle of possibilities, a circle that is
> never broken. By contrast, the openness of humans in experi-
> encing the world cannot possibly be overestimated. We have only
> to remember that we are able to direct our attention at will to

every detail, no matter how small, of the environment; that we are able at our pleasure to turn any single thing about us into an object of life-long research. Anyone who has once become conscious of this freedom of concern, this open latitude for our direction of interest, will also understand something about the most basic factor of our human uniqueness. It is the same thing as that which philosophers have sometimes designated as "openness to the world." Each one of us is capable of standing, as it were, outside himself, of observing himself from an external vantage point, so to speak, and thus gaining detachment from himself and judging himself.

We do not have the slightest evidence that anything of this kind is possible for animals. The fact that men can direct their interests at will proves that their central nervous system is regulated with a view to this "openness." We know from our own experience, to be sure, that the degree of such openness can vary from man to man, that some men soon narrow their horizons and preclude themselves from wide areas of human possibility, while others preserve the greatest creative openness to a ripe old age. Yet notwithstanding such enormous individual differences, even the man with the most paltry human equipment is marked by the most potent of all special characteristics: openness to the world. (1965, p. 40)

Just looking anew at this extraordinary quality is itself challenging. It is so easy to take it for granted. To be open to self, to others, to the world around us—by means of our senses and by our ability to transpose ourselves even outside ourselves—surely this identifies an essential quality of living as a human. Holzner (1968, p. 8) has made this clear:

The fact that others know reality is something which we never doubt; communication puts the "world in their reach" within our reach, too. A crucial prototype of this process occurs in person-to-person interaction. Here, in the direct communication between two people who attend to each other fully and speak the same language, the shared vivid present of the "We" establishes shared reality.

It comes as a shock to realize that large individual differences in this ability exist and that others are more open to experiencing the world than I. "Some men," to return to Portmann's statement, "soon narrow their horizons and preclude themselves from wide areas of human possibility, while others preserve the greatest creative openness to a ripe old age." I believe that one's usual openness, quadrant 1, can be changed. Knowledge, skill, awareness, and pleasure are determined by the magnitude of the first quadrant. Thus, to realize its existence, especially in relation to the other quadrants that are not open in one manner or another, is to establish an aspiration, if not a direction, for change.

One implication is that experience can be seen as an end in itself and as a means to an end. Certain experience enlarges this openness to the world and may be identified as true learning. Learning that closes us off is aptly described by Thorstein Veblen as "trained incapacity." The greatest single source for acquiring more openness is in the matrix of relationships to oneself and to others. Because each of us has, through experience, acquired some "trained incapacity" in functioning in this matrix, I believe that there is a genuine need to find interpersonal experiences that lead to more openness to the world. Suffice it to say, at this point, that indiscriminate or forced openness is neither useful nor desirable. Effective openness, however, takes work and some boldness because openness may be confused with nakedness.

Matrix of Interaction Between Two People

When two people interact (Figure 5.5), Person A perceives the first and second quadrants of Person B. A is aware of his or her own Q3, and though B knows of the existence of A's Q3, B is not aware of the feelings and thoughts there unless A discloses them (Figure 5.6). B perceives Q1 and Q2 of A and his or her own Q3 (Figure 5.7). A and B share awareness of whatever is mutually held in their first quadrants: behavior in the open.

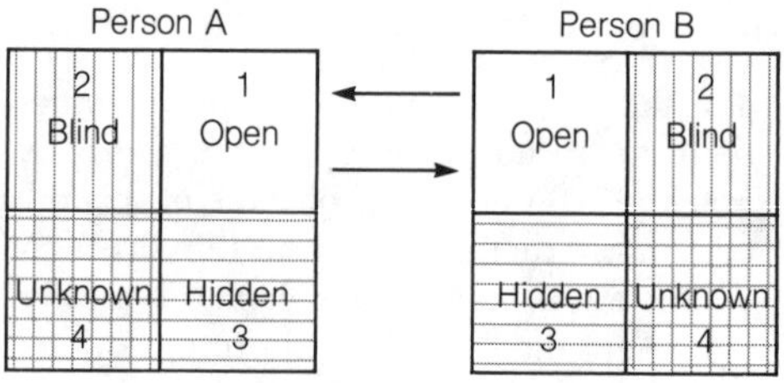

Figure 5.5
The matrix of interaction between two people.

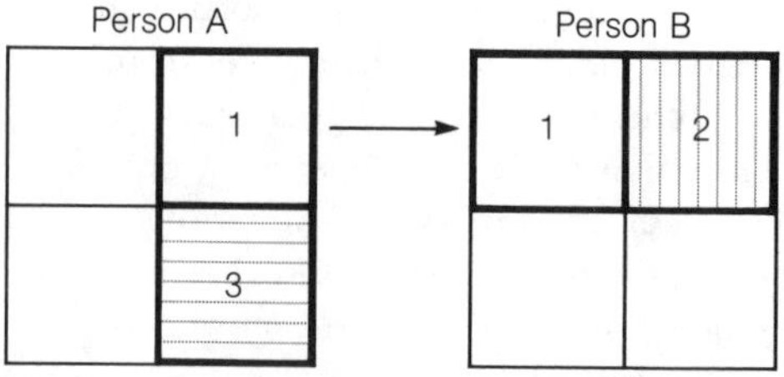

Figure 5.6
Person A's point of view.

The Johari Window: A Model of Awareness in Interpersonal Relations

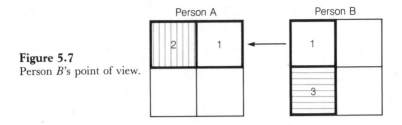

Figure 5.7
Person *B*'s point of view.

Quadrant 2: The Blind Area

How does one learn more about one's blind area, Q2? Many answers have been suggested, but nobody really knows. This is not sophistry but an accurate statement of prevailing knowledge. And there is good reason. The most complicated subject is a human being, both in relations with others and in relation to oneself. Nothing is more important, and yet systematic, confirmable inquiry has only just begun in this century. The graphic analogy for Freud was the iceberg: The human mind was mostly submerged, with only a small part appearing above the waterline.

But surely, because learning about oneself and one's blind area has been going on since the beginning of time, we must have learned a great deal. Yes, we have; but how much is valid is still unknown. Powerful suggestions come from all quarters:

1. One learns best by experience.
2. Experience is the worst teacher as well as the best.
3. Art is a good teacher.
4. "Art is but a mild narcotic; a temporary refuge" (Freud, 1929, p. 34).
5. History informs man of his true nature.
6. Literature reveals the truth.
7. Life is a mystery, and religion offers the only meaning.
8. Life is absurd, and there is no meaning, hidden or revealed.
9. Science alone discovers what the world and humanity are all about.
10. Science is limited to the simplest regularities.
11. Psychotherapy is the best way to learn about oneself.
12. Psychotherapy has failed to obtain verifiable results.
13. A good education is the best one can do.
14. Education is adapted for the past, certainly not for the present.

These trackings of our will to learn do not by any means exhaust the catalog of efforts to overcome our psychological blindness. In effect, we are compelled to take our stand in one of two ways. The first way is to continue the struggle for enlightenment by using the best of the known

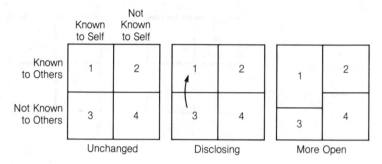

Figure 5.8
How disclosure works.

Figure 5.9
How another person sees you.

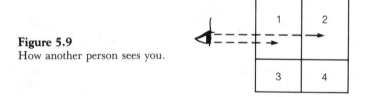

ways, adding to those ways with whatever ingenuity and originality we can bring to bear. The second is to recognize that we shall remain blind and unaware to some extent, regardless of our growth and actualization, and to develop a degree of humility in the face of this reality. Is this a pessimistic view? I do not think so, unless one is determined that both the tragic and the comic can be expunged from interpersonal experience.

Quadrant 3: The Hidden Area; and Quadrant 2: The Blind Area
One of the remarkable things about one's hidden area, Q3, is that it is an important key to one's blind area, Q2. Figure 5.8 is a schematic view of what happens in Q1, Q2, and Q3 for a typical person-in-relationship. Behavior or feelings hidden from others are disclosed, and quadrant 1, the open area, is enlarged. The other person now sees more of you in the open and also sees more of your blind area. You appear less distorted. The other person, in turn, can react more specifically and appropriately to you and thereby becomes a bit clearer in relation to you (Figure 5.9).

There is also a tendency for the other person to reciprocate by being more open toward you. With both of you now sharing greater open areas,

Q1, there is more basis for trust and less defensiveness. With less distortion and less need to protect self, you are more likely to recognize behavior to which you were previously blind, as the other person brings out or reacts to behavior and feelings in your second quadrant.

Although self-disclosure looks easy, it is actually a complex process that may be charged with serious interpersonal consequences. The crucial question is: When is disclosure appropriate? To whom do you reveal what about yourself and why?

In an earlier discussion bearing on Q3, the hidden quadrant, it was pointed out that an individual has some choice in disclosing self because the hidden area is known to self and not to others. Principles governing what is disclosed, where and when and to whom, have only recently begun to be studied systematically. These questions bear closely on the meaning and quality of interpersonal relations and are tied in with wide-ranging issues in the teaching-learning process, psychotherapy, leadership, encounter group practice, and organizational life. It is apparent that what is considered appropriate self-disclosure will vary with each individual life-style, social environment, and other important and unique variables. Still it may be of value to characterize appropriate self-disclosure through a series of hunches from which testable hypotheses may be drawn. Self-disclosure is appropriate:

When it is a function of the ongoing relationship. What one shares with another belongs in the particular relationship; it is not a random or isolated act.

When it occurs reciprocally. This implies that there is some degree of interdependency and mutuality involved.

When it is timed to fit what is happening. The self-disclosure grows out of the experience that is going on between or among the persons involved. The timing and sequence are important.

When it concerns what is going on within and between persons in the present. Some account is taken of the behavior and feelings of the participants individually and of the persons collectively. There is recognition of the relationship as an emergent phenomenon in addition to the individual selves.

When it moves by relatively small increments. What is revealed does not drastically change or restructure the relationship. The implication is that a relationship is built gradually except in rare and special cases.

When it is confirmable by the other person. Some system is worked out between the persons to validate reception of that which has been disclosed.

When account is taken of the effect disclosure has on the other person(s). Not only has the disclosure been received, but there is also evidence of its effect on the receiver.

When it creates a reasonable risk. If the feeling or behavior was really unknown to the other, it may have been withheld for a reason bearing on differences that have yet to be faced by the participants.

When it is speeded up in a crisis. A serious conflict jeopardizing the structure of the relationship may require that more Q3 material be quickly revealed to heal the breach or help in the reshaping of the relationship.

When the context is mutually shared. The assumptions underlying the social context suggest that there is enough in common to sustain the disclosure.

Robert Frost (1962, p. 27) speaks eloquently of the hidden and blind areas:

REVELATION
We make ourselves a place apart
 Behind light words that tease and flout,
But oh, the agitated heart
 Till someone really finds us out.
'Tis pity if the case require
 (Or so we say) that in the end
We speak the literal to inspire
 The understanding of a friend.
But so with all, from babes that play
 At hide-and-seek to God afar,
So all who hide too well away
 Must speak and tell us where they are.

Quadrant 4: The Unknown Area

What is not known to ourselves and not known to others is presumed to exist only by inference or in retrospect. Confirmation after the fact is one way of identifying the existence of the unknown area.

Another way of confirming the existence of Q4 is through temporary change that might occur because of the use of alcohol or drugs or during an illness. Sometimes, startling attitudes are revealed as a result of a very high fever, inebriation, or drug abuse. The individual may be surprised after recovery to hear others describe his behavior. He may be frightened, elated, or disturbed during the period of influence, and he may retain memory of specific feelings and of altered inner states after the experience. (It is doubtful that these changes provide insight, however, because a working-through stage is rarely included.) Special experimental conditions, such as sensory deprivation and hypnosis, may also elicit behavior and memories that were previously unknown to self and to others.

Irreversible brain injury may lead to marked changes of personality. The new pattern could then be seen as relatable to the premorbid state, though no one was aware of it before the injury. And projective techniques such as the Rorschach inkblot test or the Thematic Apperception Test may reveal hidden qualities in a person that had not been suspected even by those who had known the person well over time.

In everyday life, daydreams as well as night dreams may reveal or suggest Q4 characteristics.

Our perceptions and understanding of one another are always less than perfect, for we usually have spotty and limited views of one another (see Chapter 6). No wonder, then, we feel justified in resisting being told about our own behavior because the other is ignorant of so much we know about ourselves, as represented by the size of our third quadrants. There are, of course, other important psychological reasons for not accepting what others tell us about our blind spots. A person may be provoked, delighted, bruised, nurtured, and sustained by others, but he or she grows from within.

The Group as a Whole

The group, like the individual, may be treated as an entity or unit. Cattell (1956) uses the term *syntality* to mean the quality of a group analogous to the personality of an individual. Lewin conceives of the group as an organized field of forces, a structured whole. In the Johari model, a group may relate to other groups in a manner similar to the relationship between individuals. Figure 5.10 shows one way of looking at a group.

Interaction Within and Between Groups
Groups have wholeness properties. A family, for example, can be described as a unit. So can a company, a club, an office staff, a gang, a community. Groups can be arranged in terms of values, goals, functions, or whatever else it is that binds members to one another. There is no limit to the kinds of properties or classifications by which groups may be described.

In some ways groups behave like individuals. They develop lives of their own and ways of their own: talkative families, productive organizations, demoralized committees, biased clubs. Just about any quality

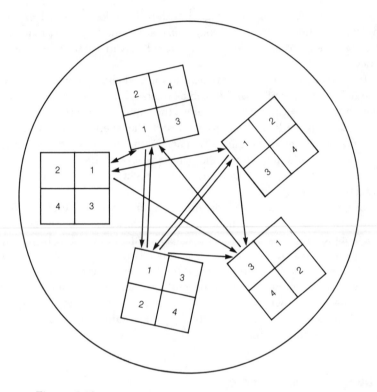

Figure 5.10
One way of looking at a group.

ascribed to an individual may be ascribed to a group, but it may not always be useful to do so. An important group quality is the extent to which members are aware of the behavior and feelings of the group as a whole. The Johari model may be used to illustrate awareness and unknowns in the behavior of groups (see Figure 5.11).

Groups also interact with other groups in an arena of openness that is less than the total area of behavior and attitudes known to the group. Some knowledge of behavior or attitude remains hidden (Q3), and some of the group's own behavior and feeling is inaccessible to the group but may be known to other groups. This is a group's blind quadrant (Q2). In short, the Johari model may be applied to intergroup relationships (see Figure 5.12).

The Johari model may be used to illustrate one of the objectives of the group dynamics laboratory: to increase the area of free activity so that

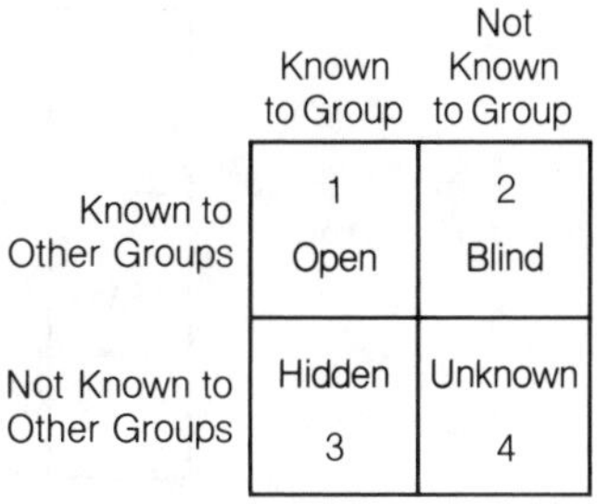

	Known to Group	Not Known to Group
Known to Other Groups	1 Open	2 Blind
Not Known to Other Groups	Hidden 3	Unknown 4

Figure 5.11
The Johari awareness model of the group as a whole in relation to other groups.

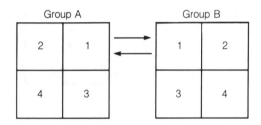

Figure 5.12
Interactions between two groups.

collaboration may progress. If follows, in terms of the model, that the work of the laboratory is to increase the area of Q1 while reducing the areas of quadrants 2, 3, and 4 (see Figure 5.13 and Figure 5.14). The largest reduction in area would be in Q3, then in Q2; the smallest reduction would be in Q4.

An enlarged area of free activity among the group members implies less threat or fear and greater probability that the skills and resources of group members can be brought to bear on the work of the group. The enlarged area suggests greater openness to information, opinions, feelings, and new ideas about each member as well as about specific group processes. Because the hidden or avoided area, Q3, is reduced (see Figure 5.14), less energy is expended in defending it. Because more of one's needs are unbound, there is greater likelihood of satisfaction with the work and more involvement with what the group is doing.

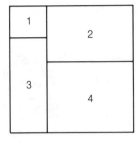

Figure 5.13
Initial interaction in a new group.

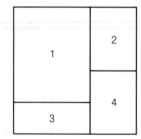

Figure 5.14
Laboratory objectives.

The Initial Phase of Group Interaction

In a typical beginning meeting of most groups, interaction is relatively superficial, anxiety or threat is fairly large, and interchange is stilted and unspontaneous. It may also be true that ideas or suggestions are not implemented and are often left undeveloped and that individuals seem to hear and see relatively little of what is really going on.

In a new group, Q1 is very small; there is not much free and spontaneous interaction. As the group grows and matures, Q1 expands in size, and this usually means we are freer to be more like ourselves and to perceive others as they really are. Quadrant 3 shrinks in area as Q1 grows larger. We find it less necessary to hide or deny things we know or feel. In an atmosphere of growing mutual trust, there is less need for hiding pertinent thoughts or feelings. It takes longer for Q2 to reduce in size because usually there are "good" reasons of a psychological nature to blind ourselves to certain things we feel or do. Quadrant 4 changes somewhat during a learning laboratory, but we can assume that such changes occur even more slowly than shifts in Q2. At any rate, Q4 is undoubtedly far larger and more influential in an individual's relationships, as suggested by Figure 5.15.

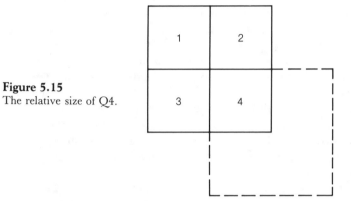

Figure 5.15
The relative size of Q4.

The Johari window may be applied to *intergroup* relations. Quadrant 1 then indicates behavior and motivation known to the group and also known to other groups. Quadrant 2 signifies an area of behavior to which a group is blind, but of which other groups are aware, for example, cultism or prejudice. Quadrant 3, the hidden area, refers to information a group knows about itself but is kept from other groups. Quadrant 4, the unknown area, indicates that a group is unaware of some aspects of its own behavior, and other groups are also unaware of this behavior. Later, as the group learns new things about itself, there is a shift from Q4 to one of the other quadrants.

When groups get into difficulty, when they bog down and fail to meet the individual or collective needs of the membership, there is a universal tendency to search for explanations at the individual level. The tendency to blame individual members is so strong that it is difficult even to consider other approaches. The model of the group as a whole suggests, nonetheless, that the sources of difficulty may lie within the functioning of the entire group. (The analogy of a family in which only one member seems to be troubled comes to mind. Nowadays, a child or other family member with problems is likely to be thought of in terms of difficulties within the family, not just within the child's psychic life.)

Groups interacting with other groups are much more likely to respond to one another according to group properties rather than the qualities of individual members. Interaction between rich and poor, blacks and whites, old and young may best be understood in terms of the images these groups have of each other. The use of a stereotype tells us that the user's perception is limited, incomplete, and distorted. The Johari model points out that the behavior and attitudes of any two groups are partially

Models and Metaphors

open, partially blind, partially hidden, and partially unknown. The relationship between the groups depends on the ways and means they develop to alter the states of awareness and unawareness within and between them.

Freud (1929) wrote of the "narcissism of minor differences" between groups. He had in mind the competitive and hostile feelings that so often exist between fairly close groups such as the Spanish and Portuguese, the North and the South Germans. It is not easy to understand or appreciate the ways of other groups. Getting outside of one's group or one's culture is not a bad way to learn about one's own ways. In ordinary intergroup relations, however, opportunities to learn about how others see your group are not easily created.

Interaction between groups is only a beginning in helping groups grow in awareness of selves and others. Even more important than the simple exchange of views between groups is the development of relations to a point that the processes of give-and-take, of impression and feedback, can be sustained. Here again we return to the problems of developing acceptance and trust, and ways of enlarging the view each group has of itself and of the other.

Principles of Change
The Johari model functions according to certain broad principles of change. The following ideas represent hypotheses about human interaction consistent with the awareness model.

1. A change in any one quadrant will affect all other quadrants.
2. It takes energy to hide, deny, or be blind to behavior that is involved in interaction.
3. Threat tends to decrease awareness; mutual trust tends to increase awareness.
4. Forced awareness (exposure) is undesirable and usually ineffective.
5. Interpersonal learning means that a change has taken place so that Q1 is larger and one or more of the other quadrants has grown smaller.
6. Working with others is facilitated by a large enough area of free activity. An increased Q1 means that more of the resources and skills in the membership can be applied to the task.
7. The smaller the first quadrant, the poorer the communication.
8. There is universal curiosity about the unknown areas, but this is held in check by custom, social training, and diverse fears.
9. Sensitivity means appreciating the covert aspects of behavior, in quadrants 2, 3, and 4, and respecting the desire of others to keep them so.

10. Learning about group processes as they are being experienced helps to increase awareness (enlarge Q1) for the group as a whole as well as for individual members.
11. The value system of a group and its membership may be noted in the way unknowns in the life of the group are confronted.

Shared Fields

In Johari terms, "mutually shared psychological fields" refers to the first quadrant, what is known or sensed by self and known or sensed by others. When Q1 is large enough there are shared assumptions about self and other and about the context in which they find themselves, indicating that the following conditions exist:

1. Behavior can be anticipated.
2. Behavior is comprehensible.
3. The common field is open to inputs of information and energy from each of the persons involved, as well as from the relevant environment or context.
4. Some experience within the psychological field is shared simultaneously.
5. Events are limited so that cycles of activity take place. The idea is that in a shared psychological field the interplay of behavior is, to a significant degree, repeated in a *predictable* manner. Hence the relationship has a distinct pattern.
6. In order to stabilize the relationship in terms of the developing pattern, which *is* the current relationship, the persons in the relationship rely upon a cybernetic process. Cybernetics involves steering or correcting the course of interaction on the basis of feedback signals. The feedback signals constitute the communication flow, both verbal and nonverbal, among the persons sharing the psychological field.
7. The mutually shared psychological field becomes an emergent whole and is governed by rules, usually implicit, that grow out of interaction (see Chapter 6 for further discussion about the nature of emergent phenomena).

Trapped in Games Without End

Within every group lies the prospect of genuine stalemate. Left alone, a group may work its way out of a stalemate, thereby enhancing its growth and autonomy. But not all groups can free themselves from the bind of their own implicit rules. Families, work groups, and organizations become caught for years in traps of their own making. One can see some of these snares working in groups designed to learn about groups.

At times the leader's interventions may stem from the freedom not to be bound by the hidden rules; thus the leader may be able to offer an opportunity to the group to move outside of its system. This principle, which has grown out of work with normal populations in encounter groups and college classes, fits precisely the experience of other specialists in interpersonal relations. Halpern (1965, p. 177) states that "for psychotherapy to succeed the therapist must avoid becoming unwittingly ensnared in the disturbance-perpetuating maneuvers of his patient." Beier, in a discussion of the information-gathering process in psychotherapy (1966, p. 43) observes that "his [the therapist's] measurements are his sensitivity to covert cues and his skill in disengaging from the social involvement which the patient tries out with him." Laing (1961, p. 21) finds that developing "his ability to shake off the 'reality' imposed by the group is the essential task of the group analyst."

Watzlawick, Beavin, and Jackson (1967, p. 234) identify the very same principle in their work with families. Unless the therapist stays sufficiently outside the rules and assumptions governing the members' interaction patterns, "we have the whole group snared in games without end." They use the term *games* according to Von Neumann's conception (Von Neumann & Morgenstern, 1944), later modified by Szasz (1961) and by Berne (1961): the creation of a relatively closed, implicit, interactional system regulating how people perceive each other. A "game without end" is one in which the prospect of working out of a bind is effectively blocked by an implicit or explicit rule. If a group has a rule stating that every decision must be endorsed unanimously, for example, no action is possible when real differences occur. Nor is it possible to change the rule, because that would require unanimous agreement, which is not possible if the minority group disagrees. Such entrapment in a game without end can be broken only if rules are changed to permit decisions even when differences cannot easily be resolved. Decisions by simple majority vote could also interfere with group functioning unless provision is made for the protection of minorities and unless rules and procedures are created for the resolution of differences.

Quadrant 2, the blind area, is characteristic of certain cults in particular that are unaware of some aspects of their own behavior, though outsiders are able to discern the cultish qualities. Or the prejudices of a certain group may be perfectly apparent to outsiders but not to the group members themselves.

Quadrant 4 applies to attitudes and behavior that exist in the group but for some reason remain unknown to the group and to outsiders. An illustration of this might be an unresolved problem with regard to the overall goals of the group. If the group is covertly split and some members want to go off in different directions — and if this fact has never been recognized or brought out into the open — then we could see the development of difficulties that remain unknown to the group members and unknown to the members of other groups. In a large scientific enterprise, for example, the physicists and engineers were having great difficulty with the machinists. Only after a long period of investigation did it become apparent that questions of status and privilege were producing bitter feelings between groups. The members of the various groups were unaware of the ramifications of this problem.

Relationships and Interaction

Another way of representing a relationship is shown in Figure 5.16, where all the information bearing on the relationship is contained in the matrix. Each person in the relationship has blind spots in areas open to the other person, and both are blind or lack awareness with respect to certain aspects of their relationship, as represented by quadrant 4. A critical factor in the relationship is the manner in which the unknowns are dealt with. Recurring interaction patterns establish the style or quality of the interpersonal tie. Every relationship can be characterized by the constraints inherent in the relationship.

The persons represented in Figure 5.16 are interdependent in Q1, and each is both independent and dependent in Q2 and Q3. Independence is defined here as awareness that is exclusive; the dependent person lacks awareness of an interpersonally relevant matter of which the other is aware. Withholding information or feelings that are interpersonally relevant is therefore a way of controlling or manipulating the other. Both persons are dependent where both are unaware, that is, in Q4.

Sketching a relationship often helps raise a variety of questions. Regarding Figure 5.16, for instance, what kinds of information or feelings are likely to be found in Q2? In Q3? In Q4?

Student-Teacher Matrix

The importance of student-teacher communication is dramatized in Figure 5.17. These questions come to mind: What kinds of interactions are needed so that learning may take place? How do the different kinds of

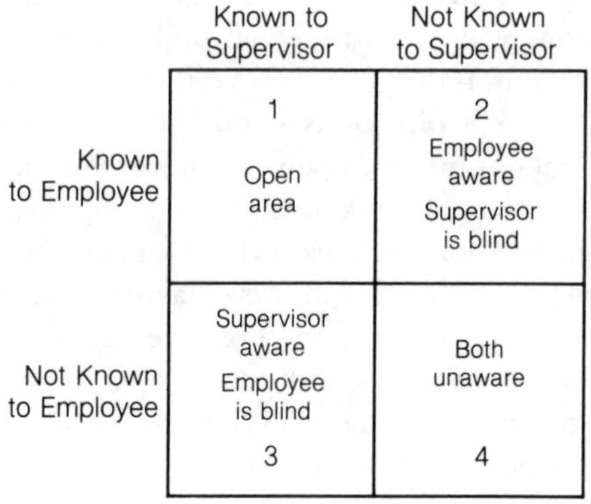

Models and Metaphors

	Known to Supervisor	Not Known to Supervisor
Known to Employee	1 Open area	2 Employee aware Supervisor is blind
Not Known to Employee	Supervisor aware Employee is blind 3	Both unaware 4

Figure 5.16
A model of person-to-person interaction: employee-supervisor.

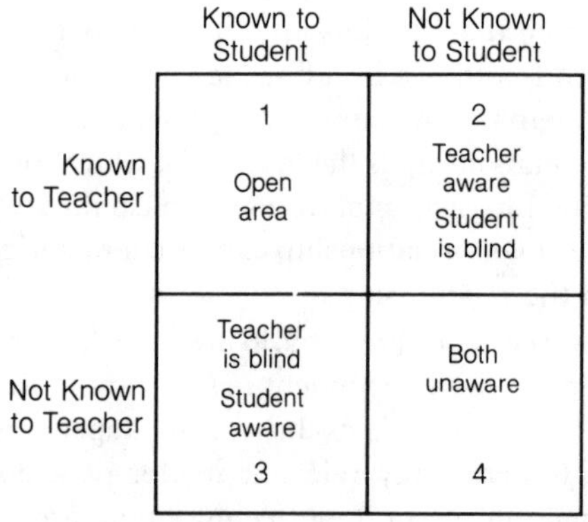

	Known to Student	Not Known to Student
Known to Teacher	1 Open area	2 Teacher aware Student is blind
Not Known to Teacher	Teacher is blind Student aware 3	Both unaware 4

Figure 5.17
A model of person-to-person interaction: student-teacher.

unawareness affect the purposes that bring treacher and student together? What group processes are involved? (See Chapter 15.)

What happens when information flows from Q2 to Q1 or from Q3 to Q1 or from Q4 to Q1? Or, regarding Figure 5.17, what kinds of interaction help to enlarge the open area? Similar questions might be raised for Figures 5.18, 5.19, 5.20, 5.21, and 5.22.

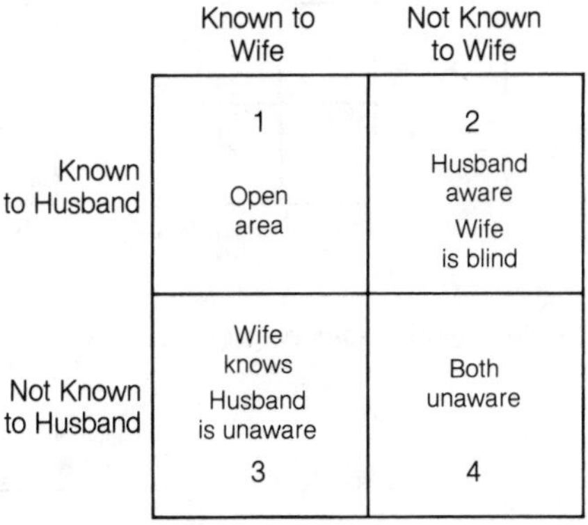

	Known to Wife	Not Known to Wife
Known to Husband	**1** Open area	**2** Husband aware Wife is blind
Not Known to Husband	Wife knows Husband is unaware **3**	Both unaware **4**

Figure 5.18
A model of person-to-person interaction: husband-wife.

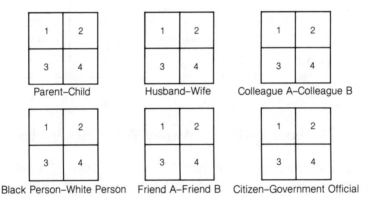

Parent–Child   Husband–Wife   Colleague A–Colleague B

Black Person–White Person   Friend A–Friend B   Citizen–Government Official

Figure 5.19
Other kinds of person-to-person interaction.

1	2
3	4

Student–College

1	2
3	4

Consumer–Corporation

1	2
3	4

Patient–Hospital

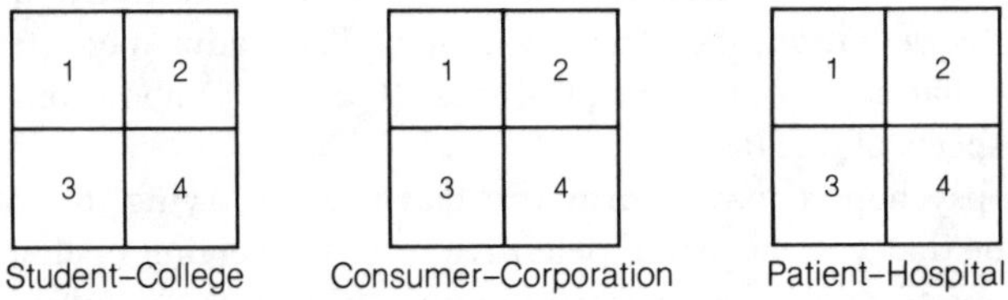

Figure 5.20
Interaction between individuals and organizations.

Figure 5.21
Interaction between organizations or groups.

	Known to U.S.S.R.	Not Known to U.S.S.R.
Known to U.S.A.	1 Open area	2 U.S.A. aware U.S.S.R. is blind
Not Known to U.S.A.	U.S.S.R. knows U.S.A. is unaware 3	Both countries unaware 4

Figure 5.22
Interaction between nations.

The Psychopest: How to Annoy Your Friends Clinically

It is rather simple to annoy your friends and relatives. Just tell them something about themselves of which they are unaware. Whether it is true is only slightly relevant. Questionable validity will rarely dissuade the psychopest, one who gives an unsolicited interpretation or judgment of another person's behavior or motives.

Psychopests purport to be specialists in the second quadrant of the Johari window. Occasionally they trespass into the third quadrant, where, by definition, they lack awareness. Their advantage stems from the fact that each of us lacks awareness (Q2 or Q4) about ourselves in some aspects of our being.

The psychopest may inform you that you are trying to manipulate others or that you are being defensive or self-deceiving or that you are acting out of guilt-laden or fearful motives. There is an endless array of tidbits like these to choose from. And the psychopest's motives are of the best; he or she merely wants to help you, whether you have asked for help or not.

It is in the nature of charges about your Q2 area that you cannot deal easily with them. How can you deny that you are trying to influence others or that you are self-deceiving? Several alternatives are, however, open to you:

1. You can ignore the psychopest (but you have to be pretty breezy to brush him aside).
2. You can ask for the psychopest's motives and credentials. It is far more comfortable and interesting to examine him.
3. You can check with others who have witnessed the same events.
4. You can request that he act like a psychopest (paradoxical prediction).

If the person carries out your request, you might compliment him or her. If you are in a group, you might invite others to keep tabs on the psychopest to see that the person's efforts are rewarded. This creates a paradox. In order to attack you, the psychopest must carry out your directive, thereby confirming your prediction of his or her behavior (for further discussion of this technique, see Jackson, 1962; Watzlawick, Beavin, & Jackson, 1967).

Should you avail yourself of this fourth alternative, it may look as if you are fighting fire with fire. The main purpose, however, is to help the psychopest gain awareness and control of this aspect of his or her behavior. This alternative would not work with people who have an inordinate need to have an advantage over others all the time. There are many strategies for fencing and fighting, and they constitute an important mode of human interaction. If the sting can be removed temporarily, a group may be able to continue its work while the psychopest struggles to gain self-knowledge.

The Floogle

Collecting floogles is neither a hobby nor an avocation. Experts in the field claim that those who collect floogles (called flooglers) have a tendency to floogle quite a bit themselves. *Floogle* is a verb as well as a noun: I floogle; you floogle; he, she, or it floogles. Floogles can be found everywhere, but good floogles are hard to come by. They are swift and elusive, and it takes experience to spot a floogle in the making. Here are a few in my collection:

1. After a long silence in one group, a member stated: "This has been such a comfortable silence I felt no need to break it."

2. In the middle of a disagreement with another member, a participant slammed his hand on the table and said, "I will not let this stupid argument make me mad."

3. A minister in a group was being heckled by another group member who accused all clergymen of being somewhat paranoid. The minister said the charge was ridiculous. He claimed he had heard similar name-calling before and ended by saying, "I'm getting sick and tired of this kind of talk. Why in the world do people keep picking on us?"

4. The leader in a group was being severely censured by one of the group members for expressing her opinion. "As the leader of this group you have no right to criticize or to judge," she was told. "Just reward those who are doing the right thing."

5. During a staff meetng, one leader criticized several of his colleagues for suggesting ideas for a lab design in which certain specific activities were to be scheduled. "I want to object to this design," he said with considerable vigor. "I will not stand by and take this point of view. You and you and you," he added, pointing to three of the staff members, "are trying to make things happen in a group, and my philosophy is to let things happen."

As you can see, there is quite a bit of variation in these floogles, and as an amateur floogler, I am rather proud to have them in my collection.

In Johari terms, a floogle is a Q2-Q1 event. At the moment it occurred, the person who said angrily that he was not going to get mad was unaware of the contradiction between what he thought he was saying and what was communicated. Each bit of behavior, both verbal and nonverbal, served to express some aspect of the individual's mixed feelings. It is clear that the nonverbal content in Q2 in this case reveals more accurately the actual state of affairs, of which the person was at that moment unaware. If this Q2 behavior (banging the table or raising one's voice) could be pointed out, the person might or might not acknowledge the discrepancy. What is particularly interesting about floogles is that few listeners recognize them when they are being made. It is hard to catch a floogle on the wing.

Studies Using the Johari Model

The Johari model was used as a basis for the construction of a test to measure openness, areas of blind self, private self, and unknown self by Esposito, McAdoo, and Scher (1978). They conclude: "These results indicate that the Johari Window Test has potential as an indirect, interesting, and sensitive instrument capable of measuring dimensions of behavior and self-evaluations that enhance or impede interpersonal relations" (p. 81).

Jay Hall (1973) describes a study using his "Personnel Relations Survey," which was based on the Johari model. The survey measures openness, whether feedback was solicited, and from whom (colleagues, subordinates, superiors) feedback was solicited. His results, used in conjunction with the managerial grid of Blake and Mouton, help explain the characteristic styles of interaction on the job. In addition, the test is used to diagnose a particular manager's difficulties with respect to each of the quadrants, thereby pointing the way toward possible correction and improvement of the manager's communication patterns.

Raymond E. Hill used the Johari awareness exercise developed by Kolb, Rubin, and McIntyre (1974) to measure openness and its impact on interpersonal communication. He found empirical evidence to support the relationship between size of quadrant and effective communication. In a paper presented at the Academy of Management Annual Meeting held in 1976, Hill stated: "In conclusion, perhaps the most important implication is some evidence, humble as it may be, that the theoretical construct underlying the Johari model has empirical validity."

From the Himalaya Mountains

A poet in Nepalganj, Nepal, wrote a song upon first learning about the Johari model. I heard the song on tape and was moved by its unusual quality and warmth. I am grateful to Prem Prakash Malla, who wrote and sang the song, for permission to reproduce the words here. My thanks also to Marion and Dick Vittitow, who as teachers and consultants working with people in Nepal as well as other countries in Asia, made it all possible.

I don't know you
You don't know me
Let us sit down together
To know each other.

Let me see into your eyes
You, please, see into my eyes
Let us tighten and strengthen
Our sensual sentimental ties
And move on further
To know each other.

Let me say something to you
You, please, say something to me
Let me know something about you
You, please, know something about me
And move on further
To know each other.

Let me sing a song for you
You, please, sing a song for me
Let me do something for you
You, please, do something for me
And move on further
To know each other.

— Prem Prakash Malla

CHAPTER 6

The Zucchini Connection: How People See One Another

In this chapter, a model of interpersonal *perception* is used to emphasize how illusions and partial truths about self and others are built into relationships. Fact and fiction blend and become stabilized. Efforts to dispel intrapersonal and interpersonal illusions tend to be resisted or ignored. The distortion most difficult to correct is the illusion in collusion, a misperception shared by the members of a dyad or a group. The Zucchini* Connection was developed to aid in appreciating the complexities and hazards present in everyday communication.

Also included in the chapter is a discussion of similarities and differences between the Johari and the Zucchini models.

Optical and Interpersonal Illusions

Everyone is vulnerable to optical illusions (see Figure 6.1), including people with excellent eyesight. Many factors influence what one sees. The arrangement of the stimulus, the setting, perspective, texture, and other physical variables can affect sight. In addition, experience can

---

*Zucchini is a thin-skinned plant of the summer squash family. "Perhaps no other vegetable has so wide a tolerance of growing conditions," say Irma Rombauer and Marion Becker, authors of *The Joy of Cooking*. They add: "Because squash is so bland in flavor, it can stand a good deal of 'doctoring' and is ideal for stuffing" (pp. 301, 302).

It is also true that the first time the Zucchini Connection was formally presented in 1978, the magic marker was green, serendipitously green.

Models and Metaphors

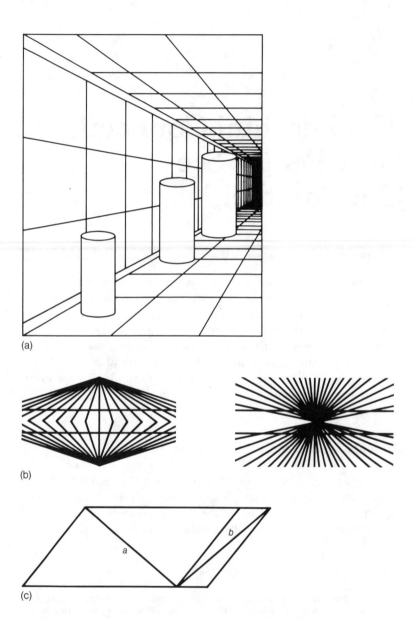

(a)

(b)

(c)

Figure 6.1

Illusions: *(a)* The three columns are of equal size. *(b)* The horizontal lines are parallel. *(c)* Diagonal lines *a* and *b* are equal in length. *(d)* Reversible figure. *(e)* The diagonal lines are all parallel. *(f)* The central circles are equal in size. *(g)* The top figure is seen as a dog, and the bottom figure is seen as a knight on horseback.

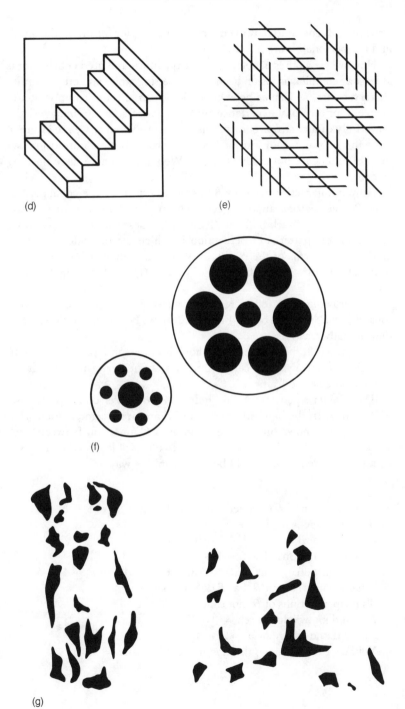

(d)

(e)

(f)

(g)

strongly influence and may even mislead the eye, for the brain, the mind, and the personality are also involved.

How we view other people, attribute qualities, and predict behavior is at least as complex as vision itself. Social setting, role, and other identity characteristics, as well as behavioral clues, can affect our impression of people. Our own past experience and our own personality characteristics powerfully influence our perceptions of others — whether we are aware of those forces or not. Our intuition is often wrong, but the impressions we form of others are not easily changed. We tend to ignore disconfirming evidence.

Human interaction rests upon less-than-perfect interpersonal perception. People see one another accurately in part, but their view is also distorted. Harry Stack Sullivan (1953, p. 29) describes this as parataxic distortion, or "patterns of perception in which the individual reacts to others not in terms of the reality of the others' behavior but, rather, in terms of fantastic personifications of others" (Hutt, Isaacson, & Blum, 1966, p. 313).

The drawings that follow represent an effort to depict how two persons, A and B, see each other. Figure 6.2 shows Person A and Person B as they actually exist.

In Figure 6.3, the square frame shows how person B perceives herself. Person B is not aware of certain realities about her own behaviors or feelings outside the frame.

The heavier square frame in Figure 6.4 covers Person A's perception of Person B. In the hatched area, A and B are in agreement about B.

Figure 6.5 shows the complete Zucchini Connection between one's self-image, another's image, and reality. In terms of Person A and Person B, the numbered areas should be viewed in this way:

A's impression of B (heavier frame) = 1 + 2 + 3 + 4 + 5
B's self-image = 3 + 4 + 5 + 6 + 7 + 8
B, the actual B = 2 + 3 + 7 + 9
B's misperceptions of self = 4 + 5 + 6 + 8
Shared misperceptions (illusions) about B by A and B = 4 + 5
What A knows about B that B does not know = 2
A's misperceptions of B, not shared by B = 1
B's valid knowledge of self = 3 + 7
A's valid knowledge of B = 2 + 3
Neither A nor B knows this about B but it is true = 9

B's misperception of self held exclusively by B = 6 + 8
What B does not know about self = 2 + 9

A's image of B is relatively organized and integrated, although A's impression seems rigidly divided among valid and invalid spaces.

For the same reason, B's self-image is organized and blended together, even though it appears as a combination of discrete parts or spaces. Thus it is not possible for either A or B to know exactly where his or her own impressions are valid as distinguished from false.

B would consider A's understanding of B to be limited *and* distorted. B might try to get A to change his impression of B by pointing out that areas 1 and 2 are erroneous. Because B is unaware of the actual existence of 2, however, she would have difficulty convincing A that 1 *and* 2 are not correct.

The relationship between A and B would be powerfully influenced by what they know of each other and the illusions they create. The veridical B, plus the perceptions of B by both B and A, constitute three images. Similarly, B's view of A, together with A's view of self and the actual person A, form three more images. This means that there are at least six different images in any two-person relationship.

Martin Buber (1957, p. 97) describes "six ghostly appearances" present in any two-person relationship.

> Imagine two men, whose [lives are] dominated by appearances, sitting and talking together. Call them Peter and Paul. Let us list the different configurations which are involved. First, there is Peter as he wishes to appear to Paul and Paul as he wishes to appear to Peter. Then there is Peter as he really appears to Paul, that is Paul's image of Peter, which in general does not in the least coincide with what Peter wishes Paul to see; and similarly there is the reverse situation. Further, there is Peter as he appears to himself, and Paul as he appears to himself. Lastly, there are the bodily Peter and the bodily Paul, two living beings and six ghostly appearances, which mingle in many ways in the conversations between the two. Where is there room for any genuine inter-human life?

Although I read Buber's description some time after developing the Zucchini Connection, there is clearly great similarity between the two models. A number of American sociologists, the social interactionists (Goffman, 1969; Strauss, 1977), have explored many different variations of self-perception and perception of others along related lines; they base

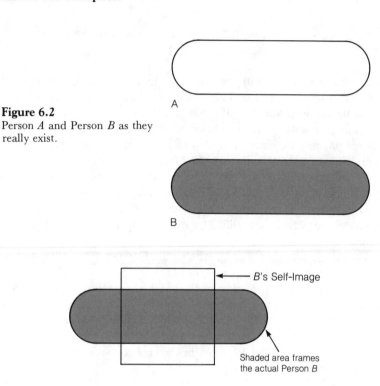

Figure 6.2
Person *A* and Person *B* as they
really exist.

Figure 6.3
The square frame shows how Person *B* perceives herself. Outside the square
frame, *B* is not aware of certain realities about her own behavior and feelings.

their theories on the seminal works of George Herbert Mead and Charles
Horton Cooley.

The Zucchini Connection is applicable to all relationships, including
persons interacting in groups. As an informal proposal, the model is
congenial with Alfred North Whitehead's observation that "in natural
science, to explain means merely to discover interconnections" (in
Kaplan, 1964, p. 334). Although no empirical data are offered, it has also
been suggested that the model emphasizes qualitative characteristics of
interpersonal perceptions (see Churchman, 1968, on selecting the right
question to study).

Supportive studies do exist. According to Laing, Phillipson, and Lee
(1966), for example, some couples who take intelligence tests separately
get higher scores than they do when they are working together. The authors claim: "This pattern reveals a destructive dyadic interaction" (p. 43)

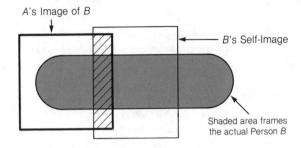

Figure 6.4
In the hatched area, Person *A* and Person *B* are in agreement about *B*.

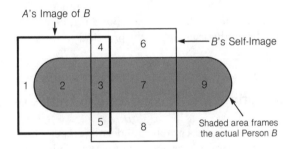

Figure 6.5
Person *B*'s self-image and Person *A*'s image of *B*, both superimposed on the actual *B*.

because, in healthy relationships, scores actually rise when couples work together.

Shrauger and Schoeneman (1979) summarize 14 different studies on the relationship between a person's self-description and this person's perceptions of how significant others describe him or her. In general, agreement is thought to exist, but there are a few exceptions, especially among children. In some 50 different studies, however, self-descriptions are *not* matched by significant others' *actual* descriptions. In other words, how a person sees self tends to differ from how others see him or her.

For the practitioners in the helping professions, it is axiomatic that "the poorer the quality of self-observation, the more difficult is the attainment of self-directed change" (Bandura, 1978, p. 352). Knowing where to look and what to look for are crucial to quality observations; hence, the need for maps and models.

The foregoing comments on how to recognize interpersonal misperceptions are intended as tentative clues to group interaction and may supplement other knowledge about group behavior. The Zucchini model may suggest sources of distortion, especially in early phases of group life. To eliminate all fantasy and illusion about selves and others is really not the purpose of this discussion, even if doing so were possible. Actually, there are studies that point out the constructive value of some illusions (Lazarus, 1979). But when an individual or a group is interested in change, it may be useful to recognize that everyone has the imagination to create illusions and that with some mutual support we can help one another learn more about our everyday organizing principles of interpersonal perception. "Because people's conceptions, their behavior, and their environments are reciprocal determinants of each other, individuals are neither powerless objects controlled by environmental forces nor free agents who can do whatever they choose" (Bandura, 1978, p. 352). Do not underestimate the aesthetic as well as the practical value of your Zucchini Connections.

Some Assumptions Underlying the Zucchini Connection

The Zucchini Connection is a graphic model of interpersonal perception. The model shows several major components involved in all two-person relationships. Assumptions upon which the model depends include the following:

1. Although each person knows a great deal about self, the knowledge or awareness is limited.
2. The accuracy of an individual's perception of another person is partial and incomplete.
3. The components that make up an individual's perception of another person are organized into a coherent whole.
4. The organizing principle guiding each person's perception of another person is relatively constant and is an important psychological function of an individual's personality.
5. The organizing principle of interpersonal perception (OPIP) serves a person's need to order and make sense of his or her interpersonal world.
6. The OPIP counters the (disorganizing) entropy principle in the systems of a person's interpersonal relations.
7. The OPIP enables a person to create the characters with whom he or she interacts.

8. Imperfections in the OPIP result in perceptions that are fictions, to some extent consisting of illusion and fantasy as well as valid information.

9. Transference and countertransference (Freud) and parataxic distortion (Sullivan) are ways of talking about errors in interpersonal perception rooted in the psychological history of the individual.

10. Distortions, exaggerations, illusions, and blind spots that the individual has about *self* are related to his or her distorted perceptions of others, but they are not necessarily the same kind of error.

11. All interpersonal perceptions contain fictional elements and over-statements of truth as products of the perceiver's experience and imagination.

12. All relationships contain some illusions that are held mutually and maintained by both parties. Shared perceptions that contain significant amounts of illusory content tend to resist correction by reality information.

13. The course of development of a relationship is governed by the interaction of the two OPIPs.

14. Distortions and illusions are a frequent source of interpersonal difficulties and disillusionment.

15. Sound relationships generate satisfying experiences that enhance the individual's development, but not at the expense of either party or of the relationship itself. Such relationships tend to affirm the utility of each person's OPIP.

Interpersonal Relationships as Emergent Phenomena

> The psychological group is a provisional being formed of heterogeneous elements, which for a moment are combined, exactly as the cells which constitute a living body form by their reunion a new being which displays characteristics very different from those possessed by each of the cells singly.
>
> — *Gustav Le Bon*

When two or more people establish a relationship, the dyad (or triad or small group) may be described as an emergent phenomenon. The emergent phenomenon arises out of the psychological event; that is, a relationship is formed. This relationship is different from the sum of the personalities; it may not even resemble the separate personalities. The emergent representing the relationship complements the activity of the two (or more) persons who have created the relationship. The emergent arises out of the way the persons now behave and feel and think with respect to each other—in the same way that personality is an emergent phenomenon growing out of the development of an individual. Personality is, of course, related to the individual as a biological organism, but it is also governed by other things: How a person feels, thinks, imagines, perceives, and behaves may include the future as well as the past and present, and these activities are powerfully influenced by culture and by social training.

In a two-person relationship, every interpersonal emergent is characterized by uniqueness; the quality of the relationship is different from any other relationships involving other persons. And the dyads reflected in their emergents have continuity and durability over time. The emergent also has wholeness characteristics; the dyad tends to become stabilized around certain structures or forms. Each emergent is both part and whole. Koestler uses the term *holon*, suggesting two faces to any system part, depending on the perspective of the observer; each system is part of another system. (See Stamps, 1980, and Anderson & Carter, 1974, on part-whole relationships involving human systems.)

In a group, we observe in two ways that this is so. We face the group as a unit and as a collection of subsystems, and we face the individual. Even fragmentary contacts between persons tend to be experienced phenomenologically as belonging to a set or category of relationships for each participant, such as colleague, friend, business associate, or family member. Hilgard (in Ericksen, 1962, p. 69) points out that "a full account of the processes of perception does well to consider the relationship between veridical perception and fantasy formation" because the qualities perceived by each participant in the emergent relationship are created by the persons. The relationship serves each participant differently, depending on the personalities involved, the setting or environment, and the participants' perception of the relationship. As a result, varying degrees of distortion are built into the relationship by each of the participants. Some of the distorted perceptions take the form of illusions, some of which are shared and held more tenaciously than they might have been had they remained unshared.

The emergent dyad is, thus, partially based on reality and partially based on fantasy. A fantasy is imaginary or unreal; an illusion is a distortion of a real image. The two terms tend to be used synonymously because distortion may be used by the imagination to create fantasy. Scheibe (in Shepard, 1930, p. 33) has expressed this in an interesting way: "To most psychological functions it is not of critical importance that cows exist and unicorns do not."

Because each participant does share some of the reality aspects of the emergent relationship, but because what is correctly perceived is not necessarily the same fragment of reality that the other perceives, emergents generate some stress and some inherent instability. It is the balance between satisfactions and stress that affects the way the dyad is experienced and the course of potential change. Persons in established relationships also tend to experience some uneasiness in the presence of a third party because the third party may not share the same illusory perceptions.

Each person in a relationship tends to influence the emergent in the direction of his or her perception of the other. One of the best ways of appreciating how an individual experiences a relationship is through attention to language. Language serves as a vehicle to convey meaning both above and below the threshold of awareness. It is interpersonal communication that best describes the dyadic emergent and reflects most clearly the way the persons perceive each other.

How to View the Interpersonal Emergent

The interpersonal emergent unites personalities into a new whole called a relationship. There are other emergents that represent groups, organizations, communities, towns, cities, nations, on up to the universe. The interpersonal emergent, which complements the physical dyad, constitutes a system of psychological processes organized according to broadly conceived principles.

The various orders of systems (personality, syntality, organization) are each made up of subsystems arranged according to patterned sequences of events and maintained by communication, shared attitudes, norms, feelings, values, and objectives underlying psychosocial ties. Like any of the other systems, the interpersonal relationship is effective to the extent that it meets the psychosocial needs and desires of the persons or subsystems and is able to sustain itself. The relationship maintains itself through cybernetic or self-correcting processes built into the communication system. The dyadic emergent is, however, more than two persons or subsystems, and it is qualitatively different from a set of two persons. The emergent has its own qualities as an organized creation. The psychological characteristics of an emergent exist even when both persons are not in each other's presence. The persons in a dyad give and take for each other and for the relationship. The emergent is carried in the mind (another emergent) of each person, and although aspects of the emergent may be held in common, certain aspects are perceived or emphasized differently by each member of the dyad.

Besides meeting, to a varying extent, each other's individual needs and desires, the emergent makes possible unique psychosocial experience. Although people can survive for a period of time with few or no relationships, the dyadic relationship enables greater fulfillment of human possibility in the same sense that culture or civilization serves larger collectives of people.

Interacting Dyads

When two pairs of persons interact, the phenomenon is different from a four-person exchange. If you assume that there is a developed relationship between the two persons in each dyad, interaction among the four becomes a group event in which the emergents of each dyad play a significant role. Each person is challenged to participate for self and to represent the dyad. The emergent quality of each dyad also has its compelling character that is then reflected in the group interaction. There is the question of sense of identity of self as a person and as a member of a relationship or emergent that represents them to the other two persons.

In addition, the two emergents face the possibility of becoming a group with the other dyad. In other words, a group emergent may be in process of being developed, which means that principles of group development and group processes are operating. The group emergent is organized as a system. Within that system, dyadic, triadic, or other subsystems may develop, grow, merge with others, or sustain themselves — as part of the group system. In effect, each interaction is now serving (in varying degrees) the individual, the dyad of which he or she may be a part, and the group. Any interaction may serve one emergent level more or less than another. The individual may serve, at one point, the dyad at the expense, say, of the group. Or one may favor the group at his or her own psychological expense. Generally, the sources of instability and distress are increased in a group setting. In a well-developed group, however, there are also many compensations for the dyads, the group itself, and the individuals. This value is attested to repeatedly in the unusual satisfactions obtained through group development, provided one is willing to endure the stress and to contribute to others by taking the groups, the subgroups, and the self into account.

Illusions and Fallacies

> The idea of infant sexuality and the Oedipus
> Complex can be accepted with a good deal more
> equanimity than the idea that the most precious
> and inviolate of entities — personal relations — is
> actually a messy jangle of misapprehensions, at
> best an uneasy truce between powerful solitary
> fantasy systems.
>
> — *Janet Malcolm*

An illusion is an erroneous perception; a fallacy is based on a misleading appearance. In a relationship, the sources for the distortions are probably distributed. When a person repeats the same kind of error with different persons, however, the source of distortion is probably with that person. To some extent, everyone tries to present a more favorable appearance, and that may be somewhat misleading. But interpersonal deception is not an illusion. It is based on misleading behavior and appearances that have been successfully fabricated.

People who misperceive others as a function of their own illusory perceptions may not realize how they could have been so blind. Hence when disillusionment sets in, blame is placed either on other individuals or on the self, and it is often expressed with indignation, with regret, or some combination of the two.

> People are punished by the reality they invent.
> — *Nicholas Nabokov*

The Function of Illusions

Illusions serve us almost as much as they trouble us. The need for systematic distortion grows out of difficulties in one's past experience or the need to work through certain stages of development. Consider the following: If a leader does not behave in a dominant, "macho" manner, he may be perceived as weak and contemptible. A handicapped person may be perceived as someone who needs support and protection far beyond his or her behavioral deficit. A person may oppose an authority figure such as teacher or manager for reasons that have nothing to do with the issues involved, for counterdependency is one form of systematic distortion. Falling in love the moment two people meet may well be a form of mutual or reciprocal illusion, familiar in song and story.

The fact that certain interpersonal illusions may have a satisfying aspect does not necessarily protect us from the consequences of interaction based on distortion. We can assume there is some psychological gain or reward in perpetuating the illusion, but there is a price for ignoring reality. Sometimes that price is repeated miscommunication. Sometimes the price is higher, resulting in seriously hurt feelings, severe disappointment, and ultimately, disillusionment.

If distortions or illusions occur in close relationships, in family, or in business, the consequences can be costly (see Tuccille, 1980) or damage the relationships. The effects on the system or organization in which the illusions are acted out can be complex.

In intimate relationships, illusions may be more difficult to identify and, hence, difficult to change. Shared illusions are most difficult to recognize and almost impossible to correct. The persons involved tend to protect the impacted theme, which is the source of the distortion, and thereby prevent each other from seeing what is actually there. Parents and child may, for example, have illusions about a child's truancy or academic or musical ability; or they may deny that, in fact, the child has extraordinary talent. Or a couple may share some illusion that one partner is sickly and needs extra protection. Both then collaborate in keeping the target person from undertaking any activity involving stress or risk.

Correction by Means of Communication

In order to change troublesome illusions, it is necessary to develop ways of introducing corrective experiences without unduly jeopardizing the relationship. The point is to sustain new or different ways of viewing behavior so that correction will take care of itself. To achieve this, it is sometimes necessary to talk about the discrepancy between what one believes and what one perceives.

Experience is probably the best way to correct distortion, but deeply held illusions may not yield to experience alone. When that is the case, corrective communication may be needed. The best kind of corrective is self-correction—in a setting that is genuinely supportive. Corrective communication generally fails because it is not clear, initially, who has the illusion. Also, because the act of corrective communication may be painful, it may be counterproductive as well. Simply pointing out discrepancies of fact may not necessarily affect the underlying feeling or attitude that sustains the illusion. It must be realized, as well, that illusions can surround the process of correction. It is generally safer and more useful to share self-feelings than to tell another what his or her feelings might be.

Sharing self-feelings has its quota of difficulties, too. It is assumed that one's intentions can be more easily changed than other aspects of affective behavior. When one is angry, the intention, for example, is to attack another, oneself, or the problem. Probably the intention when one is angry is to want to retaliate against persons, things, or the situation. (Whether it is appropriate or fair to get angry at these targets is usually not considered at the time when feelings are strong.) How can we assume the angry (or irritated, upset, depressed, or otherwise pained) individual will be moved by an intention to help the other — the other whom one may see, momentarily, as the enemy or the one who hurt or upset the individual? The willingness to disclose feelings depends on a measure of trust, confidence, or support, and that is precisely what is missing at the moment.

Fortunately, all is not lost. Despite momentary negative feeling, there is, in a developed relationship, some accumulated credit. It is based on experience that the other can be trusted, that the other will not take unfair advantage of disclosed feelings, and that there are some positive feelings toward the other. Mixed feelings (positive alongside angry or distressed feelings) then govern intentions.

There is also the realization that getting angry or showing distress may worsen one's position. In some settings, one loses face or esteem in the eyes of others by becoming overtly upset or angry. An individual concerned with retaliation may behave in a way that saves face or wins points by acting strong and in charge of self and of the situation. Some sophisticated people, when they feel put upon, do the "right" thing; that is, they acknowledge self-feelings rather than attack the other. In short, they do the right thing for the wrong reason, and the situation does not change. Such a person simply waits for another occasion to place a friend-opponent in the same kind of problem situation that he or she is experiencing. Both parties, knowing the same rules, alternately play attacker and good victim, wait for the prey to become vulnerable, and counter-attack. Neither is supposed to lose face in the process. The hurts and pains are not actually disclosed; one just maneuvers as if he or she were pained, and that is not quite the same thing because it involves battle strategy and indirect revenge.

The playwright who said "we search for love, believe in justice, and practice revenge" may have been both wrong and cynical. Because so many relationships appear to behave according to this dictum, however, it cannot be ignored altogether. Everyday observations indicate much misunderstanding and many damaged relationships. The Zucchini Connection represents but one attempt to depict interpersonal misperceptions and illusions.

Recognizing Illusions in the Zucchini Connection

Certain behavior exhibited in relation to others and seen in light of the Zucchini model indicates the presence of illusions or misperceptions. Such behavior might include the following:

1. Persistent misunderstanding
2. Particular difficulty in conveying certain kinds of information, for instance, about dependency, money, careers, illness, scheduling of time
3. Strong feelings out of proportion to what is actually being communicated
4. Drop in level of quality of thinking concerning certain topics
5. Increased anxiety for reasons not clear to persons involved
6. Both positive and negative feelings — hostility, fear, defensiveness, affection, trust, adulation, support — inordinately aroused or unrealistically based
7. Difficulty if not the impossibility of correcting distorted perceptions or erroneous communications

The Johari Window and the Zucchini Connection: Similarities and Differences

Both the Johari and the Zucchini models are concerned with interpersonal perception, how persons see each other and themselves, and with the lack of awareness of self and of others. The main difference between the models is that the Zucchini model assumes that each person has a relatively stable impression of self and of the other. This impression consists of both factual and nonfactual information, *blended together into an organized perception.*

The most important questions in any relationship are "What does the other person think of me?" "How does the other person feel toward me?" "How does the other person see me?" So crucial are these questions that Laing, for instance, has developed a system to describe sanity and madness in terms of interpersonal perception. Because every perception is also an interpretation, the objectively valid is important only to the extent that it affects the interpretation. But much of what goes into an interpretation of behavior is only remotely related to that behavior. And the same behavior may be seen differently by different people and often in opposite ways.

> I act in a way that is cautious to me, but cowardly to you. You act in a way that is courageous to you, but foolhardy to me. She sees herself as vivacious, but he sees her as superficial. He sees himself as friendly, she sees him as seductive. She sees herself as reserved, he sees her as haughty and aloof. He sees himself as gallant, she sees him as a phoney. She sees herself as feminine, he sees her as helpless and dependent. He sees himself as masculine, she sees

him as overbearing and dominating. (Laing, Phillipson, & Lee, 1966, p. 11)

Icheiser (1970, p. 51) emphasizes the stability of perceptions (as reflected in the Zucchini model):

Once the image of another person, shaped by primary mechanisms of one kind or another, is fixed in our minds, we tend either to overlook all factors in the other person which do not fit into our preconceived scheme or else we misinterpret all unexpectedly emerging factors in order to preserve our preformed misperceptions.

Another assumption of the Zucchini model is that each person would be overwhelmed with many bits of information when he or she interacts with another individual unless the flow were somehow quickly simplified and organized. We all do some processing of data whether we are aware of it or not. And we avoid overload of information between self and others by screening and cutting out much of what is there. Above all, by selectively organizing behavior, feelings and motivation, and social setting variables, we create a relatively simplified perception of the person, the setting, and the relationship (see Ross, 1977, and Mischel, 1979, for related studies).

Several illusory qualities in the way two or more people see each other are not readily apparent in the Johari model: First, in addition to *A*'s unique distortion of *B*, there will always be some illusory qualities that are made up and *shared by both* about each other. See areas 4 and 5 of the Zucchini model (Figure 6.5). Second, because a person's perceptions are organized wholes, each dyad is made up of six (ghostly) appearances, as described earlier in this chapter. Finally, the Johari model also assumes that the flood of information in an intrapersonal situation must be reduced and ordered. The emphasis, however, is on awareness and disclosure rather than on the process of organizing the perceptions.

Disclosure of self is done both deliberately and unintentionally. In effect, each kind of disclosure may be said to be organized. But inadvertent disclosures are made by everyone, by some more than others. Both models recognize that the principles governing interpersonal perception and interaction are only partially known by the people involved.

CHAPTER 7

The Circumplex Model and Bales's Interaction Process Analysis

> One of the most widespread superstitions is that every man has his own special, definite qualities; that a man is kind, cruel, wise, stupid, energetic, apathetic, etc. Men are not like that. . . . Men are like rivers, the water is the same in each, and alike in all; but every river is narrow here, is more rapid there, here slower, there broader, now clear, now cold, now dull, now warm. It is the same with men. Every man carries in himself the germs of every human quality, and sometimes one manifests itself, sometimes another, and the man often becomes unlike himself, while still remaining the same man.
>
> —*Leo Tolstoy*

The models outlined in this chapter also attempt to view relationships in terms of patterns and connections. Deeply held predispositions in each person are activated by other persons, according to the rationale of the Circumplex model. The relationship that develops is described along a dimension of dominance-submission and love-hate. Various degrees within these two sets of extreme dimensions represent how persons get along with each other. The model also offers perspectives on disturbed relationships.

And literally hundreds of empirical studies have been carried out by Bales and his associates at Harvard University using Interaction Process Analysis. Twelve kinds of interaction categories are grouped into task and social-emotional areas, and they form the basis for the study of group activity. Both models lend themselves to the quantification of interaction.

The Circumplex Model

A framework for the study of human relationships is presented by McLemore and Benjamin (1979), following the model of interpersonal behavior developed earlier by Leary and Coffey (1955). The model stresses that every person learns to induce behavior in others and that specific bits of interaction are best understood in terms of the overall implicit message that each person repeatedly communicates. The communication is successful if it gets the other person to behave in ways that will meet the security maintenance operations of the sender. Because this approach follows a theory developed by Harry Stack Sullivan, the model emphasizes psychological security and the reduction of anxiety. The important point is that interpersonal behavior consists in two or more people striving to induce particular patterns of responses in each other.

This eternal training process is aimed at the induction of either *complementary* or *symmetrical* behavior. These two patterns are, in turn, related to two basic dimensions or factors: dominance-submission and hate-love.

Behavior along the dominance-submission dimension is arranged vertically in the Circumplex developed by Leary and Coffey (see Figure 7.1). The behavior is reciprocal; that is, the one who communicates dominance tends to induce its *complement*, submission, in the other. Similarly, submissive behavior tends to induce dominant behavior in the other.

Behavior along the dimension of love-hate, arranged horizontally in the Circumplex (Figure 7.2), tends to induce similar or *symmetrical* behavior in the other. Hate induces hate, and love induces love.

When the two dimensions are brought together, they illustrate the way the Circumplex functions (Figure 7.3). A mother responds to a child's clinging, dependent behavior by offering help and by taking responsibility. The child is submissive; the mother, dominant. The mother shows love; the child responds with love.

Figure 7.1
The vertical dimension of the Circumplex model.

Models and Metaphors

Figure 7.2
The horizontal dimension of the
Circumplex model.

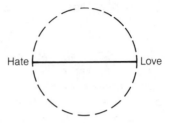

Figure 7.3
The two dimensions of the
Circumplex model together.

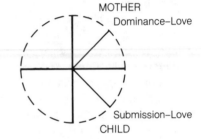

In the Circumplex it is recognized that behavior can vary from low intensity (close to the center of the circle) to high intensity (close to the outer edge). Different qualities of behavior are shown in different segments of the circle. The behavior of a teacher, a manager, or a leader in our society would, for instance, be likely to belong in the upper half of the circle but could take any left-right location from unfriendly and aggressive to tender and cooperative.

Interpersonal behavior circles appear in Figure 7.4. It should be noted that, as Carson (1969) mentions, reasonably well-adjusted people can and do show behavior in all of the categories, as called for by circumstances. The more disturbed the individual, the more apt that person is to rely on one pattern of interpersonal behavior.

Individuals in a disturbed relationship have several possibilities for improvement open to them. They can try to accommodate to each other, i.e., work through their difficulties and modify the relationship. They can try to change themselves, or they can try to induce change in others. The first option is probably the more difficult because there are limits to accommodation. Some things are too important to the self-concept to give up. Other changes are blocked by lack of awareness or simply by lack of opportunity to learn new behavior. Effort to induce change in others is the more frequent choice, as each of us knows from experience and from

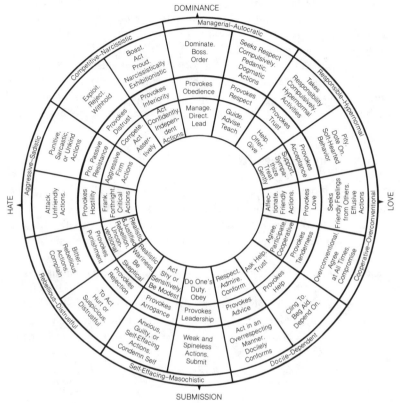

Figure 7.4

An adaptation of the Circumplex model. *Adapted from* Interpersonal Diagnosis
of Personality: A Functional Theory and Methodology for Personality
Evaluation *(p. 65) by Timothy Leary, 1957, New York: Ronald Press.*

observation. Both sorts of effort may fail. Either or both persons in a
disturbed relationship may seek more satisfying relationships elsewhere,
provided they believe that alternatives exist.

Although more complicated in certain ways, the relationships within a
group may be viewed with the same basic processes in mind. Family
structures, for example, may show the whole range of symmetrical and
complementary relationship patterns, with subtle changes over time both
within and among members. Power and control of the family members
over one another may change as some individuals grow and develop more
than others. The implicit contract then changes. New conflicts and new

resolutions may be worked out. Or children may seek satisfactions and security elsewhere. Or the family pattern may be retained, with great store being placed on its constant state, in collusion with but at the expense of some members.

For empirical evidence tending to confirm the existence of the two-factor Circumplex of interpersonal relations, see Benjamin (1974, 1979) and Lorr and McNair (1963). Studies by Schaefer and Bayley (1963) and by Becker and Krug (1964) offer similar empirical evidence on children.

Interaction Process Analysis

Robert F. Bales developed Interaction Process Analysis as a way of capturing empirically what went on in groups. In 1942 he was permitted to observe Alcoholics Anonymous group meetings "with the hope of getting some inkling of the astonishing motivational changes they seem to be bringing about" (Bales, 1970, p. ix). Later, in the 1950s, he borrowed the case study method from the Harvard Business School for his classes. Although he and his students found the case study method useful, it changed gradually into group self-analysis. The design of Bales's human relations course at Harvard University evolved, however, as a variant of the laboratory method, where he discovered that "structure is low and adventure is high" (p. xi).

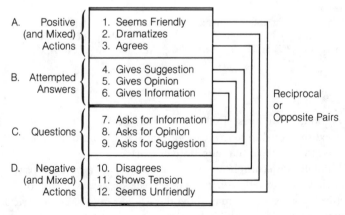

Figure 7.5
Bales's categories for Interaction Process Analysis. *From* Personality and Interpersonal Behavior *(p. 92) by Robert F. Bales, 1970, New York: Holt, Rinehart & Winston.*

In order to study the group's behavior, Bales developed a set of 12 categories. An observer can assign interaction of who does what to whom in a time-ordered sequence by marking categories on a form (see Figure 7.5).

By means of a moving tape on a machine called a process recorder, it is possible for a trained observer to pick up and record swiftly and reliably what transpires in the group. The coded data can then be summarized on profile forms, and the frequency for each interaction category can be graphically charted. The result is a frequency chart of what takes place sequentially. The data thus arranged may be used to test hypotheses about group and interpersonal behavior.

The reader interested in this method is referred to Bales's (1970) work as well as to the summaries in Hare's (1976) research handbook.

CHAPTER 8

Multiple Group Membership: The Bumblebee Hypothesis

This chapter addresses the problem of multiple group membership. Because each of us belongs or has over time belonged to a number of different groups, it is worthwhile to reflect on the way such group experiences may affect us in the present. We tend to transport attitudes, norms, values, and roles into any new group we join. Sketches are used to illustrate these invisible groups.

The Clarification Group, a procedure designed to help participants learn more about their background group identities, is also described in this chapter. The objective is better intergroup relations through heightened awareness of one's multiple group memberships.

The Invisible Network

Every group member belongs to a number of different groups, such as a family, a work group, a social group. We can assume that, by virtue of membership in these groups, the individual tends to internalize the norms and values and role patterns experienced in those groups. Even past membership in groups can influence current behavior; hence, the idea of an invisible network of groups.

In Figure 8.1, Person *A* is currently in Group 1. She is also a member of Group 2, a work group, but the other members of Group 1 may be unaware of Group 2 or what membership in Group 2 means to *A*. Each of the members of Group 1 may belong to several different groups that influence his or her behavior in Group 1.

If each of seven members of Group 1 (Figure 8.2) belonged to only four groups, there would be at least 28 memberships potentially active in Group 1. Some of the group's norms and needs may conflict with the norms and needs of its members. For example, in some families and in

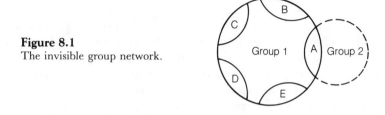

Figure 8.1
The invisible group network.

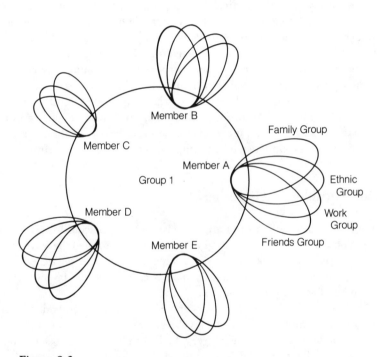

Figure 8.2
Multiple affiliations of group members.

some work groups, the expression of feelings is discouraged. In certain groups one does not openly oppose the authority person, while in other groups status is achieved by successfully defying persons with power. Some groups may be highly competitive; others may function according to norms of cooperation.

The Clarification Group

Because each group member carries with him (or her) the qualities and norms of other significant groups of which he is a member, his behavior can be understood better if we know something about what these groups mean to him. Birnbaum (1975) and Babad, Birnbaum, and Benne (1982) describe the Clarification Group (C-Group) as a form of laboratory learning that focuses on each person's multiple group membership character. They use a direct method of inquiry into the social life by exploring the group identifications (racial, religious, ethnic) of each member.

Their questions are selectively developed and used by staff and also by participants in an effort to help clarify each member's group awareness. For example, "Who am I in terms of my group identifications?" "How do others respond to me in terms of their group identifications?"

The C-Group addresses problems of intergroup relations by helping members recognize the origins of their own social attitudes and how intergroup perceptions develop. The methodology relies mostly on the structural methods of lecture and interview, but it also includes group-process development. A number of communities have used this approach to reduce intergroup tensions and improve community cooperation.

The Bumblebee Hypothesis

Engineers once studied the bumblebee to see why it could fly. In this apocryphal tale, aeronautical engineers carefully examined the wings and the body parts and took note of size, shape, and mass. After a thorough analysis, they agreed unanimously that, according to the laws of aerodynamics, the bumblebee could not fly.

Groups are like bumblebees. Communication is frequently distorted. Illusions and multiple invisible loyalties make coordination unlikely. Interminable conflicts sap their strength. Their large mass drags. Groups cannot get off the ground; they cannot fly. Group life is impossible, according to scientific analysis.

But bees do make honey and artful honeycombs and wax. And they pollinate flowers. And yes, bees do fly.

Human groups also thrive despite gravity and entropy. Groups nourish life, and although some are known to be inefficient and at times combative and destructive, others are busy cross-pollinating ideas or harvesting rice. At this moment, a group somewhere is rehearsing a symphony by Mozart.

PART THREE

GROUPS AND INTERPERSONAL INFLUENCES

In Part Three attention shifts back to questions about the nature of groups. Two of the most important aspects, leadership and communication, are discussed in Chapters 9 and 10.

Critics of the field point out that much of the research on groups is, in fact, about individuals in the group, not about the collective entity. The egocentric bias, which is said to be culturally based, makes it difficult to see and to understand group phenomena. Theories of personality vary markedly, however, in the extent to which they consider group determinants in the development of individual personalities. Theorists congenial to a sociocentric or group orientation are identified as part of the approach to this topic in Chapter 11.

Chaper 12 looks at the transient nature of our society, the current speed of change within society and its constituent groups. Accelerated changes in group norms, roles, and values dramatize the need for a better understanding of group processes.

CHAPTER 9

Leadership and Group-Process Laboratories

There is great variation in the way learning groups conduct their activities, in their goals and objectives, and in leader behavior. Such groups are called by various names. T-group, encounter group, sensitivity training group, group process group, human relations group, and human interaction group are most common, but new terms are invented from time to time.

Despite this variety, a core of activities and leader functions remains basic to most groups. In the Stanford study of group experience (Lieberman, Yalom, & Miles, 1973), nine different group technologies represented by 16 different leaders were observed. Leader behavior was measured and analyzed. The data fell into four categories:

Caring: The leader offers support, affection, praise, warmth, genuineness, and acceptance.

Meaning attribution: The leader clarifies, interprets, or explains what is happening in the group and among the members.

Emotional stimulation: The leader initiates activities that emphasize confrontation, releasing feelings, challenging, and taking risks.

Executive function: The emphasis here was on "management of the group as a social system" (p. 239). Actions include setting limits, suggesting rules, procedures, stopping, questioning, and pacing. Typically, the group is asked to explain what the actions mean.

After detailed analyses of the data concerning encounter groups and who learns what and how leaders lead, the researchers faced many inconsistencies and contradictions. The way a group leader carried out leadership functions was not necessarily the same as that espoused by the leader. Nor did other leaders who claimed the same theoretical orientation perform in that way. The researchers speculated that they may have "erred" in looking at these groups as if their major function were to induce changes in personality: "Perhaps there is a much simpler need that encounter groups are engineered to provide efficiently and effectively — that of momentary relief from alienation which some have called the most prevalent illness of our times" (p. 452).

The authors suggest that it is too much to ask of encounter groups that they make up for or repair the shortcomings and miseries of modern life. Still, they note that the "affirmation of self through the overt (rather than as in normal life, covert) comparisons with peers does provide a new dimension to ordinary human experience" (p. 454). "To experience feelings, to express feelings and to [be] *able to talk about* such feelings is a basic process for enhancing human potential" (p. 454).

The study did compel the researchers to wonder whether something went wrong. It seemed to them that *some* leaders grossly distorted and exaggerated group procedures. Operating on the notion that if some candor and frankness were good then wholesale stripping and disclosure were even better, a few misguided leaders simply went too far in their methods. Instead of participating with group members in the shaping of a context for learning, the "omniscient gurus" took over control and direction to encourage dramatic interventions aimed at instant insight and radical personality changes. The study makes a plea for moderation. My grandmother would have pointed out that "if a pinch of salt is good, a handful is not necessarily better." Experience-based learning groups can be valuable and constructive, *if* magical and unrealistic expectations on the part of both providers and seekers of training are identified and then scaled down to more reasonable expectations. Meanwhile, research continues on the study of leadership and other forms of interpersonal influence, for on matters of relationships, their growth and repair, we are all learners with vested interests.

Structure and Communication Channels

In a series of experiments initiated by Bavelas (1948) and pursued later by Leavitt (1951), Shaw (1981), and others, leadership was studied in relation to the structural arrangement of persons and channels open for communication.

Each group was given a task involving the distribution and sharing of information through a particular physical arrangement. The four most common shapes were the circle, the wheel, the chain, and the Y-shaped chain (see Figure 9.1). Many different patterns, mainly variations on these four shapes, were tried. Working under different structural

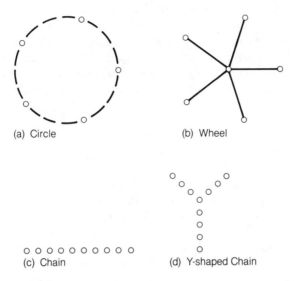

Figure 9.1
Networks for distributing and sharing information in groups.

conditions produces different effects on the work and on the persons involved.

The circle network, for example, has partitions through which members can pass messages to others, one on either side. No one person has greater access than any other person. This equal access to information results in each member's being cited as leader with equal frequency. And because the greater the access to information, the greater the satisfaction with the work, the leaderless circle group had higher morale than the more tightly knit wheel group, where the person at the center is perceived as the leader and controls all information exchange.

In the wheel arrangement, the person at the hub was most frequently seen as leader. She controlled more of the information flow because of the structure of communication channels. Structure was more important than personality variables. Similarly, the person at the fork of the Y-shaped chain was more often perceived as leader than were people in other positions.

Where structure afforded equal control over information flow, as in the circle, no one was seen as leader with greater frequency than the others. In the chain arrangement, people at the center had relatively more influence than people at the end of the chain. There was, however, less agreement about who was group leader in the chain compared to the wheel or Y, but more agreement in the chain than in the circle.

Differences in complexity of problems significantly affect the efficiency of the different arrangements. Centralized networks function best in handling simple problems, but decentralized structures work better and yield greater satisfaction when dealing with complex problems (Shaw, 1981, p. 144).

Leadership

One of the most important questions of group life concerns the meaning of leadership. In the words of Freud (1922, p. 65), "It is impossible to grasp the nature of a group if the leader is disregarded." The special influence exerted by one individual over others has fascinated and puzzled people throughout history. In the small face-to-face group, leadership has been studied in natural and in experimental settings and is invariably related to issues such as the power to reward and punish, the physical and organizational setting, the kind of problems or work confronting the group, the knowledge and special skills of members, and personality variables in the leader and in the followers. Leadership has been explored with reference to the cultural and historical conditions in which the total situation is embedded (Weber, 1970), communication or the means by which influence is expressed, overt and covert aspects of leader-follower behavior, and the psychogenesis of leadership within the family (Freud, 1922). Other studies focus on special problems in hierarchical organizations (Bass & Barrett, 1981; Fiedler, 1967; Lawrence & Lorsch, 1967), leaderless groups, distributed leadership, consensus and morale, autocratic, democratic, and laissez-faire leadership, and training for leadership (see Luft, 1969, for a leadership typology drawn from anthropology).

In a laboratory on group dynamics, where heterogeneous groups begin to function in an unstructured setting, problems of leadership invariably arise. It remains a significant issue throughout the life of the group, but particularly in the opening phases when the nominal leader clearly indicates that he or she will not assume the traditional leader role. Group members may experience considerable frustration when their reasonable expectations are not met. They soon find, however, that they can function when thrown on their own resources, and they are able, in addition, to experience and to observe leadership phenomena emerge. Soon the situation with respect to power and leadership becomes sufficiently stabilized so that members find they can work quite adequately and at the same time increase their understanding of leadership behavior.

This understanding would not be so easy to gain in a structured group with an assertive leader.

By giving attention to the leadership processes at appropriate times, group members are assisted in their understanding of these behaviors and ideas while they are actually involved in decision-making activities. As Lewin, Lippitt, and White (1939, p. 289) point out: "Recent experiments have shown that the training of leaders is to a high degree dependent upon the sensitizing of their social perception. The good leader is able and ready to perceive more subtle changes in social atmosphere and is more correct in observing social meaning."

Interpersonal Influence and the Management of Impressions

How one is led or influenced by others is affected by how one manages the impression she or he makes on others. According to Strauss (1977), Goffman (1967), and Stone (1962), each person invests considerable attention, practice, energy, and time, to say nothing of money, in learning to manage the impression made on others. And yet one is never quite certain how successfully one impresses others — along the line of his or her intentions. So one watches for clues as to how in fact the other does perceive him or her.

Even by appearance alone "a person *announces* his identity, *shows* its value, *expresses* his mood or *proposes* his attitude" (Stone, 1962, p. 101). Again the writers emphasize that self-management activities are not necessarily conscious, just as the assessment of others may not be done consciously.

Misuse of Authority

Although authority may be seen as an essential aspect of leadership and of social organization, its abuse can seriously disturb interpersonal relations. A dozen sample behaviors showing corrosion by authority are summarized below:

> *Sets up barriers:* The person with authority begins to wall himself or herself off from others more than is necessary, using secretaries, special offices, red tape, or other means.

> *Uses people as tools:* The person with authority relates to others as if they were instruments to be used in carrying out his or her will. Such behavior is impersonal and dehumanizing.

> *Does not check self:* The person acts arbitrarily and sees no need for checking because of feelings that he or she can do no wrong. The

Groups and Interpersonal Influences

validity of his or her behavior seems self-evident, and hence the person does not solicit the advice of others.

Sticks to his or her own level: The person with authority relates to others in terms of their position in the hierarchy, glorifying the elite and condescending to subordinates.

Uses special language: The person uses words, abbreviations, and labels in special ways, as in jargon or slang. He or she talks around a point.

Eliminates opposition: The person with authority does not tolerate serious disagreement. He or she demolishes or overwhelms a dissenter, with no long-range working out of differences.

Shows pseudohumility: The person is patronizing and sweet at one time and indifferent at other times.

Stresses rules and conformity: The person insists on an ever-growing body of rules and regulations, emphasizes conventional ways and conformity, and tends to avoid the risks of change.

Dichotomizes: The person considers things right or wrong, good or bad. He or she is intolerant of ambiguity.

Enjoys no real relationships with subordinates: The person selects women and men who will not rock the boat. He or she prefers adulation and seeks out sycophants.

Gets tough when anxious: The person calls for hard work, cracks down, uses power as a convenient way to deny anxieties, and buries self in work, though he or she is not genuinely productive.

Is anti-introspective: The person denies the softer side of self, that is, emotions in general and feelings such as tenderness and passivity. He or she also denies processes like defensiveness and conflict with self.

In Summary

The search for special characteristics in the personality of the leader has failed to yield convincing results. This applies as much to intelligence as to the so-called charismatic or magical quality of the leader. "The variety of traits which a leader may have is the same as that of any other group member except that the leader is usually found to have a higher rating on each 'good' trait" (Hare, 1976, p. 278). According to empirical findings, the correlations between leadership and selected (that is, "good") traits are positive but usually not very large. Sources of leadership behavior, then, must be traced elsewhere: followers, context, kind of problems, cultural variables.

Situational and organizational factors, such as the assignment of authority and the power to reward and to punish, are needed to ascertain the meaning and focus of leadership. But an important variable seems to be the ability to sense, to be aware of, what is going on in oneself as well as what is happening in the group or organization. Skill and competence to contribute to the task of the group and to the emotional processes appear to be significant qualities as well. These qualities may be distributed among different individuals in the group. There is growing interest in studying the distribution of leadership functions among the members of the group. Leaders are also followers, listeners, learners.

Qualities in followers may influence the choice of leadership. More authoritarian members may demand strong direction by one person, while more egalitarian members are apt to value leaders responsive to individual and group feelings (Fiedler, 1967; Tannenbaum & Schmidt, 1962). Authoritarian and egalitarian leaders are seen along a continuum by some writers. They suggest that it is possible to choose a leadership pattern by assessing accurately what the organizational situation requires and under what direction and freedom the individuals can best work (Argyris, 1975; Green, 1975; Likert & Likert, 1976; Schmidt & Tannenbaum, 1976).

The leader's role may even include serving as the scapegoat of the group (for a discussion of projections by members, see the section on transference in Chapter 15). One way of identifying leadership, consistent with field theory, is the idea that a member is a leader "whose pertinent frame of reference another person or group attempts to assume" (Rodgers, n.d.).

In the pioneer study on leadership in different experimental group atmospheres, Lewin, Lippitt, and White (1939) found that autocratic and laissez-faire groups were not as original in their work as democratic groups because there was more dependence and less individuality in autocratic groups. Nor was autocracy more efficient than democracy. Under democratic leaders there was more friendliness and group-mindedness. Under autocratic leaders, there was more overt and covert hostility and aggression, including aggression against scapegoats. Although this study was carried out in a midwestern American community with 10-year-old boys and the atmospheres were simulated autocracy, democracy, and laissez-faire, the results are sufficiently consistent with other knowledge of groups to encourage further speculation and experimentation.

Leadership in Organizations

Small-group leadership has some similarities with leadership in organizations, but there are also important differences. Both kinds of settings demand appreciation of task functions and social-emotional needs. In other words, both group leadership and organizational leadership require cognitive and affective skills.

The leader in an organization is, however, more strongly affected by problems and challenges related to organizational structure. Katz and Kahn (1978, p. 539) summarized the skills and abilities of leaders at different levels of a typical organization. Although knowledge and skill in dealing with people and showing consideration is needed at all levels, it is clear that middle management carries the heaviest responsibility with respect to human relations skills. The skills are affective, meaning that the leader must be able to give support and engage in appropriate interpersonal relations based on feelings, as a caring human being and not merely as a machine or part of the organizational structure.

According to empirical studies by Mann (1975), Fiedler (1967), and Katz and Kahn (1978), affective skills in the leader are related to significant influences on worker motivation and commitment, and these in turn determine to a large extent the degree of satisfaction and productivity per person. See Figure 9.2 for different leadership skills at various levels of management.

But human relations skills, though necessary, are not sufficient at any of the leadership levels. Both technical skill and insight into organizational structure at the relevant hierarchical level are important (Mann, 1975; see especially, Vogel, 1981, pp. 21-23).

At the top echelons, the leadership process calls for a perspective on the system as a whole, with special attention to the internal structure and the pertinent environmental variables. Although top organizational leaders may have access to expert information from all levels, it is only at the head of the organization that a view of the whole can be synthesized. No one else but the top-level leaders have access to the information, perspectives, and resources that enable them to visualize the functioning of the different parts and levels of the organization in relation to the purpose and overall objectives. Hence conceptual ability or skill in handling ideas is vital at upper levels of management. It follows, too, that only from this perspective can major structural changes be conceived and intitiated for the subordination of structure to the current mission and objectives of the organization. Gaining and implementing the changes are, of course, also important. But seeing the need for structural change, recognizing its timeliness, doing away with unneeded structure, and

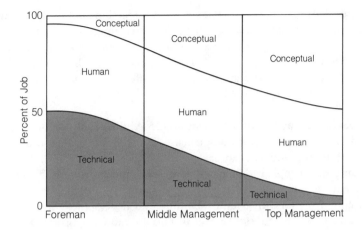

Figure 9.2
Leadership skills at different levels of management. *From* Human Behavior at Work: Organizational Behavior, *6th ed. (p. 103), by Keith Davis, 1981, New York: McGraw-Hill.*

inventing new and useful structure—these are the indispensable leader processes at the top. What makes this function so special is that, because no one else has the top vantage point, it is possible for a mediocre or poor leader to fail to see the need for structural change or to fail to make the changes and to muddle along free of blame. It might be a long while before low productivity and employee dissatisfaction alert others either in or outside the organization to the failure at the top. As Katz and Kahn (1978, p. 544) conclude: "The inability to alter and originate structure is perhaps an inconspicuous disease of leadership. . . . [I]n the long run the disease is absolutely and certainly fatal to organizations."

Intermediate Level of Leadership

Mid-level leadership also calls for a perspective on organizational structure within a larger system frame. Facing superiors above who give general directives and subordinates below on whose cooperation one must depend can be difficult and stressful. At this level, the leader or manager must recognize how much freedom is still available to fill out or modify the structure in which that person is working. Top management would not lock in the middle-range manager and deprive him or her of operational choice. How this opportunity to shape or adapt parts of the structural arrangement is used determines leadership quality. Modifying subordinates' roles, changing job descriptions, upgrading unit responsibilities, eliminating or adding positions are some ways of filling out structure within the purview of middle management. Because the lives and careers of workers can be drastically affected, the need for human relations skills becomes obvious.

Levels of Management and Leadership Abilities

Leadership in any organization consists of the ability to deal with technical, human, and conceptual problems (see Davis, 1981). Skill in working with people is demanded at *all levels* of management. Top management must be able to deal with ideas, opinions, and theories, that is, conceptual matters, in overall planning and development in line with organizational objectives. Technical skills are more important at supervisory levels. Middle management uses all three areas of leadership skills in about equal proportion (see Figure 9.2).

In addition, the leader at the middle level can tap the technical and procedural skills of those he or she supervises, as well as the knowledge and perspective of those immediately above, to help guide in piecing together the needed structures and to suggest better ways of doing things. Without good interpersonal relations, however, the middle leader's job could become even more difficult and stressful. Leaders at the intermediate level have the power, within a designated range of the system, to stagnate with poorly motivated employees or to create a cooperative, productive atmosphere.

Leadership Training

Perennial interest in improving leadership is reflected in the number and variety of publications that have appeared especially in the last half century (Hare, 1971, p. 293). It is not surprising to learn that most of these efforts have failed, for it is only in recent years that investigators have begun to learn how complex a topic leadership is.

At minimum, leadership training requires that one take into account the context or social setting in which the leader functions. Where, in the organizational structure, does he or she work? Then some understanding of the overall objectives and the requisite technical information is needed. One needs to know, as well, the personal qualities of followers or subordinates and the social-emotional maintenance needs of subordinates, taken as a group. And in terms of the work involved, the social and physical environment within which the leader and the group function is important, along with an idea of the characteristics of tasks, degree of routine, and amount of specialization. It is important to recognize the stage of development and morale of the group and of the organization within which the group may be working.

The history and traditions of various subgroups — crafts or professions, unions or guilds, or associations — represented must be taken into consideration, along with the rate of change going on within the organization, the group, and the larger environment.

It is clear that these variables must be weighed if one is to understand the scope of the leadership-training problem. Then there must be an understanding of what is meant by training or learning. Learning theory is grounded in contemporary psychology, but between theory and practice, as these are applied to particular persons and settings, there is a sizable gap. Numerous attempts have been made to combine suggestions from the behavioral sciences and from personnel practices into a variety of designs for training people who work with people. Here, too, research into the claims and promises of training programs has only recently begun to provide a coherent picture.

In practice, leadership training and organizational development are closely related and constitute parts of one overall process. Although these large topics go beyond the scope of this book, it is well to recognize the centrality of group processes.

Special programs, courses, institutes, and laboratories can serve useful purposes. But in the long run the growth and development of an organization and its people is the responsibility of all parties involved, especially managers, supervisors, executives, and others in key roles in the hierarchy. A training program can be said to be successful to the extent that it becomes an integral part of the ongoing life of the organization. With the increasing tempo of change in all phases of modern organizational life, there is no alternative to some form of continuing training and learning. For better or worse, we are all apprentices, teachers, and journeymen; learning how to learn is the underlying challenge.

Group Process: Instrument of Change

When leadership is seen as a particular kind of influence process, we can appreciate the interest in the use of face-to-face groups for leadership training.

Here, too, initial enthusiasm for the small-group (or T-group) training methods has subsided somewhat. Small-group methods vary tremendously in what, how, and by whom the work is done and with what rationale. Blanket endorsement, like blanket criticism, of such training procedures is not warranted by the accumulating evidence. Hence it will be necessary to look at group process methods for leadership training from the point of view of empirical research and of practitioner experience. In addition to a survey of practice and research, special attention should be given to newer methods (Argyris, 1975) and emerging trends (Cooper, 1975; Gibbard et al., 1974; Hare, 1962; Katz & Kahn, 1978; Smith, 1975; Zander, 1979), in applied behavioral science. See also Faucheux, Amado, & Laurent (1982).

CHAPTER 10

Communication

Communication is basic to group development, which would suggest that the more open and unrestricted the communication, the better. This, alas, is a gross oversimplification. Instead of illuminating group or organizational issues, communication can also confuse issues and muddle problems. Some increase in communication may help deal with group or organizational problems, but it may also reveal deep-seated underlying differences in values and attitudes. In order to become more effective as well as more satisfying, groups and organizations may need to limit communication by selective constraints. Both knowledge and sensitivity are required to create appropriate structure so that communication is channeled, and limited or augmented, to meet relevant social-emotional and task needs.

Psyche and Task Group Processes

There are two basic communication functions in small-group interaction: task communication and psyche communication (Coffey, 1952; Littlejohn, 1978). Task communication concerns itself with the information and ideas bearing on the work to be done. Energy is directed toward and focused on task problems, on assembling relevant information, on making decisions. The activity is primarily cognitive. Task communication tends to be rational, logical, and linear, and it relies on group or organizational structure and rules to help maintain focus. It is desirable to have constraints on task efforts in order to expedite the work. It takes knowledge and intelligence to create appropriate structure — for example, division of labor, suitable roles, sensible rules, and useful procedures. These constraints help to free the members of the group and help them to get on with their work. It is necessary, however, for participants to keep task structure in good repair. Whenever people work together, some facet of structure may not function well. Constraint, though generally useful in a working group, may be out of phase with participants' feelings or attitudes, and psyche processes then interfere with, instead of being integral to and supportive of, work efforts.

Psyche communication refers to feelings and attitudes of people who are interacting, to how people relate to one another. It is emotional and apt to be less rational (or even nonrational) and less logical. Feelings tend to come in wholes, and they are less predictable and very often ambivalent or inconsistent. This type of communication is more difficult to manage and may prove to be highly idiosyncratic.

Although the nominal leader may serve both task and maintenance functions, that person is ordinarily preoccupied with task efforts. Who, then, is in charge of psyche functions? Someone else in the group may recognize the need to call attention to the psyche processes. If one person or a subset of persons is particularly attuned to this aspect of group life, the person (or subgroup) is identified as a leader of the maintenance function.

And how does a group work on psyche processes? First, different ground rules apply. Participants are encouraged to express their feelings, usually the ones that are restrained while the task rules are in operation, especially negative feelings, dysphoric moods of boredom and frustration, and disturbed attitudes.

The psyche process may consist of a brief interlude in the group's work, or it may be of a recurrent, episodic nature. This depends on the aims and focal themes of the group and the personalities of the members. In certain groups — family, friends, and social and therapy groups — the primary activity is the psyche process, but the socio- or task processes are primary in other groups. In business, industrial, professional, classroom, and service groups, people join together to produce, to give service, to earn a living, to make a profit, or to learn. *Psyche processes are present in all of the interactions involved*, but they are supplementary to the principal work mentioned.

In a work group or class group it is sometimes difficult if not impossible for psyche processes to be expressed. As a result, they spill out indirectly, or they may be misplaced, or they may immobilize a member or the group itself. Some members may tie up their feelings, bring them home, and share them out of context with family or friends. It is equally true, of course, that feelings generated at home or among friends can remain unresolved and carry over to the job site. Emotions may be aroused during work or class that have very little to do with the event at hand. Feelings of competitiveness or hostility may be aroused. Participants may suddenly become upset or embarrassed or fearful and then withdraw from active and constructive work. It is not easy to understand what is happening, and what is more important, it may be counterproductive to guess or to try to diagnose what is going on. There may, on the other hand, be value in encouraging the expression of feelings and in supporting persons who are holding back defensively. Now the emphasis is on the *subjective*, on what is going on here and now, not on what one thinks but on what one feels. Task efforts may concern the past or the future, and they could involve people and groups not present. On the other hand, psyche processes dwell on what is now existing, with the ongoing situation and with people and events in the present. Also, to express oneself *spontaneously* is characteristic of the way psyche processes unfold — in contrast to the more careful deliberation of task activity.

The social-emotional *climate* may be crucial to enabling group members to be more open with one another. The climate consists of degrees of tension and harmony (Lieberman, Yalom, & Miles, 1973) that determine the psychological safety felt within the group. A supportive climate is one in which participants might be more willing to risk self-disclosure. In other words, sanctions, criticism, or other punishments by the group, its leader, or individual members will not be imposed for expressing feelings. In fact, if leadership is at all enlightened, the psyche process will be encouraged because it is seen as a natural concomitant of human effort and as necessary for sustaining participant motivation and commitment.

The psyche process is important to the group as a system because it is part of a natural *feedback* function. As mentioned above, feedback is communication back to the individual (or the group) about the course the person (or the group) is taking.

During the psyche phase, it is particularly important to let the person know he or she is being listened to and being heard. Usually, one can tell if others are attentive, but if a person is upset or preoccupied, it is a good idea to be a bit more specific about the fact that he or she is being heard with appreciation. Offering attention, taking the person into account, is an indispensable support to a troubled group member. That member needs at least some minimal personal reaction to help him or her in self-guiding what is being expressed. Then if others also express themselves, the person feels supported and is encouraged to continue the process more freely.

But even in psyche or maintenance work there are some limits. It is hardly necessary for the group to invoke constraints during this time because constraints or inhibitions are built into one's personality as a function of individual development. According to Georg von Békésy, Nobel prize recipient in medicine and physiology, "sensory inhibition is as important as sensory excitation, in filtering information, to prevent overload and permit adaptive responding" (1973, p. 128).

People, like groups, tend to regulate themselves, and this holds true for maintenance function. Having exchanged feelings and repaired interpersonal relations, the group as a whole may gain new energy as well as new information about its work and its collaborative efforts. Psyche pro-

cesses may enhance group feelings of cohesiveness and deepen appreciation of each member's individuality. Afterward, the group may take pride
in its work (task) efforts that were not feasible before the maintenance
process had time to unfold.

Metacommunication Theory

A point of view now emerging in the study of human interaction and
group processes focuses on ideas and concepts about communication,
which is viewed as dealing with any behavior, verbal or nonverbal, that
may affect another. "Metacommunication" is still in its infancy as a
science, yet its impact is already being felt in various social and physical
sciences. In its concern with the lawfulness of communication patterns, it
breaks with current psychodynamic and behaviorist traditions.

Each of us knows a great deal about communication that we do not
know we know, in the same way that we know how to speak our native
language with skill and fluency without necessarily knowing the basic
grammar. Metacommunication is essentially a search for the underlying
rules governing interaction. The intention is to break through some of
the reifications and conceptual biases that have grown in contemporary
social science.

Ideas used in metacommunication theory have come from many disci-
plines over the last two decades, but most originate in feedback theory or
cybernetics, in particular, and from systems theory, in general. The word
cybernetics was invented by Norbert Wiener (1954). It comes from the
Greek word *kubernetes*, meaning "steersman." Watzlawick, Beavin, and
Jackson (1967), along with systems theorists Ashby and Bertalanffy (see
Buckley, 1967), have worked in this area. The reader is referred to
Watzlawick (1977) for a more recent account of their work.

To provide some sense of the range and significance of metacommunication theory, it is contrasted here with prevailing ideas of psychodynamic psychology. The brevity of the following list exaggerates the
differences, and this is done intentionally, for purposes of clarification:

Psychodynamic Theory	*Communication (Feedback) Theory*
Group consists of the psychodynamics of its members	Group is a self-regulating system
Key concept is energy	Key concept is information
Basic dynamics are intrapsychic	Organism interacts with environment

Search for personality dynamics	Search for interaction system
Search for cause-effect relations	Search for feedback patterns
Search for linear reactions	Search for circular loops
Based on determinism (Freud) and vitalism (Jung)	Based on pragmatism
Study monadic phenomena	Study dyadic phenomena: groups, larger systems
Study the unconscious	Search for interaction rules rather than degrees of awareness
Study the past history of individual	Study the present
Study utility and survival functions	Study exploration, creativity, and play
Search for symbolic meaning	Search for present patterns of interaction
Search for discharge of tensions and for need gratifications	Search for spontaneous activity
Symptom is outcome of unresolved intrapsychic conflict	Symptom is constraint or rule of interaction
Ask "Why?" regarding behavior	Ask "What for?" regarding behavior
Search for stable qualities and states	Search for repeating patterns of communication
It is possible to not communicate	It is not possible to not communicate
There are chains of behavior with beginning and end	There is no beginning or end, only feedback patterns
Abnormality and insanity refer to syndromes	Abnormality and insanity are terms of doubtful value
Patient's condition is a function of inner attributes	Patient's condition is a function of context and observer's bias
Pathologies are in individuals	Pathologies are in interaction
Study closed system; individual best described in terms of intrapsychic dynamics	Study open systems; individual best described as person-in-communication-with-others
Study variables one at a time	Study ensemble of variables

Structure and process are different things in personality as well as in society	Structure and process are part of the same holistic phenomenon (morphogenesis)
Individual and environment are separate entities	Environment and other parts of interaction system may be divided into subsystems, but the division is arbitrary
Factors in research can be varied one at a time	Systems are wholes and are not amenable to study by varying one factor at a time

Content and Relationship in Communication

According to metacommunication theory, any communication conveys both content and information as to how the content is to be taken. How the content is to be taken is strongly influenced by the relationship of the people who are communicating. A stranger who asks, "Do you have a dime?" means something quite different from a spouse who asks, "Do you have a dime?"

Sometimes the relationship can be undestood only through the context in which communication takes place. The simple question, "What is your name?" may mean one thing in a courtroom and another thing at a party. And the same message may mean something vastly different when a third person joins a dyad.

Watzlawick, Beavin, and Jackson (1967) point out that the relationship part of communication is rarely defined or well understood by the persons involved. In a group process laboratory, the relationship part of communication receives much more attention, particularly when difficulties develop within the group.

Verbal and Nonverbal Communication

Taking biological processes as a model, Watzlawick and his colleagues use the all-or-none function of the neuron and the discrete chemical substance of the humoral system to identify two basic kinds of physiological communication systems. The neuron either fires, or it does not fire. Thus it conveys yes-no, digital information. The humoral system functions in terms of the amount of a specific substance in the bloodstream. *Digital* computers use the all-or-none principle to register information with electronic equipment. A digital computer program is abstract and arbitrary and can refer to anything that can be arranged as yes-no bits of information. Similarly, words are abstract and are used according to a particular order in language, essentially a conventional arrangement.

Analogic messages, in contrast, are conveyed by nonverbal behavior, such as body movement and posture; voice tones, rhythms, and inflections; and gestures and other expressions, particularly of the human face. Edward Sapir (in Brown & Keller, 1979, p. 156) expresses this idea differently: "Nonverbal behavior is . . . an elaborate code that is written nowhere, known by none, and understood by all." Nonverbal patterns, because they are more deeply rooted in the evolution of the human race and in the history of the individual, are much more difficult to measure. There are, however, analog computers that operate according to specific amounts or magnitudes, as do pressure gauges and thermostats. The context, that is, the social and physical environment, also conveys analogic communication. Although the context tends to be taken for granted because it seems to be rather obvious, contextual cues do constitute critical aspects of communication systems, and it would be a mistake to overlook this source of information.

Interpersonal communication takes place digitally and analogically (verbally and nonverbally) simultaneously. Verbal language is well adapted to the content part of communication, but it is far less adequate for the relationship aspect. Nonverbal language conveys relationship information more adequately, but it is less precise in defining the content of the relationship. Translation between these two languages is necessary but very difficult. Information may be lost or distorted, and curious inconsistencies can develop in relationships.

Symmetrical and Complementary Patterns of Communication
In symmetrical patterns of communication, each person mirrors the behavior of the other. For example: If I am docile, you are docile. If I assert, you assert.

In complementary patterns, each person's behavior complements the behavior of the other. For example: If I am assertive, you are compliant. If I am compliant, you are assertive. Complementary behavior is not to be considered right or wrong, good or bad, strong or weak. The interactions form an interpersonal Gestalt, and their fitting together may be according to a social pattern such as mother-child or employer-employee relationship. Or the interactions may develop simply as a unique relationship of a complementary nature.

Disturbances in communication may be noted, however, if complementary interchanges become rigid and fixed or if symmetrical patterns escalate too rapidly. An example of escalation is a dispute during a committee meeting on parking arrangements that turns into an argument and then a fistfight.

Disturbed Communication
Survival depends on adequate communication, and the development of uniquely human qualities requires patterns of communication in which

the individual's conception of self is accepted and confirmed. In literature, religion, the arts, and folk wisdom through the ages, people have known this intuitively. Recent research into sensory deprivation supports this idea, just as many studies of normal individuals and schizophrenics do. Again see the work of Watzlawick, Beavin, and Jackson (1967) as well as that of Laing (1961), Rogers (1970), Buber (1957), and Erikson (1959). Awareness of self and others is impossible without adequate communication. Much everyday activity may be understood as part of a process in which people struggle to define and redefine themselves. The all-important defining behavior can only occur in developing relationships through a feedback process in communication.

The power to confirm or accept another's self-conception is matched by the capacity to reject it. Such rejection, though it may prove unpleasant and even painful, nevertheless recognizes the individual, provided that dialogue is sustained. Change in the relationship may occur in the face of such rejection, and along with this change there may be some new learning about self. It is doubtful if any new learning about self could occur if the other person were not sufficiently accepting. The process of rejecting, continuing dialogue, and learning is complicated by disturbances in the communication process and by limitations in the self-awareness of the partners in a dyad or of members in a group.

Disconfirmation

Watzlawick, Beavin, and Jackson (1967) concur with Laing (1961) on the significance of disconfirmation for pathological communication. The individual in a relationship is disconfirmed when he is treated as if he did not exist, as if behavior and feelings were stripped of their meaning, their intention, and their consequences. The self-definition is systematically invalidated. The process can be subtle and sustained, with mystifying as well as devastating effects on one or both partners in communication. Such patterns are usually characterized by partners with limited self-awareness, and the patterns follow repetitiously over time in vicious circles (Watzlawick, Beavin & Jackson, pp. 95, 238). There is not much hope for change unless the participants become able to communicate about their communication, that is, to metacommunicate. Yet it is apparent that lifting themselves out of the frame of reference is extremely difficult. Each considers his or her view of reality as the only possible one, when each in fact has created his or her own reality with limited information and partial awareness. This is not to say that "insight" is necessary before change can occur. Actually most changes occur without insight or before insight.

Any experiences that enable a person to learn more about his or her own patterns of interaction could be useful. Feedback processes in a context that sustains the relationship would inevitably play an important part in developing change.

Developments in Metacommunication Theory

Proponents of metacommunication theory hope to achieve significant breakthroughs in behavioral science. The theory, broadly taken, is in some respects discontinuous with prevailing theories, although it does not purport to reject or invalidate earlier knowledge. The hope is that it may serve to reorganize what is currently known about interpersonal phenomena and group processes into a larger and more coherent whole. The emphasis on organization and on wholeness properties is consistent with Gestalt psychology and field theory.

Metacommunication theory discusses feelings in particular ways, for instance, as part of the communication process rather than as intrapersonal states. The theory does not deny living subjective experiences. It simply assumes that feelings enter all messages and are crucial to an appreciation of interaction rules underlying relationship systems. As feelings are expressed in communication, they become available for consideration, and inferences about a system of interaction may be made from them.

Another important property of the theory is its research orientation. Many important psychological and social issues have simply not been amenable to past methodologies that focused on research designs that manipulate one variable at a time, on questionnaires and the like. In clinical psychology and psychiatry, the efforts devoted to uncovering unconscious determinants using ingenious psychodiagnostic devices have not lived up to expectation. Metacommunication theory attempts to invoke the attitudes of post-Einsteinian relativism and indeterminacy, as expressed by such contemporary psychologists as Koch (1981), Maslow (1966), Coan (1968), and Watzlawick, Beavin, and Jackson (1967). Systems theory research dwells less on precision of instruments and statistical rigor and more on observation and the search for the way things are interconnected. In short, it lends itself to the subject matter and the problems of group processes.

Groups and Cybernetics

Cybernetics is a young but promising discipline, particularly for group psychology. Cybernetics deals with relations between means and ends, with regulatory functions, and with the acquisition and transmission of information in general (Piaget, 1979). Hence all biological and psychological processes might be viewed as modulated by principles of cybernetic functioning.

A familiar example of cybernetic self-regulation is the thermostat. Small-group processes contain many self-regulated patterns of interaction. The kind and number of group interactions appear to be governed by self-regulated patterns related to a group's short-range and long-range goals.

However, groups are also involved with the regulation of regulations. Resetting the thermostat, for example, might change the range of function, but the resetting process itself might follow a different pattern, such as the social needs of the people doing the resetting. In group functioning, the pattern of regulation may be changed by the group itself, either as a function of learning or by group development.

Example: A group consisting of subgroups was involved in a struggle for control. Action by members of one subgroup were blocked systematically by members of the other subgroup. Much of the polite fighting was outside the awareness of group members. The discussion leader encouraged members to express their feelings about what was happening. Feedback to the group about its own behavior helped the group become aware of the underlying conflict and move toward resolving the struggle. New alignments and interaction patterns began to emerge.

Cybernetic Hierarchy

Systems are influenced and controlled by information. As Hare (1962, p. 15) has indicated, "a unit containing information will be able to control a unit containing raw energy." The body energy is controlled by the personality, which in turn is regulated by social patterns and by culture. In a group, the specific behavior or action (energy) of a group is controlled by that aspect of a group concerned with the maintenance of pattern. If, for instance, a group member breaks a rule regarding norms about speaking, responding, seating, or movement, others in the group will attempt to reassert the "correct" pattern. The latter, those concerned with maintaining certain established ways, will in turn be controlled by social or cultural norms and patterns. In general, subsystems at each level in the hierarchy of systems are controlled by those who have the information and knowledge of how the system works. Just as a computer processes information and, hence, may control a series of manufacturing operations, further up the hierarchy the subgroups that design the software and program the computers control the computers and their operations.

CHAPTER 11

Individualism as Reductionism: The Search for a Group-Level Paradigm

> We must conclude that the psychology of
> groups is the oldest human psychology; what
> we have isolated as individual psychology, by
> neglecting all traces of the group, has only
> since come into prominence out of the old
> group psychology, by a gradual process
> which may still, perhaps, be described as
> incomplete.
>
> — *Sigmund Freud*

In the very beginning of this book it was stated that one of the major difficulties in understanding groups stems from the overemphasis on individual personality in our culture as well as in contemporary psychology. Donald Campbell (1975), in his presidential address to the American Psychological Association, charged that the egocentric bias permeates the principal theories of behavior across a wide spectrum of studies, including those of Skinner, Freud, Jung, Piaget, and the existentialists. He shows how trends favoring the individual over community (or society) follow broad historical and cultural developments. Bias is reflected in what is valued implicitly and explicitly. In our time this has meant the neglect and loss of social institutions, social customs, and traditions that have profound value for survival. Campbell goes even beyond this. He believes that our theories and research suffer because of the way we approach the subject matter. In Figure 11.1, he offers a balance model to dramatize how we have underemphasized altruism in favor of selfishness.

135

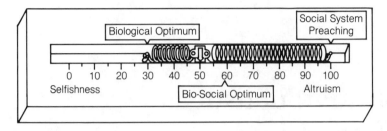

Figure 11.1
Meter illustrating conflicting tensions on a dimension of selfishness-altruism.
From "On the Conflicts Between Biological and Social Evolution and Between Psychology and Moral Tradition" by Donald T. Campbell, 1975, American Psychologist, 30, *p. 1118.*

Note that the biological optimum is not at the extreme selfishness level, based in part on studies of other social vertebrates. The current level of moral behavior is estimated at 50, which is below the biosocial optimum. A little more consideration for others would shift the indicator closer to the optimum for both the individual and for the various social groups that make up our society.

Campbell (1975, p. 1104) states: "Psychology and psychiatry not only describe man as selfishly motivated, but subjectively or explicitly teach that he ought to be so." The meter, above, is being pulled too far to the selfishness side, he argues, without considering the necessary evidence. For Campbell, traditions approving the altruism side of the meter deserve favorable consideration because of their proven value for survival in societies throughout history.

The Skewed View

Individualism as ideology began as a protest against medieval society, according to Robert Hogan (1975). The social ties and customs of the Middle Ages were seen as undesirable restraints, and in his words, the *"remaining structures of shared existence* [italics added] are assaulted as unjust obstacles in the way of liberty, as impediments to the free assertion of the self" (p. 533). Hogan traced historical and psychological developments in what he terms "theoretical egocentrism," identifying four different forms of individualism:

Romantic individualism: associated with the liberal philosophy of Rousseau

Egocentric individualism: associated with the conservative philosophy of Hobbes and of Nietzsche

Ideological individualism: associated with the academic and scholastic tradition and resting on the belief that, in the final analysis, what is valid depends upon "one's personal vision of the truth" (p. 534)

Alienated individualism: associated with the nineteenth-century sociology of Weber, Tönnies, and Durkheim, and characterizing the role of the thoughtful person in an industrialized and bureaucratized world

The responsibility of the intellectual, then, is to repudiate society and its customs, structures, and norms (p. 534). Thus the position of egocentrism asserts that the individual is natural, good, and self-regulating; society and its collective entities are unnatural and altogether suspect.

A prevailing bias stemming from an ideology of individualism is the belief that groups are unnatural, unhealthy, and bad. Such a climate appears to affect students of group behavior who may start inquiry into groups but often end up with observations, data, and ideas about individuals in group settings. The fact that the individualism bias is a strong, implicit group attitude held in collusion by members espousing individualism is worth noting, even if it lacks irony.

Evidence against the individualism bias is compelling, and it comes from a variety of sources. According to anthropologists S. L. Washburn (1962) and E. Mayr (1963), early man lived in small face-to-face groups as hunting bands:

> Thus, human society throughout pre-history consisted of small groups literally struggling for survival, and survival was promoted by the quality of the group rather than the accomplishments of individuals. Specifically, an adaptive advantage was conferred on those groups that developed an efficient social organization defined in terms of leadership structure, division of labor, communication systems, transmission of knowledge, etc. Reasoning of this sort leads to two conclusions: First, culture or social organization rather than brain size was the key to man's evolutionary success; and second, the individualism assumed by many psychologists is probably an inaccurate reflection of man's biological nature. Rather, man seems to have evolved as a group-living, culture-bearing, norm-respecting animal whose survival was closely tied to his social institutions. (Hogan, 1975, p. 537).

Moral development is also seen in social rather than individual or intrapsychic terms. In Durkheim's view, one's moral conduct and psychological health depend upon "acquiring a sense of respect for the rules and values of one's society" (Hogan, 1975, p. 537). Serious personality disorders follow the breakdown of social traditions and institutions, resulting in alienation, anxiety associated with normlessness, and weakening of one's sense of identity.

Children Naturally Seek Social Involvement

Citing a series of studies undertaken at Johns Hopkins University, Hogan (1975) finds empirical support for spontaneous social interaction through the observation of infants in the first year of life. Hogan drew the following conclusions:

1. Children at birth appear to be "preprogrammed" to accept social risks and interaction.
2. Children's behavior, both verbal and nonverbal, shows sensitivity to a concern with one another's motives and behavior.
3. Role repertoires (for example, of family members) are acquired in early childhood. Children find these roles rewarding and intrinsically satisfying and may become upset if role patterns are violated (p. 538).
4. Very young children appear to seek out and value interaction for its own sake. They quickly learn social roles and the rules that accompany interaction. The rules of play, for instance, become so important that some children will not play if the rules are not observed. (This idea is closely linked to habeas emotum, which is discussed in Chapter 12.) Hogan suggests utility value in the reliance on rules because they provide some control and predictability in social interaction.
5. On the basis of many different ethological studies, Bowlby (1969, 1973) claims that human beings are "genetically biased" to avoid being alone or with strangers. He offers documentation to show that stable social relationships *are* natural and help the child overcome fears of isolation and unpredictability.
6. Children do not have to be trained to fit into society. Hogan claims that because the child is naturally sociocentric, the problem is to learn what is done to alienate him (p. 538).
7. The disturbed or alienated individual may be helped by integration into a social or cultural group. Hogan claims that the secret to the success of such groups as Alcoholics Anonymous (and others) lies in getting the person to accept the group standards. To the extent that the group becomes important to the deviant and the deviant believes that in some way his or her own actions are tied to the well-being of the group, the deviant can, and in fact does, make progress.

The issues of socialization and alienation, of individualism and sociocentrism, are large and complex, and they extend beyond the purview of this book. In the field of psychology, the effects of the individualism bias are especially evident in clinical and social psychology. Albert Pepitone (1981, p. 972), who recently surveyed the history of social psychology in the United States, finds a pervasive "individuocentric bias," that is, favoring the individual over the group. "I conclude," says Pepitone, "that theories based on intraindividual processes are inadequate to explain social behavior." When difficulties and problems are attributed to the individual, to intrapsychic life, there is a tendency to ignore the reality of "groupness." Group theory suffers; group practice becomes limited to a narrowing focus on the individual. Theory building in small-group research is all too often theory of individuals within groups.

Kurt Back (1979) insists that group dynamics has changed from being a science to being a profession in the service of helping individuals, and he speculates that the study of groups "is not dead, but perhaps merely asleep" (p.284). He was referring to the surge of group research that followed Lewin's work in the late 1940s and to the recent drift toward individual emphasis. Zander (1979, p. 423) notes that "the theories that do exist, moreover, seldom aid in understanding groups as such, or even the behavior of members in behalf of their groups, because the theories often are based on ideas taken from individual psychology, and these are primarily concerned with the actions of individuals for the good of those individuals."

Difficulty in perceiving and thinking about group-level phenomena may be a function of the complexity of the subject as well as a matter of cultural and intellectual bias. To acknowledge the possibility that overemphasis on the individual constitutes a special kind of obstacle in pursuit of a theory of group behavior may, however, be a step forward.

Person in the Context of Relationships

> Many blind spots of psychoanalysis were the consequence of the fact that Freud himself was never "socioanalyzed" and did not realize the influence of his historical background upon his own theories.
>
> — *Gustav Icheiser*

In the West, the individual is seen as a distinct and separate entity, and the experience "of interpersonal intimacy is precarious or scarce," according to anthropologist Francis L. K. Hsu (1971). To break out of this "intellectual prison," Hsu proposes changes implied in the concepts *psy-*

chosocial homeostasis and *jen*. These terms refer to the individual's ties to other persons, usually kin and close friends, in intimate relationships. It is meaningless to attempt to describe the person without these relationships for they are as important to one's well-being as "food, water and air" (p. 29). The key to understanding psychological soundness, stress, change and stability, and social action is the homeostasis characterizing one's intimate relationships. The Chinese word for *man* or, as Hsu prefers, *personage*, is *jen* (in Japanese, it is *jin*), and it refers to "an individual's transactions with his fellow human beings." In contrast, the Western term *personality*, Hsu continues, "puts the emphasis on what goes on in the individual's psyche."

Rejecting the term *personality* as misleading and inaccurate, Hsu states that the Yiddish word *mensch* comes close to *jen* in meaning. Leo Rosten (1968, p. 234) defines a mensch as "an upright, honorable, decent person . . . someone of consequence, someone to admire and emulate; someone of noble character." The further definition of *mensch*, which Hsu also finds similar to the meaning of *jen*, is "to be a *mensch* has nothing to do with success, wealth, status . . . [it has to do with] a sense of what is right, responsible, decorous. Many a poor man, many an ignorant man, is a *mensch*."

Hsu (1971, p. 42) also notes that concern with individuality is reflected in Western literature and art. Artists in the West are preoccupied with ceaseless probing and "exploring the mind and feelings," and this is "in sharp contrast to their Chinese counterparts." In other words, individuals in the West have been removed from a proper human context. Only occasionally do they experience "illusions of intimacy," but the sense that something is missing haunts them. They turn to literature and the other arts to help them find out who they are and what went wrong.

Hsu believes Westerners will never find themselves by endless inner search. Instead, the anthropologist suggests, it will be necessary to change Western culture so that person-in-relationship will become the true basis for personality—something similar to jen. For students of human behavior in general and of group processes in particular, the idea of relationship as context appears to be significant and challenging, for both the practitioner and the theorist.

The price we pay for overemphasizing egocentrism also shows itself in the way we think about collective behavior. Whether we are attending to dyads, face-to-face groups, or larger communities, we tend to seek explanatory ideas by referring to individual personalities rather than to group characteristics. Individual traits, personal styles, values, habits, intelligence, and everyday kinds of individual psychopathologies are invoked to account for what is happening in groups at home, at work, in schools, and in communities.

Individualism as Reductionism: The Search for a Group-Level Paradigm

In an issue of the *Journal of Applied Behavioral Science* (1979), group researchers and practitioners were criticized for utilizing observations and theories on individual personality to discuss group phenomena. One attempt to study families as entities, rather than as collections of individual personalities, was developed at the Mental Research Institute at Palo Alto, California. Don Jackson (1962) realized that the constraints growing out of cultural bias and out of his own training as a psychoanalyst limited his perspective. Preoccupation with personality affected what he saw and how he thought and made it impossible to deal with family as family or even with married couples as two-person relationships. Paul Watzlawick (1977, p. 23), in a discussion of family rules between married people, claims that "whatever transpires between two such captives — that which is neither clearly "I" nor clearly "Thou" — is a mystery for which we have no language or understanding."

Jackson proposes that relationships consist of arrangements between and among members (couples or families) on a quid pro quo basis. The idea is that, in order to achieve their broadly defined goals, each member will behave in a way that reflects "something for something." Many things must be done on behalf of the couple or family, but the rules governing who does what grow out of the patterning of relationships. A division of labor is generally used to emphasize differences between persons (in the case of couples), but how those differences will be exploited depends on the interaction rules. Typically, rules evolve without awareness and are repeated over and over. The supraindividual entity, the relationship, functions according to these rules and the redundant patterns of interaction. In fact, Jackson defines norms as consisting of rules in use.

An important finding, according to Jackson, was the realization that conventional sex roles had little influence on how the couple interacted within the context of their marriage relationship. Robert Leik (in Jackson, 1962, p. 26) found that, while the couple tend to act out traditional roles with strangers (the man is more task oriented and shows less emotion; the woman is less task oriented and more expressive of feelings), the cultural stereotype patterns do not hold in the context of their families. Jackson warns that rules, not roles, are the key to understanding a particular relationship.

These embryonic theories of Jackson and his colleagues were developed most frequently in the family setting, but they apply equally well to groups in general. Face-to-face groups vary greatly in terms of goals or purpose, composition of membership, and context within which they exist. But the principle of quid pro quo and the patterning of interaction according to underlying rules offer a promising approach to the study of group processes based on a group psychology rather than on individual personality dynamics.

Critique: Self or Others?

Is the individual or the social group more important? Recent debate (*Annual Review of Psychology*, 1982) by philosophers, public officials, and psychologists has reopened an ancient and important controversy: Are we placing too much emphasis, too high a value on the individual? Does society, and the groups of which it is made up, suffer as a consequence? Does a bias exist favoring the individual in building theories of personality and theories of social groups? Which position is more important, more basic?

I believe both positions are important. In fact, I believe that they are inseparable parts of one large question. The study of groups calls for attention to the person, to relationships, and to the group as a whole. The study of an individual must take into account development in a social setting of family, work group, friends, community, and so forth. Focus on the person brings out the perennial tension between independence and interdependence. As the individual matures, the groups to which he or she belongs are more apt to mature. Conversely, as a group grows and develops soundly in terms of both pragmatic and ethical values, so, too, do the group members. The individual who grows toward self-actualization also gains respect for the integrity of others. And as groups mature, they become more sensitive to and respect the integrity of the individual as well as the integrity of the group as a whole. A mature group is also better able to recognize the needs and values of other groups and remains open to influence by others.

In a sense, the question of which is more important or more primary is similar to the nature-nurture controversy, which means that it is philosophically speculative. The implication is that there are more useful and important questions to be raised so that work toward better theory and more effective resolution of problems can continue.

In the history of psychology attention has also shifted from one emphasis to another. At times there is new interest on some aspect of person; at other times new ideas emerge regarding collective human activity. Trends in the social sciences often reflect the large cultural interests. The 1930s and 1940s witnessed great concern for cooperation versus competition in view of the tremendous collective problems raised by economic depression and mobilization for global war. The 1960s and 1970s were preoccupied with "me-ism" or egocentrism, according to some critics. The 1980s seem to be a time of change requiring greater self-awareness and individual development and reorganization within both public and private group activities at a time when society is becoming more interdependent. As Erikson (1964, p. 233) has stated: "Truly worthwhile acts enhance a mutuality between the doer and the other — a mutuality which strengthens the doer even as it strengthens the other."

Ruth Benedict (in Waterman, 1981, p. 771), in describing cultures with high synergy or mutually reinforcing acts, observes:

> Societies where nonaggression is conspicuous have social orders in which the individual by the same act and at the same time serves his own advantage and that of the group. . . . Nonaggression occurs (in these societies) not because people are unselfish and put social obligations above personal desires, but when social arrangements make these two identical.

Whether we can combine both interests (individual and group) in an ethically just society is the challenge of our time.

Covert Rules of Interaction

The difficulties involved in seeing relationships as relationships (or groups as groups), rather than as collections of individuals, is matched by the lack of language adequate for the job. A new vocabulary is suggested, in line with the following observations:

1. Interaction in a group or family is organized.
2. A family is a system governed by rules (Watzlawick, 1977, p. 6).
3. When a collection of people becomes stabilized as a group, the group is defined as a rule-governed system.
4. Behavior among group members is patterned by repeatedly following the rules of the system.
5. Families (and groups) are idiosyncratic in style of life, as reflected in their patterns of interaction.
6. There is division of labor and a relatively fixed distribution of power.
7. Rules are inferred from observation of patterned interactions.
8. Because any act can potentially convey meaning in a relationship, behavior is treated as synonymous with communication.
9. Every communication conveys two functions, report and command. Report is the content or information, whereas command refers to "how this information is to be taken" (Watzlawick, 1977, p. 7).
10. How the relationship is perceived and what the relationship means are conveyed in the command aspect of a communication. Implicit in the command is "This is how *you* are to see *me* in relation to you" (Jackson, 1962, p. 7).

A message may be communicated in any one of a number of ways, but the way chosen reflects on how the relationship is perceived. In a group, the communication will reveal something about how the person sees the group and his or her own place in it, as well as how he or she expects to be perceived. If, for example, the content to be conveyed refers to the idea that progress of the work in the group is too slow, there may be many different ways of expressing this information.

11. Response to the communication will indicate whether the implicit definition of the relationship is accepted, changed, rejected, or ignored.

12. It is assumed that "the individual in this relationship with this other" comprises an indivisible whole (Jackson, 1962, p. 8).

13. When relationships are important, then there can be no escape from the process of rule stabilization; otherwise, the relationship would end.

14. Relationship definitions contained in the command aspect of communications become relationship agreements in families or groups that have become stabilized.

15. Relationship agreements control and organize interaction into a more or less coherent system.

16. Group or family rules consist of relationship agreements.

17. The process of developing rules and the rules of relationship are generated without awareness of the people involved.

18. Rules are metaphors conceived as abstractions by observers to help explain observed interactional patterns. For example, the father may make demands, but the mother controls decisions.

19. It takes but a few rules to bring out the meaning of the interpersonal relationship. This does not mean that it is easy to infer the rules that best fit the relationship.

20. In a group or a family, the range of behavior becomes narrowed by implicit mutual agreement about what is acceptable. After a while, it takes very small cues to signal what is not acceptable and what it takes to keep the interaction within bounds.

21. Norms or rules are enforced by "homeostatic mechanism." It is a way the system corrects deviation from the acceptable pattern. For example, a group may suddenly become quiet and tense and engage in unsuccessful changes of topic when someone or some subgroup violates a basic rule.

22. It may be easier to infer a rule when someone transgresses. One can then observe behavior mobilized to bring about rule enforcement.

23. Values that are generally overt and public may be invoked ex-

plicitly to curb rule infractions. Norms are actually covert and idio-syncratic to a particular relationship.

24. Values are held by individuals. In a group or family there may be agreement about a value, and the value may be invoked explicitly to deal with violations of interactional rules. Values, from this point of view, may serve as homeostatic mechanisms, but the covert relationship rules govern the system: "values are used as interpersonal tactics which affirm or enforce a norm" (Jackson, 1962, p. 15). An example of an espoused value is "Everyone has an equal share in making a (family or group) decision." In practice, however, interactional rules determine who controls decisions, and these decisions are not based on equal sharing.

Personality Theory and Group Processes

The study of personality lies at the core of contemporary psychology. As mentioned at the beginning of this chapter, theories of personality have been fueled by the tremendous preoccupation with individualism, personal freedom, and self-development. However, personality theorists do vary widely in their concern for group phenomena and for concepts bearing on group processes. How personality theorists have treated group-relevant issues is made clear in Table 11.1.

Of the 24 dimensions used as a basis for comparison by Hall and Lindzey, four are particularly important for group theory. They are group membership determinants, field emphasis, psychological environment, and social science emphasis. Five of the 19 personality theorists stressed these qualities in their theories. They are Erikson, Sullivan, Adler, Lewin, and Murray. Fromm, Horney, Freud, Angyal, and Binswanger and Boss stressed these qualities a little less, but the emphasis was still strong.

Freud is rated high in terms of psychological environment and social science, medium in terms of group determinants, and low in terms of field emphasis. Jung is rated low on all of the group-relevant variables except psychological environment, where he is rated high. At the far end of the scale, Skinner's operant reinforcement theory and Sheldon's body structure typology are rated low on every one of the four qualities related to group psychology.

It is worth noting that the theorists with high ratings on *all four* group-relevant characteristics, Erikson and Sullivan, are designated as psychosocial theorists or social-psychological in emphasis. In other words, for them the social setting and the individual are both important for the creation of an adequate theory of personality. "Erikson says that people must

Table 11.1 Emphasis on Group-Relevant Qualities in Contemporary Theories of Personality. *From* Theories of Personality, *2d ed. (p. 92, Table 17-1), by C. S. Hall and Gardner Lindzey, 1978, New York: Wiley.*

Theorist	Field emphasis	Psychological environment	Group membership determinants	Social sciences interdisciplinary emphasis
Freud	L	H	M	H
Erikson	H	H	H	H
Jung	L	H	L	L
Adler	H	M	H	H
Fromm	M	M	H	H
Sullivan	H	H	H	H
Horney	M	M	H	H
Murray	H	H	M	H
Goldstein	M	M	L	L
Angyal	H	H	L	L
Rogers	M	H	M	M
Binswanger and Boss	H	H	L	L
Eastern psychology	M	M	L	L
Lewin	H	H	H	M
Allport	M	M	L	L
Sheldon	L	L	L	L
Cattell	M	L	M	L
Miller and Dollard	L	L	M	H
Skinner	L	L	L	L

Degree of emphasis: H = High   M = Medium   L = Low

find their identity within the potentials (for stability or change) of their society, while their *development* must mesh with the requirements of society, or suffer the consequences" (Hall & Lindzey, 1978, p. 108).

Sullivan's position, high on the list of theorists with interests in group interaction, comes as no surprise, for his viewpoint is called the interpersonal theory of psychiatry. As Hall and Lindzey note: "Sullivan insists repeatedly that personality is a purely hypothetical entity, 'an illusion' which cannot be observed or studied apart from interpersonal situations. The unit of study is the interpersonal situation and not the person" (p. 183).

In terms of personality theory, Lewin emphasized the psychological environment (or the world of experience); group membership determinants; interdisciplinary anchoring (concern with findings of sociologists and anthropologists); diversity and multiplicity of motivation; the uniqueness of the individual; the importance of the field (situation or setting within which behavior occurs); and contemporaneous variables, that is, what is going on in the present rather than past events. He deemphasized hereditary factors, unconscious determinants, early developmental experience, continuity of development, biology, the ideal personality, and abnormal behavior.

CHAPTER 12

The Speed of Social Change and the Effect on Human Interaction

The Effect of Transience

Groups are influenced by their physical setting and by their social environment. Recent changes in the way people live, their interpersonal relations, and their expectations have been rapid and significant. This inevitably has affected the behavior of groups. Changes in family structure and relationships; changes in women's economic, social, and political status; changes in the status of minorities; changes in attitude toward work, government, education, sex, parenthood, having children; and, above all, changes in regard to self-development and self-direction have swept across the country and a good part of the world since the end of World War II.

Public opinion has been surveyed by Gallup, Roper, Yankelovich, Harris, and the institutes at the Universities of Michigan and Chicago, covering the pre- and postwar periods up until the present. In his review of these surveys, Yankelovich (1981a) finds that some of the changes occurred at an "explosive growth rate." The number of single households, for example, has increased by 66 percent in the last two decades.

Three out of four Americans now agree "that it is morally acceptable to be single and have children" (p. 69)—a sharp contrast from just a few decades ago. Many other changes affecting relationships have occurred, together with mixed, often troubled feelings about what has been lost. Self-improvement efforts of all kinds, physical, mental, and professional, have increased markedly as more people insist on self-directed choices. Yankelovich believes that the basic underlying rules of living—what people expect implicitly to give and to get in return—have changed. This applies across the board from responsibilities as parents to expectations from work and from government, or some other source.

How much self-denial and postponement of gratification is acceptable now is also rapidly changing. Of college students around 1965, about 72 percent believed that "hard work always pays off." By the early 1970s, that number had dropped to 40 percent. In the general population the change went from 58 percent down to 43 percent.

This trend has affected attitude toward work and the meaning of success. Yankelovich and his associates claim that more workers insist upon a job and a career that pays off psychologically as well as economically. Employees want work that is more interesting and more meaningful, and they demand more real power to participate in making relevant decisions. The fact that these attitudes are basically more effective motivators is not yet fully appreciated, except perhaps in the high-technology and specialized service areas. There is respect for these newer work attitudes in some of the more experimental units of large companies and in various industries in Western Europe and Japan.

Self-improvement and the attempt to meet personal needs and desires may, according to Yankelovich (1981a) be thwarted by drastic economic changes of the 1980s. But closer to our interests is the dilemma created by imbalance between self-searching, self-development, and deterioration of social and interpersonal relations. On the basis of his interviews, Yankelovich finds that "self-fulfillment seekers focus so sharply on their own needs that instead of achieving the more intimate relationships they desire, they grow farther apart from others. In dwelling on their own needs, they discover that the inner journey brings loneliness and depression" (1981b, p. 40).

The surveys over the years of people's thinking and feeling reveal an underlying malaise and distress. Whenever there is a failing economy, increase in unemployment, and disabling inflation, social institutions (schools, mental institutions, prisons) tend to become increasingly dysfunctional and disorganized. The drive for self-actualization, despite its usefulness and psychological value, is simply self-defeating if the commitment to human community is not also present. For personal fulfillment and for essential productivity, it is necessary to create and to sustain social and interpersonal ties at all levels of life, and that cannot be done by introspection and self-development alone.

Yankelovich predicts that the self-absorption and self-indulgence of recent years will give way to some extent as individuals awaken to the realities of cultural and economic changes and to the shortcomings of egocentricism. The prospects, he adds, are movement "to a higher stage of civilization or to disaster" (p. 44). And, he concludes, "the outcome is uncertain." A shift toward the sociocentric side of the continuum could help achieve a new balance, a balance emerging out of shared meanings based on appreciation of both individuality and community. Individuality and community would be stronger; each would cultivate the other.

Only a century ago there was concern in various parts of the world about vehicles that moved too swiftly. We now look back with amusement as we read of laws forbidding vehicles from moving faster than five or ten miles per hour because these speeds were thought to be the limits that humans could bear. These limits turned out to be false, alas, and the race to increase speed was on. There has seemed to be no limit. Now airplanes can move at twice the speed of sound, and rockets can travel at more than 20,000 miles per hour.

But unexpected difficulties did develop. "Jet exhaustion," for example, is felt by pilots and travelers. Fatigue and decline in efficiency, malaise, poor judgment, and an increase in the number of accidents are some of the things experienced as people travel great distances in too brief a time. Biological and behavioral patterns are disturbed in ways not fully understood. A regular, daily pattern of psychobiological functioning, now known as "circadian rhythm" (from the Latin *circa dies*, about a day), has been identified. Circadian rhythm influences a wide variety of important physiological conditions, such as body temperature, heart rate, blood pressure, metabolism, blood cell count, the number of cell divisions, urine chemistry, and kidney function. These inner conditions can have a significant effect on behavior: judgment, job competence, stamina under stress, response to surgery (Luce & Segal, 1966). Though most people are unaware of these conditions, human beings become upset when inner timing is disturbed. There are, in short, real limits to human beings' adaptability, and circadian rhythm happens to be only one area of limitation.

Accelerated changes throughout society—in the structure of family life, in communication and transportation, in art, in environment, in politics, in sex patterns, in community, and in values—challenge the capacity of people to adapt. So many changes coming so quickly have already precipitated problems that we have not yet begun to grasp and identify. But their disturbing effects are felt and suffered.

According to Toffler (1970), "trying to comprehend the politics, economics, art or psychology of the present let alone of the future without the concept of transience is as futile as trying to write the history of the Middle Ages without mentioning religion." Widespread feelings of irritation, apathy, confusion, anxiety, and senseless violence are symptoms of transience, that is, a disease of experiencing too much change in too short a time. Other symptoms include a sense of continual harassment from the physical and social environment, accompanied by a panicky feeling that one is no longer able to control what happens in daily life. Irrational feelings ensue, from profound withdrawal to running away to drastic changes in jobs and life-style.

Changes are occurring so rapidly that one often feels like an alien in one's own culture. When neighborhoods, roads, buildings, clothing, customs, styles of interaction, and social rules change too quickly, people feel disoriented, things lose their meaning, familiar cues are gone, and there is no place to which one can return. Toffler uses the term *future shock* to describe the sense of loss and disorientation that is experienced when one's culture is too rapidly replaced by another culture to which one cannot adapt.

The main issue in future shock is the limit of human responsibility. Although historians can point to many periods when fast and profound changes have occurred, the sudden acceleration of contemporary change is of a different order. It is discontinuous with the past, there are no precedents, and it is irreversible.

A profile of some of the factors reflecting accelerated change that have had a radical impact on humans and society follows:

Population: "The time required to double the world's population has dropped from 1,000,000 years to 200 years, to 80 years, until now. At present accelerated rate of population growth, the earth's population will double in 35 years" (Ehrlich, 1969).

Production: The gross national product of goods and services in the 21 advanced nations of the world is doubling every decade and a half.

Scientists: Between 85 and 95 percent of all scientists who have ever lived were alive in 1970.

Energy: Approximately half of all the energy consumed in the last 2,000 years was consumed in the last 100 years. The rate of increase in consumption is itself increasing at an accelerated pace.

Speed: The top speeds of transportation never exceeded 20 miles per hour until the middle of the nineteenth century. Rockets now take man at over 20,000 miles per hour, and commuter speed for many exceeds the speed of sound.

Innovation: The innovative cycle between a new idea and its application has shortened from as much as a millennium to a few years. Combinations of inventions, including those using computers, have drastically speeded up new inventions.

Moving: Approximately 36 million people move from one place to another each year in the United States.

Books: In four and a half centuries, the publication of new books has increased from 1,000 a year to 1,000 a day.

Scientific literature: The number of journals and articles appears to be doubling every 15 years, with a current output of some 20 million pages per year.

Information: The number of words and ideas taken in daily by the average adult from newspapers, magazines, radios, and television has risen sharply, and new technologies to increase the speed of information flow proliferate at a rapid rate.

These changes constitute just a partial list. Significant and irreversible environmental pollution, for example, is integrally related to the changes noted and exacerbates their worst effects.

Transcience is defined as the cultural and psychological concomitants of change. When change occurs too rapidly, then people, places, organizations, and ideas impinge on us in ways that are unsatisfying and unsettling. The quality of human ties, the presence of commitment and involvement, the nature of friendship, the process of education, and the ability to communicate—all seem to suffer decline. An uneasy feeling of temporariness pervades people. These conditions are essentially psychological, but few studies and few theories dealing with them currently exist.

Two points may be made. The first is that although these changes probably cannot and perhaps should not be stopped, they need to be subject to enlightened, humanizing social controls. The second point is closely related to the first, and here the end can be stated more clearly than the means. The quality of human interaction needs to be elevated so that a sense of meaning and worth is restored. Temporary groupings are one means to this end. Such groupings are becoming more important, even in large organizations, to deal with fast-changing problems and policies. As the older, more rigid bureaucracies attempt to deal with new technologies, new products, and new methods, they will rely more on the power and flexibility of specially composed temporary groups of people. As Miles (1963), Bennis and Slater (1968), and Davis and Lawrence (1977) have pointed out, these temporary systems will increasingly influence education, social and cultural affairs, and industry. The shortcomings of fluidity and temporariness of these *ad hocracies*, to use Toffler's term, will be balanced against the supportive values of the relevance of the group and its concern for persons. Basically, these values rely on an appreciation of the power and worth of group processes in face-to-face interaction.

Flight from depersonalized and ephemeral society has taken nostalgic and romantic forms. The good old days cannot be brought back; nor can we return to nature and quiet pastoral ways. Though it is of vital importance to have parks and wilderness areas, it is doubtful whether communes in the country can have a significant bearing on the transience problem in general. There are too many problems related to poverty, housing, and urban decay that demand attention and work. Thus there is a great need for change even as we become aware of and begin to inquire into the psychological implications of accelerating change.

On the job, more time and attention will have to be shifted to a concern for people. This need not reduce productivity — quite the contrary. People problems, poor communication, and deteriorating relationships seem to characterize most organizations, but particularly the inefficient ones. The image or model of efficiency itself will change as concern for individuals takes its rightful place at work, in the community, and in the school.

Temporary groups such as Alcoholics Anonymous and halfway houses for former patients will increase in number and kind. The number of people perceived as having problems of adaptation to stress and change increases greatly if we include those in life-and-death crises (maternity and postpartum periods, various illnesses, advanced age, the death of a spouse). Added to these are people undergoing social-psychological stress through losing a job, getting married or divorced, having trouble involving law and the courts, or being involved in community conflicts.

A principal approach to such normal crises is to bring together people who can share experience and who have a feeling for what it is like to be in the crisis state. There is a growing body of evidence that nonprofessional helpers are more effective than professional ones for many kinds of psychological disturbances.

There also will be increasing numbers of exploratory groupings; that is, individuals will have opportunities to find themselves in different groups and to help one another come to terms with what is going on in the world around them and within themselves. The cocktail party and the social club are social inventions that have had some utility on this score, but they certainly could bear improvement. Utopian ideas of the past and the present could be usefully studied in the search for more livable ways.

"Western civilization may not be able to survive long without utopian fantasies any more than individuals can exist without dreaming," according to F. E. Manuel and F. P. Manuel (in Nisbet, 1979, p. 31). But they also warn that the utopian spirit reflected in some of the great minds of Greek, Hebrew, and Christian history should not be confused with "prognosticators, divine or human, inspired or insipid, [who] have a way of leaving out the crucial unknowables, the vital unpredictables, while they befuddle us with inconsequential knowables" (see Nisbet, 1979, p. 30).

One of the significant qualities of group process laboratories is that they quickly develop a subculture of their own. The emerging group seems to take hold of time and to modify it. Here is one place the rat-race syndrome and the feeling that events are out of hand may be subdued. Arrangements are civilized in the sense that what transpires takes serious account of people as individuals working together. The study of group processes may be in its early stages as a science, but a world wracked by accelerating change may already be looking in that area for some assistance in organizing itself on a more human scale.

Habeas Emotum: On the Search for Fair Play in Human Interaction

Habeas emotum is a quasi-legal metaphor about fair and just transactions in interpersonal relations. Every person, every group member has a right to his or her feelings and a responsibility to others for the same right. This dictum echoes habeas corpus, a basic tenet of common law that applies to the lawfulness of restraining a person physically. Habeas emotum applies to a person's emotions and fair regard for the feelings of an individual or of a group. It is noted that group discussions often resemble a trial with a complaining party, charges, witnesses, jurylike observers, and a judge. Roles and proceedings change as testimony and feelings are expressed. Habeas emotum is closely tied to a group's ethics in practice.

One step marking human advance was the evolution of the writ of habeas corpus, around the twelfth century. In its earliest form it enabled a person to avoid trial by battle and to obtain trial by jury. Later, habeas corpus was firmly established in English law to end all forms of illegal custody. Meaning literally, "you shall have the body," the words are the opening of the legal writ that had as its object the bringing of a party before a court or a judge. In the United States we inherited the idea of habeas corpus, along with a legal system based on common law, and the idea became established in the federal Constitution and in the laws of most states.

But that writ applies to a person's physical freedom. It prompts another question: Do we need to assert the principle of psychological freedom in a writ of habeas emotum? Today the courts deal with problems of civil, economic, political, and physical rights, and the realm of emotions is left as a private matter — as it should be. But human beings seem to long for some sense of justice in the exercise of their psychological freedom, particularly now that major institutions involving family and community traditions are changing so rapidly (Yankelovich, 1981 a & b).

Where can one get a fair hearing, to say nothing of an unhurried reaction to the blend of thoughts and feelings that are so close to one's own selfness? Is it not true that all human relations implicitly rely upon some code of justice? Fairness is a way, after all, of showing that we do care, and this accountability is important for feelings of belonging with others and for being one's self.

The Speed of Social Change and the Effect on Human Interaction

I once suggested that a training group is, at times, a trial, metaphorically speaking. It is a trial in which each member, including the leader, serves as prosecutor, defendant, witness, judge, and jury. Not all at once, but eventually, each member performs every role. Behavioral incidents are freely provided, charges are made, indictments are offered, countercharges are developed, evidence is ascertained, witnesses testify, judgments are passed and then rescinded as more data are gathered and rules are generated, implicit laws are agreed upon, and a form of justice is acknowledged.

The leader of a group is first seen as judge, then jury, and then as an expert witness. Later the leader is seen as a special member of the group who is himself or herself judged by common law.

Interpersonal and intrapersonal conflicts generate the most significant charges and countercharges. The members divide and take sides, sometimes overtly, often covertly. What makes judgment so significant is that members are being judged by scales made, at least in part, by their own efforts. Everyone has erred and failed before. Now everyone has a second chance. Although each falls short of his or her own standard and is so judged, everyone is acquitted.

The most frequent "crimes" are emotional misdemeanors against others. The most serious malfeasance is a violation against oneself. The victim in the latter instance usually sets up the most stringent standards for evidence and for justice. The prosecution and the defense happen to reside in the same person.

It is a paradox that this kind of trial and judging takes place only after a nonjudgmental atmosphere has been established, which means only that the more superficial customs of the common culture are swept aside or taken for granted. There is a search for psychological order, and a kind of universal constitutional law is finally recognized: a fundamental law of humans and their feelings. The mark of a group is its concern for human emotion. The right to one's own feelings and the right to express them constitute the keystone. Awareness of the feelings of others has a high premium. The exercise of these rights, so based, creates a profound sense of freedom. And individuals find themselves learning and changing as their implicit and explicit expressions are noted, pondered upon, and reacted to. Little wonder then that strangers participating in this process quickly become significant persons.

Even simple, everyday contacts between people are highly complex and often yield a residue of misunderstandings and emotional debris. By common, unverbalized agreement, we ignore many of these minor incongruencies. From experience we know that extraneous problems carry over to unrelated situations. For example, Mr. A is greeted in a cool or gruff manner by his colleague. Mr. A is puzzled but ascribes the coolness to something that may have happened at home or perhaps on the way to the office. But there is always the prospect that these simple incongruencies are significant and pertinent to the people in interaction. Where and when can one ever become enlightened about them? Even with people we know well, there are always large areas of inconsistencies or unknowns in our interactions. And these misunderstandings yield a quota of miscarriages of justice.

If we can get away from the association of judging and justice with relation to law and the courts but think of their pertinence to everyday life, we can immediately note innumerable ways in which judging and justice are called for.

Certain kinds of children's play call for more judging and justice than others, sandlot baseball as opposed to exploring an anthill or playing house, for example. Children seem to have a keen sense of what is just and unjust. Without straying too far afield, a person on a job also invariably searches for and expects a fair evaluation as well as recognition for everything he or she does. Obviously, the person is not going to be judged or evaluated on every single act. This is neither feasible nor desired. Yet deep within the person is a longing for fair acknowledgment.

What is, however, more germane to habeas emotum is that feelings, unlike work, are not planned or expressed deliberately. By their nature they are spontaneous and often occur without warning. And yet each individual longs for an acceptance of those feelings, particularly the negative or difficult ones, on fair and just grounds. This requires an opportunity for an unhurried hearing and an examination of contingencies as necessary. And in everyday life, as noted, there is usually neither the time nor the inclination and often not the ability to accord full and fair acknowledgment to the expression of feeling. Thus all of us, and especially men, hide, disguise, or control our natural tendencies to express ourselves as integral whole beings, feelings and all. The way we temper and control feelings depends upon the reality and the fairness accorded by others to their expression. Watch how children seethe with indignation when they are constrained for reasons they neither understand cognitively nor grasp intuitively.

Perhaps the longing for fairness or justice is an archetype in Jung's sense that it derives from the experience of the human race and is present in the unconscious of the individual. It is perfect in no one and has of course many variations in different cultures. But basically this sense of justice seems to exist in all humans in one form or another. Where the sense is seriously warped or stunted, it is seen as a major pathological symptom for the individual as well as a problem for society.

Perhaps the decay of a society coincides with disregard for the emotional rights of others. Psychological injustice can be found throughout history, and there is little doubt that where it has been widespread, society has been in serious trouble. In plays, novels, and poetry we often find the clearest distillation of the meaning of emotional violation. Because many people continue to experience and to think of feelings without regard for emotional rights, it is not surprising to find fairly widespread emotional barbarism today. Emotional interchange need not be reduced to bland, mild, restrained affairs. Authentic feelings are invariably rugged. But there is a time for the kind of informal hearing and quest for fair play wherever people interact emotionally. After all, life is for people, people with feelings.

In this book, discussion has been limited as much as possible to the special kind of trial phenomenon that transpires in a basic laboratory group. It is obviously not the only significant thing that happens in a training group. Invoking the metaphorical writ of habeas emotum means that a group lays aside its other activities for a while and gives precedence to the claimant who demands a fair and open hearing. This implies the right of the individual to have his or her own feelings; it also means he or she has a right to express those feelings freely unless it can be shown that, by so doing, he or she limits the emotional freedom of others. Conflicts are inevitable and deserve a fair hearing commensurate with the significance of the feelings for the individuals concerned. The broadest latitude is accorded the litigants. In the pursuit of psychological justice, new interaction precipitates additional data and evidence, and the processes of gathering and weighing impressions and observations are of prime importance. The trial calls for both deep involvement and objective observation, a most difficult combination. The quality of consensus varies with the caliber of the persons in the group, but more crucially with the nature of the processes employed. As a group becomes aware of its own behavior, it tends to develop a sense of integrity and feelings of self-worth. Interpersonal fairness is one of the more certain indicators of a soundly developing group.

PART FOUR

Applications

The final part of this volume surveys current applications of group-process theory to different kinds of groups. Because organizations consist of networks of groups, large and small, the first chapter examines group theories on which these applications are based. Highlights of organizational psychology covering a hundred years are outlined.

For the consultant who works with groups, there is a discussion of structural interventions. These interventions are designed to emphasize group-level variables rather than interventions that focus on particular people.

The relevance of group processes for teachers in the classroom covers another large area of applications. In clinical psychology and related fields there is increasing recognition of the value of group-level work to supplement a more traditional psychodynamic approach to personal, psychological problems. By attending to these problems where they originate, in natural group settings such as the family, the work place, and the community, the prospects for primary prevention may be significantly improved.

Finally, the apparent discord between theory and practice is discussed. Despite differences in style and methodology, theory (viewed as behavioral science) and practice (viewed as behavioral art) complement each other in a partnership that is as stormy as it is potentially prolific. The book closes with a Viking myth about the god Thor, who sets out to investigate a problem and winds up with a surprising discovery.

CHAPTER 13

Groups, Organizational Behavior, and Structural Intervention

The meaning of work has changed over time, and it continues to vary because it reflects cultural values. Historians inform us that, to the Greeks and the Romans, work was not highly esteemed. Work was for slaves and the poor. Free citizens were not expected to work. After the Reformation, it was morally proper to work hard, to be frugal, and to defer pleasure or leisure. To be idle was sinful. Those who did not work were subjected to social disapproval and suffered guilt feelings. Working hard indicated that one's fate was being favorably judged.

According to recent surveys of public opinion (Yankelovich, 1981a), the meaning and value of work is again shifting. In 1969, for example, almost 60 percent of Americans agreed that "hard work always pays off," compared to 42 percent only seven years later. Also, in 1978 only about 12 percent agreed that "work is at the center of my life," compared to 35 percent in 1970.

Theories about organizational behavior have changed markedly since Weber's thesis regarding rational planning and the bureaucratic model (see Table 13.1). Taylor's "scientific" management proposals found a ready response in an expanding technology; it made sense to the engineers and builders, matching people to machines with some precision. But social and psychological factors were rediscovered in the Hawthorne Studies, and they continue to demand a central position in organizational theories. During the first part of the twentieth century, personality theories proliferated. James, Pavlov, Freud, Jung, Skinner, Erikson, Piaget, and Lewin, among others, attempted to explain why people behave the way they do. Their ideas were conflicting and fragmentary as far as the organizational theorist was concerned. McGregor contrasted the older traditional organizational ideas with a more enlightened image of the modern worker.

Table 13.1 Organizational Behavior Viewed over the Past Hundred Years

Time	Leading theorist	Theories or studies
1880s	Max Weber	Bureaucracy Rational organization Protestant ethic
1910	Frederick W. Taylor	Traditional organization "Scientific" management
1920s	Elton Mayo	Hawthorne Western Electric Studies Import of social and psychological factors
1930s	Ivan Pavlov B. F. Skinner Sigmund Freud	Behaviorism Behavior modification The unconscious Intrapsychic conflict Work and love
1938	Kurt Lewin	Leadership and organization Autocracy Democracy Laissez-faire
1946	Kurt Lewin	Group dynamics Tavistock Institute Formation of National Training Laboratories
1943-1950	Abraham H. Maslow Carl R. Rogers	Human potential Self-actualization studies

With the advent of systems theory, important insights about people and organizations began to emerge. Now a language appropriate to organizational matters was evolving, and it focused on information flow and cybernetic control as the important data. Likert's fourfold schema showed how organizations could theoretically and profitably change from authoritarian to participative systems. Central to these ideas was the study of group processes that had been triggered by Lewin's research and powered by the Gestalt view of psychology and environment. Organizations became networks of groups, with organizational structure and process opening new possibilities for intervention and modification. Quality circles, for example, are a modified form of team building developed in Japan (see Ouchi, 1981; and Pascale & Athos, 1981).

After enthusiastic forays into various conceptions of organizational development, it soon became evident that planned change was elusive and difficult, often complicated by unanticipated consequences. By the

Table 13.1 *continued*

Time	Leading theorist	Theories or studies
1953	David C. McClelland	Achievement motive Drive measurement Challenge
1953-1954	Ludwig von Bertalaffy Norbert Wiener	General systems theory
1960	Douglas M. McGregor	Human side of enterprise Theory X and Theory Y
1967	R. and J. G. Likert	The human organization Fourfold systems Authoritative-participative systems
	D. Katz and R. L. Kahn	Social psychology of organizations, a holistic perspective
1980s		Eclectic organizations Intrinsic motivation Adaptive strategies Implicit bargaining Job enrichment Organizational development Quality circles Redesign of work Selective participative systems Quality of work life

1980s, the attitude had become a bit more cautious. Although assessments of durable change (Porras, 1979; Porras & Berg, 1978; Walton, 1975), were not encouraging, there was, nevertheless, a feeling among both practitioners and theorists that a fair start had been made. The major segments and dimensions of organizational behavior had been at least roughly identified, and the grounding in personality theory and group processes was being strengthened. In practice, organizational specialists developed adaptive strategies on an eclectic basis, taking note of the social and the technological subsystems and their interconnections.

W. Edward Deming (1980, p. 30), an American economist, for example, helped the Japanese to advance quality assurance methods after World War II. When he was asked recently to discuss quality circles, he said, "The quality circle is a name given to the fact that the Japanese work in groups. They like to work in groups and always have worked in groups. The quality circles are groups of workers who study the local system and have the authority to change it." Deming concluded: "The Japanese worker has much more freedom on the job than does the American worker. He can modify anything. The Japanese have a democracy on the job that we can't appreciate."

Group Processes and Organizational Behavior

> When someone is honestly 55 percent right,
> that's very good and there's no use wrangling.
> And if someone is 60 percent right, it's
> wonderful, it's great luck and let him thank God.
> But what's to be said about 75 percent right?
> Wise people say this is suspicious. Well, and
> what about 100 percent right? Whoever says he's
> 100 percent right is a fanatic, a thug, and the
> worst kind of rascal.
>
> —*An old Galician*

One of the most important studies to call attention to the significance of informal groups in a large organizational setting was the pioneering work of Mayo (1933) and his associates. Beginning in 1927, Mayo tried to find relationships between physical conditions of work and the productivity of employees at a large electrical manufacturing plant. He set up a control group and an experimental group and proceeded to vary systematically the physical variables of light, heat, and humidity. Production rose as these conditions improved, but when he restored the original condition, he was surprised to find that worker output remained at a high level. Only then did the researcher probe the attitudes of this group of workers. He found morale to be quite high, partly because the workers were relieved of the usual supervision and partly because they enjoyed being singled out for special attention by the experimenters. This change in attitude among the workers seemed to be more important than changes in physical conditions. The results called attention to the significance of small-group processes that exist informally outside the formal structure and organization of the factory.

Another of the Mayo findings came from the depth interviews of large numbers of workers. The researchers learned that, in spite of a seemingly fine set of personnel policies, many employees had all kinds of grievances and complaints. It appeared that a subworld of important attitudes and feelings existed that was unknown to the supervisors and executives. Furthermore, levels and standards of production were determined more by informal groups than by management. Workers sought acceptance and approval by their informal groups rather than risk social rejection and ostracism. At times, the pressure to conform to the group's standards, to win the group's acceptance, was more important than financial rewards.

Change in Industry

Industrial managers began to discover anew that workers were human and that their feelings and attitudes could not be taken for granted. This essentially was the meaning of McGregor's (1960) X and Y theory of management, which had significant influence in the field. The industrial employee was no longer a special kind of machine, neither a slave nor a serf, but an individual whose social and psychological needs reflected the political and philosophical values of society in which he or she lived. Industry turned to sociologists and psychologists to learn more about these informal groups, how their attitudes were formed, and how decisions were made. While some managers merely sought new ways of manipulating and controlling employees with knowledge gained from the social scientists, managers, in general, sought a better understanding of their industrial organizations (French & Bell, 1978; Lorsch, 1979; Margulies & Raia, 1972; Porter, Lawler, & Hackman, 1975). Workers, too, through their trade unions began calling in interdisciplinary experts to help them understand problems affecting union management and the process of collective bargaining.

Various universities throughout the country have tried to meet these needs by turning more attention to research on human resources in industry. The *Harvard Business Review*, for example, publishes many articles and studies in this field. The Society for the Advancement of Management cooperates in various ways with social scientists, including the organization of workshops and seminars to learn more about the art and science of working with others.

School System Innovation

All institutions now feel the pressure for change, but none more than school systems. Frequently the different subgroups within a system agree on the need for change but disagree strongly on methods. Change may mean threat, and it is understandable that people's defenses may be aroused. It is not enough to rework the vocabulary and call for "problem solving" instead of "change." The most important thing in promoting real change appears to be organizational and interpersonal climate.

Climate is important because the process of solving problems is as significant as the solutions. Good ideas alone are not enough. Concern for people and their feelings is crucial. Parliamentary procedure according to *Robert's Rules of Order* may seem efficient, but the rules often create a win-or-lose situation.

Large-group meetings require some structure but not more than is necessary. Usually too much structure is imposed, thereby increasing the chances of proper form at the expense of individual feelings. The subtleties of group processes are active, even if never mentioned. Feelings of insecurity that seem to permeate most face-to-face interactions in faculty meetings can become transformed into anger and defensiveness rather quickly. The university is harder to reorganize than a cemetery, according to Warren G. Bennis. It takes time for ruffled feelings to be expressed and for face to be saved. This is the same as saying that it takes time to build a psychological climate for real collaboration. People learn quite soon whether dissent is tolerated; innovation without the feeling that it is all right to dissent is as insubstantial as cotton candy.

Interpersonal relationships throughout an organization affect the general psychological climate, and the attitudes of the organization affect interpersonal relations. Parts and wholes influence each other.

In one large study covering eight school systems in Wisconsin, the investigators found that the ability of a school system to innovate successfully depended on the psychological climate of the system. As reported by Hilfiker (1969), real innovativeness in school organizations is related to the quality of interpersonal behavior: people's interest in and concern for people. The research points up the importance of "interpersonal process norms and problems solving norms that characterize professional staff meetings" (p. 39), and the investigators note that "awareness of the degree of openness and trust" (p. 39) is among the most significant variables bearing on the soundness of change. Although the investigators emphasize that more research is needed on social-psychological climates, their findings indicate that, for those interested in successful change, "efforts should be undertaken to increase awareness of the importance of human relations skills in classroom as well as organizational settings" (pp. 39-40).

In an important English study on the quality of education in London, Rutter et al. (1979) discovered again the importance of social climate and staff relationships. The clue to better education and superior academic achievement, plus a significant reduction in vandalism, truancy, and school disorder, turned out to be good organization in the school and genuine concern for people. Children's previous records of delinquency were not predictive of subsequent problems — if the headmaster and staff built a warm and effective organization.

Likert and Likert (1976) and Likert and Bowers (1969) discuss the promise and the difficulties of organizational research. They find that studies of business and industrial organizations can contribute valuable principles for solving societal problems. In general, their data and results are in line with the trends found in the school system research toward "establishing cooperative interaction and problem solving among conflicting parties" (Likert & Bowers, 1969, p. 592).

The Tavistock Way: A Sociotechnical System Approach

The Tavistock Institute in England developed its own theory and practice of group and organizational behavior. Trist and Bamforth (1951) , Rice (1963), Emery and Trist (1965), and others at the Tavistock Institute saw the problem as sociotechnical, that is, the *integration* of the social-psychological issues with the technical. They reasoned "that organizations can avoid much of the conflict between productive efficiency and alienated workers by examining the various possible work arrangements for given tools and machinery" and "since a sociotechnical system includes people as well as tools it is appropriate to ask how well it utilizes tools and how well it utilizes the abilities of people and meets their needs" (Katz & Kahn, 1978, p. 277; see also Bridger, 1978).

The old industrial psychology took account of the person-machine equation; individual differences and physiological factors guided engineers and managers in creating industrial equipment and procedures. But the sociotechnical approach considered group processes as basic for taking into account the social-psychological system together with the technical. As Rice (in Katz & Kahn, 1978, p. 701) expressed it: "The technological demands place limits on the type of work organization possible, but a work organization has social and psychological properties of its own that are independent of technology."

It was assumed that social and psychological needs could be met by arrangements that offered some *independent* judgment and decision making by the worker; *group* and *interpersonal relationships* that were satisfying; and some work in which workers contributed a *meaningful* part, which meant that the work had to be recognizable as a completed unit or a phase in a sequence of steps.

A major contribution by the Tavistock investigators was recognition of the primary work group as crucial to the system. When employees could decide among themselves (within technical limits) how the work was to be arranged, productivity increased, followed by job satisfaction, and absenteeism decreased. It was in the small group that a sense of task meaning, as well as a feeling of autonomy, developed.

The sociotechnical system practitioners did not limit themselves to the basic work group. They recognized that the same social and psychological needs pertained to the managerial units. It would be a mistake to overlook the peer-group needs of supervisors, foremen, and managers, as well as their ability to come up with ideas and methods through small-group processes that help integrate the social-psychological systems with the technical systems. The opportunity for satisfying relationships, the

sense of belonging to a team or a unit, as well as the need to be autonomous, are at least as important as recognition for task ability. And this
would appear to hold for employees up and down the whole organizational structure.

Groupthink and Counterproductivity

The old proverb about too many cooks is obviously true for organizations. In fact, the field of group processes as a behavioral science has
grown because of the increasing realization that groups, in and out of
formal organizations, can be terribly inefficient. Irving Janis (1972)
writes of *groupthink* to describe lowered intellectual effectiveness, especially in certain political and governmental decision areas. Reality
testing and moral judgment also may suffer, even among officials who are
highly intelligent and capable leaders, as a result of group conformity
pressures.

Janis states that shared illusions about group unanimity were disclosed
after the failure of group actions (for example, the Bay of Pigs fiasco)
became known. Still, other groups have clearly benefited from the
increased skills and resources of members for productivity and problem
solving. According to researchers at the University of Michigan (Kahn et
al., 1964, p. 394), "all coordination involves costs; to require that even
two persons somehow synchronize their activities takes time, effort, and
some psychological costs of accommodation." Their recommendation
was to keep the organization "decentralized, flat and lean." Then, to
avoid the equally costly effects of competitive individual achievement, it
is essential to tie in rewards to the success of collaborative group efforts,
teamwork that actually achieves organizational goals.

Individual Versus Group Productivity

Is a group more effective at solving problems than are individuals
working alone? A number of experiments on group versus individual
effectiveness have failed to resolve this question. Kelly and Thibaut
(1954) have summarized research on "experimental studies of group
problem solving and process." Although research reports go back about
35 years, no systematic principles have yet emerged.

Covering a wider range of relevant studies, Hare (1976) offers the interested student results on individual and group problem solving and
effectiveness with varying combinations of populations, tasks, and productivity criteria. While noting that groups can be spurred on in certain
obvious as well as more subtle ways, Hare says that "productivity in the
task area is often achieved only at the expense of member satisfaction in
the social-emotional area" (p. 330).

It is obvious that many physical, structural, and process problems pertaining to groups are involved in this issue. Variables such as size of group, nature of task, composition of membership, time and quality factors, motivational forces from within and from outside the group, imposed goals versus self-determined goals, intragroup communication, conformity pressures and morale, and processes of interpersonal influence have been studied in scattered researches and have a direct bearing on the question of productivity. But no comprehensive theory has been developed to link these variables in a way that would permit definitive answers. In a sense, the question of the superiority of individual productivity as against group productivity is less important than an understanding of what takes place when people work together. Even when we work alone, we are involved with the contributions of others. For example, consider the borrowing and lending of ideas and techniques among scientists and artists. Also, our present ability to work alone is a function of our past learning.

Frequently, individual and group efforts supplement each other. Executives and administrators need to know what other sectors are doing, if only to avoid working at cross-purposes or causing duplication. Every decision maker is, however, faced by the problem of uncertainty inherent in the lack of knowledge about, or the known unpredictability of, the environment in which he or she acts. The amount of uncertainty to be dealt with probably increases with an increasing rate of social change, but the problem exists in all societies. Techniques for the handling of uncertainty are developed that supposedly reduce it to manageable scope. There does always remain an irreducible residue, however, and the possibility exists that the failure to control uncertainty, or an especially low tolerance for uncertainty, may produce reality shocks (Holzner, 1968, p. 13). A group effort is a necessary evil for some people, inhibiting and hampering freedom, reducing quality to mediocre levels. But is this the inevitable result of group effort? The American Declaration of Independence and the Constitution are group efforts; it is doubtful whether a single individual could have done a superior job. On the other hand, how would a committee have fared working, say, on the Moses sculpture by Michelangelo? Obviously the nature of the work is important, as well as personal preference.

A deeply integrated society with pluralistic aims calls for the expression of diverse, individual needs and for the resolution of differences in the solution of certain problems. Planning a new transit system, changing the tax structure, or building a factory calls for broad awareness of needs and demands and the advice of the technical expert. Learning itself seems to progress best for most people when there is an appropriate balance of learning with others and studying alone. Unless we prefer a job (or a society) that tells us what to do and how to do it, we are committed to a belief in interpersonal consultation. Within this belief, however, there should be ample room for an optimal balance between individual and group productivity. Perhaps an enlightened self-interest can best guide us in deciding when a group effort is required. And it is a wise group that knows when to cease and expire.

Summary

When a problem demands a single overall insight or an original set of decisions, an individual approach may be superior to a group effort. The greater the group members' desire for individual prominence and distinction, however, the lower will be the friendly sharing or group morale.

Problems demanding a wide variety of skills and information or the cross-checking of facts and ideas seem to need a group approach. Feedback and free exchange of thinking may stimulate ideas that would not otherwise have emerged. If goals are shared, then there is greater likelihood for cooperative effort; when the group goal is not shared by members, morale and productivity may suffer. Consequently when the goal is decided upon by group discussion and participation, there is greater likelihood of full-member involvement. When members decide on the need for group effort, the smaller the size of the group, the better it will function, provided that the necessary diversity of skills and group maintenance resources are present.

A group may be a source of strong interpersonal stimulation; a group will also generate its own conformity pressures. In order to decide between group and individual work, these two sets of forces (stimulating and binding) should be kept in mind. A society that places highest value on the worth and freedom of the individual also encourages the strongest independent thought, independent work, and independent responsibility. An inherent goal of a sound group in such a society is the reaffirmation of true independence while at the same time meeting group needs concerning tasks and morale.

> A hundred times every day I remind myself
> that my inner and outer life depend
> on the labors of other men, living and dead,
> and that I must exert myself
> in order to give in the measure
> as I have received and am still receiving
> —*Albert Einstein*

Structural Intervention in Organizations

A particular kind of consultation activity is known as structural intervention. I do not plan to dwell on the working through of process changes that are inevitably involved in such interventions. Nor do I plan to go into the development of initial contact with the client organization, the establishing of contract and working conditions, or the building of relationships with individuals and with groups with whom I might be working. These considerations are all important in organizational consultation; there is no consultation without them. I will go further and say that the purpose of a particular structural intervention is in the service of process. In practical terms, this means that the intervention itself grows out of a need for the client group to study itself, to learn how it is functioning, to become aware of interpersonal and group processes that underlie the way life is lived in that organization and how work gets done.

In a discussion of organizational consultation, Edgar Schein (1969) lists four basic kinds of intervention: (1) agenda setting, a large category involving all kinds of questions or issues to be looked at and processes to be explored; (2) feedback of observations and data; (3) coaching or counseling of individuals or groups; and (4) structural suggestions. Schein goes on to say that the likelihood of using these interventions is in descending order. He would rarely use a structural intervention because the "consultant is rarely in a position to suggest how work should be allocated, or communication patterns altered, or committees organized" (p. 118).

This is a very different kind of structural intervention from the kind I am trying to explore. I would agree with Schein that suggesting changes in organizational structure is not within the purview of the psychologist as process consultant, though he or she may examine, with management, the meaning and consequences of their intended structural changes.

I can see structural intervention as a way of freeing communication patterns for exploration by the client group as the need arises. A department in an organization may have difficulty talking about how members work together. Ordinarily, the consultant may use a number of different ways of proceeding, each of which requires an appreciation of the readiness of the group to gather observations, to share impressions, and, in short, gradually to get on with the study of their own processes.

A major assumption underlying structural interventions is that every organization and every unit within an organization undergoes a differentiation process and that interaction patterns reflect this differentiation. Particular psychological constraints characterize each group and each relationship just as they do each individual. And most of the time the sources of the constraints function outside the awareness of the person or the group itself.

A structural intervention in one unit of an organization was a suggestion by the consultant that the members divide themselves into two groups, either as newcomer or old-timer. Difficulties had arisen frequently over the need for and resistance to change in the organization. Assuming that the timing was right, the members were invited to move to opposite sides of the room on a self-selected basis; that is, each individual had to decide for himself or herself whether he or she was a newcomer or an old-timer. The results were surprising. Some members who were with the unit for less than a year classed themselves as old-timers, and some who had been on the job for as long as six years felt they were newcomers. Of course, more than chronological time was involved, and during the intense discussion that followed, all kinds of new and important information and feelings emerged. Questions of power and influence, standings on chronic issues affecting the unit but never clarified, allegiance to the boss, insecurities, and friendship patterns were some of the things brought out. Many meeting hours were used in exploring the effects of this one intervention because it touched on so many patterns of interpersonal and group functioning and on how people saw themselves and one another.

It is obvious that a structural intervention can be too revealing, too powerful, too threatening for productive processing and, hence, should not be used. Here, again, the judgment and skill of the consultant is needed to decide when and how to intervene, if at all.

Bringing people into contact with one another can produce many possible structural interventions. In one school, the consultant expressed interest in having teachers from different class levels come together with the vice-principal and the consultant to discuss a complicated problem of a younger child. It was evident that many of the teachers had never talked together before, and they seemed delighted with the opportunity to get to know one another. In a large housing project, tenants were brought in by management on issues dealing with routine maintenance. This minor change resulted in a quite different kind of meeting, and participants and consultant obtained a rather different view of problems and interaction. What is so striking in these instances is also true of just about every organization, particularly large ones and those involving marked status differences. Invisible guidelines and boundaries seem to determine who talks to whom and who attends what meetings and gets involved in which decisions regardless of operating rationale. In addition to status differences, there are all kinds of attitudes about territoriality and privileges, stereotypes, bureaucratic pigeonholing, and 57 varieties of interpersonal and intergroup distortions. In most organizations and institutions there just does not seem to be enough time to check things out and learn about genotypical patterns of work. Besides the time shortage, it is difficult to create a setting that makes it possible to learn about human interaction, production, and service problems.

Structural interventions grow out of a need to deal somehow with invisible constraints and boundaries. Each group and organization generating its own climate and miniculture will probably vary considerably in ability and readiness to deal with the effects of its organizational mechanics on its groups and individuals. At best, change in attitude toward facing psychological realities is a very slow process.

Here are some characteristics of structural interventions: They do not place the onus on the individual. Implied in the action is the group-relevant quality. A department or unit may struggle with morale problems of an intragroup and interpersonal nature only to discover that a change in relation to the organization as a whole, for example, may markedly affect the state of mind, as well as the unit's effectiveness. Structural interventions may also lead to a structural change. As a result of a particular intervention, a group may discover that its working processes improve after the devising of closer ties or new linkages to another part of the organization.

The most important structural interventions stem from the participants themselves. Unless the consultant can help the members become aware of the manner in which contraints operate, there is small likelihood that organizational changes will be useful.

Structural interventions, like every other form of intervention, serve to aid participants and groups to learn about ongoing functional processes within organizations. Processes such as communication, influence patterns, decision making, and collaboration are affected by the kind of formal and informal structures that exist in an organization.

Reflection on structural interventions draws one to search for notions that throw some light on the relationship between structure and process. Much has been written on basic organizational concepts such as structure and process, but I have selected only a few that may be of interest to the organizational and community consultant.

Hunches for Intervention
The few ideas that follow are offered in the hope that they may be of interest in speculating about structure and about intervention. They are only suggestive, representing certain fragmentary aspects of organizational theory or process.

The narcissism of minor differences. Freud (1929) notes that "communities with adjoining territories," such as the Spanish and the Portuguese, the English and the Scotch, the North Germans and the South Germans, who are engaged in constant feuds and embarrassing each other, indulge in a relatively harmless expression of aggression which Freud calls "the narcissism of minor differences," but he also points out that the same force may increase cohesion of members in a community. It is not unusual to see the same kind of behavior in social agencies or in closely related professional groups. The consultant would do well to note the existence of these realities in planning a structural intervention.

Communication networks. Structural intervention may be based on a theory of communication networks (Leavitt, 1951). In several studies, the investigators found that by arranging persons in particular configurations, such as in the shape of a star, a wheel, a circle, or a chain, differentiated patterns of communication resulted. (See page 115.) Information traveling in a direct line back and forth from Person A to Persons B, C, D, and E, all in a fixed order, created effects on relationships, morale, and efficiency that were conspicuously different from those of a wheel arrangement. The wheel network required that every person send information to and receive it from a central point. The central person became highly important because he or she had more information and controlled more flow of information than anyone else. Thus each form of network produced its own effects on individuals and on the system as a unit.

Pseudomutuality. Wynne and his associates (1968) found that some families of schizophrenic patients attempted to maintain an illusion of complementarity at the expense of individual needs. The extent to which organizations sacrifice individual differences and uniqueness of persons for the "good of the group" may offer a clue to the consultant planning intervention. From a systems point of view, such an organization is preoccupied with its boundaries and the preservation of structure rather than with the purposes for which it was originally formed.

Group entrapment. Closely related to pseudomutuality is the phenomenon of group entrapment. Actually, Wynne's schizophrenogenic families illustrate a particular kind of entrapment. Watzlawick et al. (1967) developed the idea that any set of relationships may become entrapped in such a way that no escape is possible. Entrapment usually involves implicit or explicit rules that prevent working through the impasse. Insistence by some decision-making bodies on absolute majorities or on unanimity, for example, may foreclose conflict resolution. And yet the group may be unable to change the rule for the very same reason that interferes with its decision making. It is even more difficult to free oneself when the constraints are implicit. The consultant makes a contribution when, through his or her structural intervention, he or she breaks the entrapment and makes apparent the covert rules.

The linking pin process. Empirical studies in organizations (Likert & Likert, 1976) support the idea that the effectiveness and morale of subgroups depend in good part on the way they overlap with, and are linked to, the rest of the organization. Particular emphasis is placed on the value of occasional meetings over two hierarchical levels so as to become aware of any breakdown in the linking pin process.

The subsurface organization. Organizational theorists recognize the significance of informal groupings in every organization, especially since the work of Mayo (1933) and Roethlisberger and Dickson (1939). From a consultant's point of view, an appreciation of the life and influence of the subsurface groupings is crucial to understanding of the organization and to the effectiveness of intervention. Even if one cannot immediately tap into these groups, it is necessary to respect their existence and the role they play in motivation within the organization. For example, a structural change may disrupt a social network and cause distress, even though everyone may recognize the technical effectiveness of the move. The people will not complain about the loss of social ties, but they may gripe about some irrelevant technological issues.

Temporary systems. Rapid social and technological changes have subjected organizations and communities to unprecedented pressures. As a survival tactic, many important minor changes have developed in a way that Miles (1963) has identified as temporary systems. He shows how temporary systems have spread throughout society and identifies the many different patterns and life spans that shape their existence. The more rigid bureaucracy is giving way to more flexible systems, many of which are temporary and everchanging. Structural intervention, leading to appropriate structural changes, fits well with this contemporary trend (Reed, 1965).

The open systems idea. Broadly conceived, systems theories may be useful in the search for and the implementation of structural intervention. Every organization is seen as a more or less open system with no limit to the kinds of components that bear on the well-being of its people and the effectiveness of its functioning. The consultant is freer to examine real and imagined objectives, the varieties of motivation in work and in relationships, and the planned and unplanned consequences of change. The individual and the group are the contributors to and the inheritors of change. Ultimately, the open system idea may help us to appreciate more of the realities of organizational behavior and to make collaboration with an outside consultant more comprehensible.

Crisis and confrontation. A special pattern of structural interventions is identified in the work of Maxwell Jones and Paul Polak (1968). They see crisis as "an intolerable situation which threatens to become a disaster or calamity if certain organizational and psychological steps do not take place immediately" (p. 114). What they propose essentially is an immediate structural intervention consisting of a face-to-face confrontation with major crisis participants, led by a professional skilled in group methods, in a setting that encourages open communication of feelings. Social learning and the emergence of new perspectives in the daily work life of all concerned may result from this process, according to the authors, who draw on their experience in therapeutic community practice.

The morphogenic model. Morphogenesis is a system concept that attempts to explain the growth and decay of organizational structure. The model rejects homeostatic or balancing notions and, instead, conceives of organizations as "systems of interacting components with an internal source of tension, the whole engaged in continuous transaction with its varying external and internal environment" (Buckley, 1967, p. xxiv). "Information is the central organizing element of a social system, and communication, or information exchange, is how parts organize into a system" (p. xxiv). "Selective mapping grows out of these transactions and becomes part of the structure in the form of meanings and tendencies to act in certain ways" (p. xxv). There is, then, a source of variety that may contribute to sets of alternative actions as well as constraints within the formal structure.

Morphogenesis takes account of personality dynamics but considers it a reductionist error to use psychodynamics to account for organizational behavior. Emergent phenomena, such as roles, norms, authority, power, expertise, interaction networks, ecological settings, and decision-making processes are considered to be more compatible with a system approach. Roles, for example, undergo continuous change as the structured demands of others conflict with the individual's subjective view of his or her role in a more or less fluid setting. The extent to which such morphogenic propensities are free to resolve themselves will determine the soundness of the changing order.

In this model of change, the consultant's role is to help liberate these propensities in the organization in whatever ways he or she can. Structural intervention is one such way — by temporarily removing or modifying an organizational constraint so as to accelerate the inherent change process. How much and what kind of intervention would, of course, vary with the particular need for change, that is, the psychological state of affairs in particular and of organizational life in general.

In preparing this discussion, I have felt less than satisfied with what I could do with the topic. Nevertheless, the realization that structure lies at the core of organizational development remains an exciting one, appealing to the imagination as a question of design.

Some current views of organizational structure, while conspicuously logical, suggest only a first approximation to the inner design of the organization. Porter, Lawler, and Hackman (1975), for example, tally these dimensions: (1) size of organization, (2) tall or flat organizational shape, (3) centralized or decentralized shape, (4) number of organizational levels, (5) line and staff hierarchies, (6) span of control, (7) size of organizational subunits.

Other investigators would include ecological dimensions, behavior settings, behavior characteristics of milieu inhabitants, and psychosocial characteristics and organizational climate (Moos, 1975). All of these appear to be important and relevant areas in the study of organizational structure.

But there is also an artistic view. As Herbert Simon (1969) has observed, the aesthetics of natural science and mathematics is at one with the aesthetics of music and painting in that "they inhere in the discovery of partially concealed pattern" (p. 2). Perhaps the same may be said for the search for form and design in human organizations.

While that search continues, the most promising source of organizational forms and configurations would appear to derive from functional analyses. A good illustration would be the sets or ties that connect employees who depend on one another for information, ideas, or services in order to get the work done (Katz & Kahn, 1978). Empirically tracing these natural linkages and identifying the interdependent nets is still the most likely source for the exploration of the shape of organizational structure.

CHAPTER 14

The Teacher and Group Processes

Almost a century ago, William James told teachers that the science of psychology had little to offer that would aid them in their daily work.

> I say moreover that you make a great, a very great mistake, if you think that psychology, being the science of the mind's laws, is something from which you can deduce definite programmes and schemes and methods of instruction for immediate schoolroom use. Psychology is a science, and teaching is an art; and sciences never generate arts directly out of themselves. An intermediary inventive mind must make the application, by using its originality. (1899, p. 3)

The volume of research and publication has increased tremendously since then, but teachers have not been overwhelmed with knowledge they can use. They stand pretty much as they did then—each stands alone. The comments offered here are not designed to show the teacher how to teach; rather they are intended to call to the teacher's attention certain group-relevant characteristics of teaching. By emphasizing group processes in teaching and learning, the teacher may find it useful to reconsider some basic problems that arise daily.

Unfortunately, many people think of group dynamics as a collection of techniques and methods. As mentioned earlier, group dynamics is the study of behavior in groups. One may study riot mobs or church congregations or a team of scientists or a teacher conducting a class. Group dynamics does not tell us what a group should or should not do. It does not advocate doing things in groups; nor does it mean sweetness and light in group behavior.

A colleague once told me that he was opposed to group dynamics because he personally disliked committee work. He might just as well have said he opposed biology because he hated raw green vegetables.

Here are some questions that a teacher may ask because they have a bearing on teaching and on group processes:

1. How can I get my pupils to work harder and to learn more?
2. What about discipline? Are disciplinary actions related to group behavior?
3. How can I communicate more effectively with my class?
4. To what extent should my pupils determine what is to be studied and how they are to be evaluated?
5. To what extent do I follow a predetermined plan for my class? To what extent do I permit changes in my overall plan and changes in my daily plan?
6. Is classroom morale any of my business? Or does it take care of itself so long as I keep to my teaching?
7. What relation is there between how I get along with my school superiors and my classroom work? What about the same question in connection with my colleagues?
8. Should I have a hand in setting school policy? Or is this just not the teacher's job?
9. What about curriculum? Is it the teacher's concern, and if so, how do I go about influencing curriculum change?
10. Does it help to think of oneself as a leader in the classroom? What kind of leader should a teacher be? How do I find out what kind of leader I am?
11. What about parents? How do I learn to work more effectively with them?
12. What about my own improvement in my field of specialization? Are my own studies and intellectual growth a personal matter, or are they also a function of group processes in the school?
13. Should I carry special responsibilities outside of school? Who decides about the role of the teacher in the community?
14. Is it possible to improve my skill in working with groups without becoming a manipulator of people? What about ethics in group dynamics?

Some of these are age-old questions that still cannot be answered. Others are beyond the scope of this book. But all have some relation to the teacher and the group, and the discussion that follows attempts to highlight this relationship.

Teachers are both participants with the class and observers. They need to explain, give information, ask questions, challenge, listen, think, recognize individual and group differences, stimulate, give support, and inspire, among other things. And they hope to follow some overall plan so that their work with their pupils ties in with what went before and what will follow.

Then, too, teachers must recognize the needs and demands of their school superiors, their bosses, and their colleagues, to say nothing of parents and their questions, problems, and demands. But perhaps most important is teachers' knowledge and awareness of themselves, their strengths and weaknesses, their own needs and blind spots.

This adds up to a tremendous order. And from all quarters we find people eager to criticize the teacher, to point out shortcomings. But what can be offered to help? More specifically, why add to the burden by calling attention to group dynamics? If, as James pointed out, teaching is an art, what should the teachers know about groups in order to improve their skills?

A group may be thought of as a developing system with its own structure, organization, and norms. Classes may look alike from a distance or on paper, but actually each class is as unique as a fingerprint. Each class develops its own internal procedures and patterns of interaction and its own limits. It is as if imaginary lines were guiding and controlling behavior within the group. In spite of day-by-day variation, there is a certain constancy in each class that emerges from its individual history.

The teacher may be able to recognize qualities, such as interdependency, that characterize the way the pupils work. And the teacher might speculate about what it is that one does to enable the group to become more independent and more interdependent. How can one encourage individuality in pupils while at the same time teaching them the value of consideration for others? This is another way of looking at the goals of the group. Pupils cannot learn independence and interdependence by merely reading books or listening to lectures. That comes from working with other people as a supplement to working alone. What a person learns from infancy on in the family is of course fundamental to what that person is. *Because each family is, in fact, another group with particular qualities, the child carries over certain expectations into the classroom group.*

The main point to be emphasized here is that group life, per se, is an important reality; that a growing body of scientific knowledge exists concerning principles of group processes; and, finally, that through particular kinds of experience it is possible for the teacher to become more effective in working with groups.

There could be considerable value for teachers in learning more about their own behavior in groups. It is possible, of course, to learn this from experience. Or the teacher may participate in group laboratories or workshops especially designed to encourage awareness of characteristic interactions. Some reasons for laboratory learning about groups include:

To take the time to explore the factors influencing the teacher's own motivation in learning and in teaching: In a permissive group, it becomes possible to clarify deeper motives. In learning about one's own tendencies to "dress up" motives, the teacher might better appreciate the same problems in pupils.

To recognize the development and power of group norms: By experiencing the development of a group norm and its power to guide or restrict the individual, a teacher can more intimately grasp the significance of these norms in pupil groups. Pressure toward conformity and hostility toward those who violate group norms have an important bearing on classroom learning.

To learn about social and personal obstacles to learning: Groups can be cruel or gentle with a sensitive or an atypical pupil. To learn something about blocks to learning, it is useful for the teacher again to experience group response to unusual individuals, but this time in a group where the experience can be identified, clarified, and understood.

To distinguish between the surface appearance of groups and the covert life that may not be apparent but still is highly important: In other words, a group may seem to be working very well—orderly, quiet, and going through the correct motions. Only nothing really happens, nothing changes, nothing is learned. A sound group, a class in which pupils are working and learning, may not always look very productive to an outsider.

To learn more about the value of self-determination in groups: As a class learns to guide itself, to take on more responsibility, the pupils learn more out of intrinsic motives. Each pupil does more to learn and to acquire knowledge and learns to work with others at the same time.

To become more aware of the variety of leadership functions: The teacher as a special kind of leader should understand the different kinds of leadership patterns, such as centralized or distributed functions, formal and informal leadership, the emergence of pupil leaders and of leadership in subgroups, and the effect of these patterns on the teacher's work.

To recognize the teacher's power as a leader so that his or her use of rewards and punishments is in line with the learning goals: At the same time, the teacher needs to learn about the group's power to reward and to punish its own members and its ability to influence the teacher.

To learn about the evolution of status and role within a classroom group: The basis for status may be school grades and intelligence, but it may also include social skills, physical prowess, ability to defy authority (Lippitt, Polansky, & Rosen, 1952), and other emotional capacities that have little direct relation to academic learning.

We take for granted that teachers are well informed, particularly in their field of specialization. Knowledge and the ability to acquire continually new knowledge are basic to their work. But what is less well understood and less well appreciated are the more subtle skills required to work with a classful of 20, 30, or 40 young people.

Standing alone in their classrooms, teachers have little to guide them except what they know, what they observe and understand, what they sense and feel. Superiors, colleagues, parents, and the community look over their shoulders. They must be sensitive to what is going on while they work, somewhat as artists, in moving toward learning-teaching objectives. The rules and plans of the school can seem quite remote and abstract; here are pupils reacting intensely, with strong curiosity or apathetically at any given moment. Teachers must learn to trust their own senses, their own observations. They must recognize the realities of group life as well as the complexities of individual personality. If they are well aware of their own impact on others, they can work to influence the class in a desired direction. If they are blind to their own motives and to their own behavior, they may work hard and yet defeat their own purposes.

In effect, this amounts to asking the teacher to "know thyself," that ancient appeal which is so widely known and even more widely ignored. For to learn more about oneself in relation to others is not only difficult and time-consuming, it is apt to arouse unsuspected anxiety.

When self-awareness is limited, we often see rigid, authoritarian methods imposed on teachers and pupils. And on the other hand, mistakes of an equally flagrant sort occur when well-intentioned but misinformed teachers loosen all controls and a misguided permissiveness in the classroom results. This can be recognized by an atmosphere of indifference diffused through the class; very little is learned, and pupils tend to become bored or merely mischievous.

Like the artist who steps back frequently to observe more clearly an emerging work, the teacher needs open and effective communication with a class to perceive more clearly what is going on. The teacher needs to stop, to observe, and to listen. If the atmosphere is sufficiently free, the teacher will obtain an adequate picture of what is going on and what needs to be done. If one can accept some of the negative feelings in oneself, one may be better able to accept pupils as they are. And one may be better able to tolerate and to deal with group hostility and classroom anxiety, for these feelings are bound to develop as pupils, with their diverse backgrounds and expectations, learn to work together in an educational setting.

If teachers can be more aware and more open about their own abilities and limitations, they may help generate more trust in their pupils.

They will have less need to hide behind their official status. They may be more open to new ideas and new information from their pupils and from others as well. By dispensing with the spurious privileges of status, they may be freer to concentrate on the subject matter and on the learning process. Pupils, sensing this more authentic atmosphere, may respond with greater curiosity and effort in their work. The results may not be as neat and as uniform as some critics would like, but the new atmosphere will further the achievements of the individual and of the class as a whole. By accepting pupils' dependency needs and by encouraging participation and involvement, the teacher will help the class grow in ability to govern itself and to work more on its own. This implies that the teacher is willing to work with each collection of pupils as a unique group. Going through the motions of group participation and group decision-making but subtly retaining all control is simply manipulation. A teacher who cannot or will not trust pupils to have a real voice in class work or class decisions could at least be open and aboveboard about it.

On Groups and Methods

Thus far, nothing has been said about group methods and techniques. Frequently, teachers want to know specifically what they might do under particular circumstances. The main point to be made here is that learning "methods" of working with groups can be rather futile or worse if the methods are not based on understanding. (Parents also ask, "What do I do when . . . ?" questions. It is difficult to impress upon them that a specific situation may be far more complicated than it seems — or it may actually be different from what they perceive.)

Teachers may want to know what to do, for instance, when there seems to be an outbreak of restlessness or apathy among the pupils. It is simply not possible to indicate what should be done without knowing what produced these widespread feelings in the class. But the teachers can learn to find out. They might inquire and observe and attend to what is happening. They might express a willingness to become more aware of what is going on — without judging too critically. There are many different ways of reducing tension and resolving conflicts, and a teacher may learn to sense what method would be appropriate for him or her under these circumstances. One teacher might be able to change the group atmosphere by asking the class what is going on and what it is they feel so that all can face the ongoing reactions more openly. Arithmetic or reading lessons may stop temporarily so that pupils can express themselves and thereby work on meeting or resolving emotional needs.

Another teacher might achieve equivalent results by suggesting pupils join in smaller groups so that they can work and talk more informally and more freely. Children frequently work out their own problems of interpersonal relations and may be encouraged to do so. Of course, the teacher may need to establish limits, but these should be broad and realistic.

Viewing the class as a working group may change the teacher's perception of the classroom itself. The chairs, the tables, and the floor space should serve particular work needs. Sometimes the work will demand that all pupils discuss and plan together, and this may call for a circular or rectangular arrangement of chairs and tables. For smaller planning groups, the tables may be distributed around the room. Sometimes the work will call for a chair arrangement without tables, or some other variation. In short, once the teacher frees himself or herself from a conventional teacher-centered approach to class work, he or she may think of many different teaching methods as well as different uses of physical facilities to aid the teaching-learning process.

Often, a teacher will respond intuitively to a change in the atmosphere of a group, and this is fine. However, when his or her intuition does not work, can the teacher find out why? How, in other words, can the teacher improve on his or her intuition?

Teachers learn a great deal by discussing their classroom experiences with others. Unfortunately, many teachers feel it is not wise or discreet to talk over their work frankly, for fear of adverse reactions. Consequently, they impose a quiet censorship over their classroom problems and experiences. Teachers need to be able to discuss these matters freely and frankly with persons who are skilled and sensitive to their problems.

It would be fine if every teacher could have access to nonjudgmental experts who would listen and clarify and instruct. But because such a resource does not usually exist, the next best thing is to be able to discuss these matters with colleagues. And free discussions with colleagues and with superiors calls for an atmosphere of mutual trust in which the teacher can admit weaknesses, errors, or anxieties without fear of negative appraisal. It would be even more effective if the teacher could sit in on other classes occasionally and observe how other teachers handle problems and how they apply methods. Then the observer and the ones observed could get together to discuss what went on as each one saw it.

There is probably no limit to the number of ways in which teachers can improve their teaching skill. It would be naive to underestimate the complexities of the problems involved in the large organizations that schools have become. What is emphasized here is the reality of group life, how group processes affect the teacher and the pupils, and some opening ideas about what might be done in order to become more aware of the learning-teaching experience. Also emphasized are the significance of classroom atmosphere and the underlying variables that influence group and individual motivation.

Motivation to learn may be seen as a function of the needs of the individual child and of the needs of the group. Pupils may have a need to understand the world around them and the world of ideas, that is, an intellectual need. They also have social or group needs: the need to belong—to be accepted by peers, the need to be understood, the need to express oneself, and the need for esteem and for status. They have basic emotional needs that also affect their learning: the need for affection, the need to be dependent, to be nurtured, to be assertive, to be alone, to be creative, to be secure, to take chances, to explore, to change, and to grow—among many other basic needs. Although it is obviously impossible for either the school or the teacher to meet all these needs, they nevertheless exist and have some bearing on classroom behavior and learning.

A class as a group may have a need to participate with the teacher in setting goals and establishing structure, in developing its norms for behavior, and in finding its channels and means of communication. A group may need to build or reduce tension, which is related to strength of motivation. A group may need to test the limits that govern its behavior and to test before it trusts its teachers and its leaders. A class as a group may need to make its own mistakes, to learn by its own experience as well as by the experience of its teachers and the recorded experience of others in books.

Lewin, Rogers, and others have emphasized that learning requires a change in perception. If punishment is heavily relied upon to motivate the pupil, then the learner's field may be restricted, but that does not assure that the learner will acquire new knowledge or new insight. If the pupil's efforts are met with friendly interest so that the pupil finds it satisfying to consider small changes in his or her own perceptions, the pupil may be making progress toward reexamining and restructuring the whole context under consideration. In short, the pupil will entertain new perceptions; that is, the pupil will learn. He or she will develop questions that will stimulate newer inquiries. Intrinsic motives, learning because one wants to know, will replace extrinsic motives. When a group of pupils develops norms such that new perceptions and new questions are part of the group's own purpose or goals, then the learning process will have been greatly strengthened for the individual learner. As Lewin's work has shown, a group attitude toward change can often be more powerful in supporting new learning in its members than individual, isolated efforts.

The teacher's task is to develop an atmosphere conducive to new group perceptions. Methods and techniques devised by the teacher to encourage a pupil's participation in the work of the class will increase the learner's readiness for new ideas and new attitudes. New knowledge must be absorbed and integrated with what the pupil already perceives and understands, and this can be done better by participating with peers and with the teacher so that questions and directions are integrated with the work of the class. The pupil will feel not only like part of the class instead of a passive observer but also like a contributor to its goals and procedures.

Though a common base of knowledge and ideas will be shared, pupils will vary in their learning depending on their ability, their needs, and their experience. Each child will have a shared frame of reference and a shared body of knowledge, as well as a unique context and a unique learning achievement.

The teacher's awareness of the phenomenon of group cohesiveness will point up the value of meeting the pupil's need to be accepted and to belong. At the same time, the teacher will be alert to the pressures on the pupil to conform to the prevailing code of the group. If, in the development of group norms, minority voices are not permitted, then the class will have lost its potential for new change and new ideas. And a rigid uniformity could result. Very small incidents in the early life of the group can serve to indicate whether it will be safe and acceptable to express original, dissenting, or deviate ideas. The teacher can be sensitive to these events if he or she understands how groups develop and how group standards and group atmospheres are formed.

A Word About the School as a Whole

The school itself is, of course, a large organization. The interactions and structures of the school have an important bearing on the individual teacher and the individual pupil. Greater awareness of the group processes in a school as a whole can help individual teachers to understand what is going on. They can relate the fluctuations of morale of teachers and pupils to the various group-relevant behaviors of persons and subgroups in the total school setting.

By working toward the clarification of processes when necessary, the teacher may be able to influence the school as a whole, at least to the extent that it has implications for teaching. Cynicism in the teaching staff, for instance, may be seen more clearly in relation to some misapplication of power than to a defect of one person's character. Awareness of group interaction in a school may counteract the tendency to ascribe difficulties on the job to personality weakness. Unfortunately, the search for a "flaw in character" seems to be a fairly common practice in schools, as it is in too many large organizations.

A teacher's effectiveness depends to a considerable extent on relationships with fellow teachers and superiors. Just as pupils are able to spot petty defensivness and the playing of favorites in the classroom, so, too, can teachers quickly sense the misuse of authority by their superiors. But the superiors are also dependent on the teachers. Teachers' sensitivity to the needs of the formal authorities may help superiors to feel more accepted by the staff. A teacher can help the head of the school become more aware of the school's group processes. And it would help everyone to be able to discuss these things in nonjudgmental terms.

Although the specific content is different, the goals of the larger group in the school are similar to those of the classroom group: greater independence and interdependence in the teaching staff, distributed leadership functions between the school head and teachers wherever this is appropriate (Benne & Muntyan, 1951; Schmuck et al., 1972), the clarification of the principal's role and responsibilities, the improvement of communication between administrators and teaching staff, the application of the principal's power in a fair and realistic manner, and the encouragement of individuality and creativity among the teachers within the broadly defined goals of the school. Relations between the school and the community can be strongly influenced by staff collaboration, so that the teachers are supported in their efforts and protected against unnecessary interference with their work. These are only some of the tasks and goals of group relations in a school setting.

The Teaching-Learning Paradox

Members of a freshman class once were asked by the author to describe their best teaching-learning experience. Surprisingly, their written descriptions fell mainly into two categories. The best teachers were described as either "warm, friendly, like a member of the family" or "well organized, clear, strict." One student seemed troubled and soon raised his hand. He wanted to know if he could give two descriptions because he could not decide for himself which was best. Permission granted, he described one as "like my mother, warm and tolerant; I could do no wrong." The other, he said, "was a strict disciplinarian." The student was not asked what his father was like. Other classes responded in about the same manner.

Teachers throughout time have been puzzled by the difficulties involved in pinning down precisely what it is that works. Many, such as William James (1946) and Gilbert Highet (1950), have declared that teaching is an art and that's that.

Bad Teaching and Good Learning

Many would agree with Hilgard (1966, p. 3) that the problem is far more complicated and slippery than heretofore thought. After commenting that careful studies such as those by W. J. McKeachie and Nevitt Sanford show few clear results and that most studies show small differences in effectiveness relative to size of class, lecture versus discussion, the use of teaching aids, and the like, Hilgard goes on to say that one of his best learning experiences in high school occurred with a teacher who did not understand her subject matter. The students got together and tried to teach the teacher, who turned out to be quite ready to learn. In another illustration he describes a very poor teacher who was nevertheless very effective. The teacher would really get mixed up presenting his materials, and the students would help him out. Hilgard also tells of his experience with students who got together to work out subject matter that the academic department failed to offer. Each of these failures in teaching led to successful learning.

These stories suggest that appearances can be misleading in teaching and learning, that things are not what they seem to be on the surface. If we equate good teaching with good lecturing, we miss the essentials from the learner's point of view. Transfer of information is only part of the process. Other important behavior includes the encouragement of an active rather than a passive attitude, of reflection and critical thinking, and of idiosyncratic exploration. Varied opportunities to make mistakes and to try out ideas that are new or different also are important. There is nothing wrong with lecturing or audiovisual aids or programmed textbooks, provided that learning conditions and a learning climate are present. If there is a classroom atmosphere that suggests that students have the freedom to find their own way and that what they think and feel and do is important to the whole educational enterprise, then learning will be successful even if formal teaching is inadequate. The skilled teacher is one who can create this kind of learning environment, a psychological state in which teacher and students participate. And, one might add, it is an environment to which the really effective administrator lends support.

In brief, the necessary interpersonal relations within the total classroom grow out of the group process that the teacher knowingly or unwittingly helps to set in motion. As Bruner puts it, "Children appear to have a series of attitudes and activities they associate with inquiry. Rather than a formal approach to the relevance of variables in their search, they depend on their sense of what things among an ensemble of things 'smell right' as being of the proper order of magnitude or scope of severity" (1965, pp. 288-289). Although Bruner is referring more to the intellectual structure of learning, he does acknowledge the importance of attitudes and nonformal characteristics. He also recognizes the significance of self-directed learning: "the most uniquely personal of all that man knows is that which he discovers for himself."

From Passive to Active Learning

It is difficult to find studies that delineate the qualities of group processes within which effective learning occurs. Two studies are described below. The first deals with certain specifics of the teaching-learning process, and the second, with the overall social-psychological climate as a function of implicit expectations of results.

Grib and Webb (1968) did a two-year study that tested the notion that one learns by teaching. They recalled that once "a group of psychologists were sitting around . . . talking about teaching and some of the difficulties they had, when somebody made the observation that he never really understood certain material until he had to teach it" (p. 1). Their study consisted of varied arrangements of classes so that in small groups the students presented lectures and taught one another through discussion. In general, the results showed that students learned more than usual and were more enthusiastic about these arrangements. Comparing the arrangements to other teaching methods, 97 percent of the students (control group design was used) agreed that "the discussions placed more emphasis on comprehension and understanding and less on memorization" (p. 6), as well as increasing their interest in the subject. They were also able, during discussion, to see several other points of view. The students noted "greater freedom and a relaxed atmosphere" as characteristic of these student meetings. The teachers provided the general design of the arrangements, were available for consultation, and did the evaluation of the study. They felt that communication between students and teachers inproved. Grib and Webb state, "Perhaps the main shift in the role of the student was from a passive, receptive attitude to a more active, responsible one. Accompanying this more active role was a change in the students' expectation of courses" (p. 11).

The subtlety of influences that affect social-psychological climate is dramatically illustrated in the work of Rosenthal (1968) and Rosenthal and Jacobson (1968). They call attention to the interaction effect between the experimenter and the subject, whether the subject be a rat or a child. This effect tends to elicit the results the experimenter wants. When teachers were told that a group of *randomly selected* children were brighter ("intellectually blooming"), the pupils actually learned more. *Somehow the teachers changed their ways so that their expectations were fulfilled.* Variations of this study were carried on in several cities and in different socioeconomic classes. The results were essentially the same. Bright, average, and slower children all seemed to improve if the teachers expected them to. Even intelligence quotients rose when children were expected to be brighter. And those children who were brighter than they were expected to be tended to be seen by their teachers as *less well adjusted*. Rosenthal and others found that the same kind of results were attained in a nonintellectual task such as swimming.

In everyday life we can be quite sure that all kinds of interaction effects influence behavior, just as they do in school. Rosenthal (1968) draws from his research five categories of interactional effects: (1) *biosocial* (sex, age, race); (2) *psychosocial* (status, warmth, authoritarianism); (3) *situational* (effect of earlier results, experience of investigator, familiarity with subjects); (4) *modeling* (investigator's inadvertent use of his or her own behavior or judgment as a criterion); and (5) *expectancy*, as mentioned above.

One clear result of these studies is the need for experimental designs and controls that take expectancy effects into consideration at all stages of research. Perhaps a more important conclusion is the need for teachers to learn more about influence processes in general and their own influence effects in particular.

Interaction Effects and Professional Training

I have taught an advanced course for students who were about to become junior college teachers. The group was small and the format of the program sufficiently flexible so that atypical approaches could be used. The method used was a more or less unstructured group experience in which the students could talk about any aspect of their work and concerns. The students were practice teaching in different junior colleges in the subject matter of their majors. A half-dozen different majors— mathematics, English, business administration, art, the humanities, and psychology—were represented among the 10 students.

Although all the students showed psychological scars from too many years in school, from too much evaluation, and recently from too much red tape in working for large school systems, most of them appeared able to use the course for their own growth. In addition, they could share experiences: learning from one another, laughing and agonizing over their mistakes, and often finding that others suffered lonely anxieties just as they did. At times they talked of physical symptoms, such as gastric problems, headaches, and sleeplessness, that accompanied their first efforts to teach a class.

A kind of cadre spirit arose as they talked of their work on the firing line facing their students. After some wrangling, polemics, and strenuous intellectualizing, they eventually managed to be a little more open than usual with one another. Even so, much remained undisclosed, as the student's paper below clearly shows.

In this experience-based learning seminar, one could begin to see some relationships between a student's interaction in the group and that person's work in practice teaching. Problems of leaving the student role, of taking over new responsibilities, of being liked but also of being respected by one's own students and one's classmates permeated the seminar. Each in his or her own way struggled with problems of evaluating and grading students' work, of having suddenly to appear as an expert, a professional, an authority.

It would be difficult, through extended generalizations, to do justice to these concerns and how the new teachers were coming to terms with them. Instead, it seems wise to present parts of a paper written about the course by one of the students, Carol B. Olszewski. It is used with the permission of the author. In her paper she was able to set down what was going on within her, in her classroom, and in our seminar, and just how the interaction of all these things at once was experienced by a single person:

> I have delayed writing this paper in the foolish hope that a magic outline of the "ideas, questions, and dilemmas of teaching and learning that have bearing upon this course" would suddenly flash before me. Now, due to necessity rather than revelation, I have begun to write. As I said in class, this seminar has given rise mainly to dilemmas rather than solutions for me. It has made me more aware of some of the basic issues that I have so far largely been able to conceal from others and, to a lesser degree, from myself. When I first started the course, I had not yet begun to teach; and I did my best to subdue the pure fright and anxiety I felt about teaching behind an attitude of unconcern. Everyone else in the class already had been teaching for a couple of weeks before we met, and although they talked of the nervousness they had felt during the first few days of teaching, their nervousness seemed to be a trivial matter to them and their expression of it almost insincere. I suppose what was most important to me was that they had been through it, had survived it, and could discuss it calmly, while I had the secret hope that perhaps something would happen, and I really would not have to face it. At this point I felt incapable of discussing teaching calmly and objectively — it meant only terror to me.
>
> I lived in real agony right before my time to teach, but to my surprise, I did begin. Subject matter or class reaction was of little

importance to me in the beginning—I had all I could do to stand in front of the class and keep noise coming out. I was afraid to bring these matters up in class, mainly because it would mean exposing myself to the others and hurting my pride, but also because it seemed that they were all so very far from my situation. Discussion had long since passed beyond mention of that initial twinge of nervousness they had all experienced to more rational and "sensible things." It was about this time that one of the members of the class said he thought I "couldn't care less" about the course. This made me angry and hurt. It was as if all those calm, self-assured people had not appreciated my rationalized attitude of "not burdening them with my problems," but were picking on me instead.

I did get over most of my nervousness in my class, although sometimes I still feel frightened before I come in. After a couple of weeks, I became extremely concerned with the reactions of my students, for they were reacting strongly. Some days there would be almost a discipline problem—I mean there would be quite a bit of talking going on among the students; other days they would all be very quiet and attentive. I could never quite figure out why they differed so in their reactions on different days. I know they had been very quiet, very inhibited, and very bored when my master teacher was teaching. One thing I was most concerned about was that they would not be bored in my class. I wanted them to react, to be alive, and to feel that something vital and meaningful to them was happening in school. This seemed to be a totally new conception to them, and at first they had no idea how to handle this freedom. Some reacted belligerently, some eagerly, others very timidly. I changed the class from a tightly structured, teacher-oriented, lecture hour to an almost unstructured, student-oriented, discussion period, at the loss, I am afraid, of some subject matter. However, I'm very glad I did it—I couldn't really have acted differently. It seems that my students did as well as and, in most cases, better than the students in my master teacher's other two classes on the same tests. What is more important to me, my students opened up tremendously by the end of the course; all discipline problems were gone; and the students really seemed to become interested and even excited about the class.

I could go on for dozens of pages discussing my class and giving you specific examples of the really amazing things that happened. I wish we had spent more time in the seminar discussing our individual classes. I suppose we could have if we had wanted to, but several people in the seminar have told me that they felt guilty talking about their classes in the seminar. This was certainly the case with me. I always felt that my problem was unique in that I seemed to be the only one so restricted in what I had to teach and how I had to teach. Therefore, it seemed selfish to talk about something with so little bearing on the other members of the class—to simply sit back and receive the sympathy and well wishes of others. This situation, coupled with my natural hesitation in speaking in class, kept me from talking as much as I might have about my class.

Much of the discussion in the seminar concerning group interaction and perception was very pertinent to my situation. I do not feel that many of the ideas in this area were new to me, but it was very gratifying to hear them expressed and reinforced by others. Also, as the course continued and I became looser and freer and more sure of myself, I began to really consider some of the ideas mentioned earlier in the semester. A prime example of this concerns your suggestion that I might tell the class that I didn't enjoy grammar either and that we should just get it over with so that we could get on to more interesting things. When you first suggested this, right after I had begun teaching, I was horrified and could not imagine doing such a thing. But about three weeks ago, I found myself using almost those same words in talking about the grammar assignment. I do not know if I would not have said this without your suggestion, but I do know that I felt much better and less guilty about saying it. In these small ways I can at least show that I disagree with the system until I am in a position to buck it more successfully.

I suppose the most important thing that characterized this semester for me was a general loosening up of my personality and a certain increase in self-assurance. I honestly feel that both the student teaching and the seminar were largely responsible for this. In student teaching, my students and I developed together in our loosening up and loss of inhibitions. I could feel that the freer and more open I became in the classroom, the more warmly they reacted and the freer they became. Similarly, when they would show interest and openness, the less self-conscious and more free I would become. As I have said, the class, meaning both the students and I, has developed into a kind of group open to exchange and discussion of ideas; I hope very much that the students and I can retain some of this atmosphere. In the seminar I feel I have also become more free and open. I am not nearly so frightened to say whatever is on my mind, or for that matter to say anything, as I was before, although I cannot say I have lost all my hesitancy. I don't know if this change has been so obvious to the members of the seminar. Some have told me they have noticed a difference, although I'm not sure how great. Anyway, judging from my behavior in all the past seminars I have taken, I speak more than I have before, and I feel much more a part of what is going on than I usually do.

CHAPTER 15

Group Processes and Clinical Psychology

> I have made a ceaseless effort not to ridicule,
> not be bewail, nor to scorn human actions,
> but to understand them.
>
> — *Baruch Spinoza*

Ever since Freud's *Psychopathology of Everyday Life* appeared in 1901, there has been a change in the way we see the garden variety of human idiosyncrasies. Illustrations such as the following one are commonplace, and nearly everyone can recall a similar instance. At the beginning of a meeting of a conservative women's club recently, a prominent radical was introduced with the following slip of the tongue: "It gives me a great pleasure to prevent . . . I mean to present, the distinguished speaker." What Freud contributed was a rich new source of ideas, new hypotheses, to explain human behavior.

Errors, slips of the tongue, lapses in memory, and many other kinds of foibles can be interpreted in a more meaningful way consistent with the unconscious, underlying, purposive behavior of the individual. There is a hazard here, of course, because not everyone has Freud's skill and sensitivity in making interpretations. If interpretations are seen as hypotheses that can be checked and tested against other observations and evidence, however, then a genuine contribution has been made to the understanding of behavior.

Clinicians in psychology and in psychiatry deal constantly with major and minor deviations of human activity. It has become increasingly clear that the differences that exist between the normal and the abnormal are differences in degree rather than in kind, and the social context may have a more significant bearing on the unconscious than has heretofore been suspected.

The large and growing experience in studying and treating the disturbed, the anxious, and the pathological has improved our understanding of the entire population. This does not mean that every human act can or should be viewed from a clinical orientation. It means, rather, that we are becoming increasingly free of the tendency to see behavior as right or wrong, sick or well, good or bad. It is viewed simply as human behavior. The clinician's understanding of behavior is moving farther from the categories and types that preoccupied clinicians until fairly recently. The expert tries to comprehend the full complexity of what is called the "psychodynamics of behavior" rather than attaching a label—a diagnostic category—onto the patient.

The major divisions of the work of clinical psychologists consist of diagnosis, therapy, and research. Like specialists in group dynamics, they are painfully aware of the tremendous gaps in knowledge and of the tentativeness of much of present understanding. In a comprehensive appraisal of the field of psychotherapy covering the last 40 years, Garfield (1981, p. 181), states: "The issue of the effectiveness of psychotherapy has been questioned, debated, reformulated, defended, and still not conclusively settled." That is why clinical psychologists place high emphasis upon the need for further investigation, study, and research. It is still necessary to try to assemble the best ideas and to form the best understanding of the present, even though tomorrow's findings may invalidate the ideas or change the understanding.

The work of people involved in group dynamics can be divided into roughly the same categories—diagnosis, therapy, research—as the work of clinicians. Diagnosis then means observation (usually as participant-observer), measurement (attitude scales, sociometric devices), and assessment of the behavior in the group; it means trying to understand, with whatever tools and techniques are available, the interactions of group members. The end product of diagnosis of group behavior is precisely comparable to that of the modern clinician—a better understanding of the dynamics of group life.

For the clinician, the second major division of work is psychotherapy; for the group dynamics specialist, it means helping the members of the group find out more clearly what they want to do and the methods by which they might move toward their own goals. This is particularly true of laboratory groups. In a work or task group the goal is to increase effectiveness, while at the same time increasing the satisfactions of the individual member. Just as the modern clinician knows that his or her job is not to make the plans or decisions but to aid the patient in working through his or her own problems, so, too, the student of group dynamics recognizes that group members themselves can best establish goals, work through problems, and make their own decisions.

Interpersonal Diagnosis

The official *Diagnostic and Statistical Manual of Mental Disorders* (DSM-III) is currently used by clinical psychologists and psychiatrists to diagnose psychological problems. Readers interested in this schema may want to read an appraisal by Schacht and Nathan (1977). A number of psychologists have criticized DSM-III because it fails to accord full importance to psychosocial variables. McLemore and Benjamin (1979) argue that a diagnostic procedure should emphasize interpersonal relations and interpersonal behavior.

Interpersonal diagnosis is preferred because the behavior on which diagnosis is based can be observed in interaction. There is less need to infer motivational states or attitudes. Because psychotherapeutic intervention consists of client-therapist interaction, the interpersonal diagnosis can serve as a guide for the therapist's treatment plan.

The use of interpersonal description also reduces the clinician's reliance on a medical model for psychological disorder and "is relatively free of stigmatization" (McLemore & Benjamin, 1979, p. 28). The trend toward interpersonal diagnosis is still in an early stage of development. The prospect is promising, however, because rather than intrapersonal disorders, there is greater likelihood of developing useful preventative and psychotherapeutic theory and practice.

In the 1960s and the 1970s many new methods were developed to improve psychotherapy and to speed up the process. Most of these innovations failed and have quietly disappeared. Although the older standard methods still prevail and may be the best for certain psychological disorders, the challenge to find new ways continues strongly.

As Ford and Urban (1967, p. 366) noted following their review of research on the effectiveness of psychotherapy:

> The king is dead, long live the king. The picture of psychotherapy as a condition in which two people sit privately in an office and talk about the thoughts and feelings of one of them with the expectation that changes in these will automatically produce changes in overt behavior outside that office has been shattered. A new generation is emerging in the field of psychotherapy. A much wider range of procedures is being used by people with a variety of theoretical persuasions. Out of this innovative activity will undoubtedly come major theoretical change.

Evolving Ideas

Freud's theories have had enormous impact on the social sciences, and it would be beyond the scope of this book to attempt a summary. The psychoanalytic point of view has, however, been applied fruitfully to the study of face-to-face groups and will be briefly touched on here. Psychoanalysts tend to make few distinctions between the activity of psychotherapy groups and other kinds of collective behavior. The basic model is, of course, the family. All groups are seen as modifications of family life. Leaders are viewed from the point of view of the psychodynamics of parent-child relationships. Unconscious strivings of group members are given greatest importance. Love and hate, pain and pleasure, and the strictures of the superego versus the demands of primitive impulses are the basic motivations and sources of conflict.

The development and capabilities of the ego constitute the coping mechanism of group members. The growth and dissolution of inappropriate psychological defenses are important processes in the group. Transference and countertransference (see p. 200) among group members account for many of the "irrationalities" and conflicts. Although cultural pressures and external work requirements are acknowledged as significant forces in group processes, the emotional factors in intrapersonal and interpersonal dynamics are seen as the most important determinants.

Unstructured groups are veiwed as arousing latent, unresolved, unconscious conflicts in group members. Progress consists in working through these conflicts in a permissive atmosphere so that more energy and ability can be applied to the realities of the group situation.

Many psychologists, such as Rogers (1970), after acknowledging their indebtedness to the germinal work of Freud, depart from the psychoanalytic tradition and take strong issue with orthodox Freudians, particularly on the question of unconscious motivation, transference, and the directive activities of the therapist.

Rogers holds that the individual is basically guided by inner needs for growth, health, and self-actualization. Personality problems develop when individual freedom is threatened or hampered. These negative pressures distort the individual's perception of self and of others and result in the loss of self-esteem and some decrease in feelings of security. To the extent that individuals distrust their own feelings and perceptions, they retard their potential for growth and self-actualization. In addition, they feel alienated within themselves and may develop various physical and psychological symptoms of anxiety.

The problem of the therapist is to encourage communication between client and therapist, so that the client may be able to rediscover (through insight) those thoughts and feelings that are really his or her own. The therapeutic process calls for the closest kind of listening on the part of the therapist so as to see things as the client sees them and to identify feelings that the client is actually trying to express. The therapist does not guide or direct the client's thoughts, feelings, or plans. As the client feels more secure in the permissive situation, he (or she) can bring out more real feelings, although initially he finds himself permeated with critical feelings toward himself and his own worth. As these are accepted, without valuation or interpretation by the therapist, the client is encouraged to bring out more painful or hidden feelings, until a more balanced picture emerges. Emphasis throughout is on respect for the independence of the client; Rogers and his associates have found that the client does not experience the disabling dependency that accompanies more directive kinds of therapy.

In any group situation, whether it be a committee, a task force or work group, a seminar, or a therapy group, the basic phenomenological principles are essentially the same for Rogers. The emphasis is on the self-directiveness of the group, on permissiveness so that threat is reduced and communication freed, and on sensitivity to feelings and the importance of listening to what is actually being expressed rather than dwelling on the interpretation of behavior. These principles, greatly condensed here, are seen as the prime matters of group life and, if faithfully carried through, will enable a group to develop its own goals and move toward their achievement.

It should be noted that both theorists are psychodynamic in orientation to personality and to psychotherapy. This is true for all neo-Freudians, such as Horney, Fromm, Sullivan, Rollo May, and Maslow. As contemporary theorists emphasized the social environment and the here-and-now interaction between persons, they evolved away from orthodox psychoanalysis and moved toward communication theory (see Chapter 10). Communication theory, which is still emerging, constitutes a radical departure from psychodynamic traditions, relying less on intrapsychic variables and more on cybernetic and general systems models.

Group Dynamics and Group Psychotherapy

If we restrict ourselves to the laboratory method for studying group dynamics, we might profitably consider in what ways group-dynamics courses differ from group psychotherapy. (Similarities and differences are discussed by Weschler, Massarick, and Tannenbaum, 1962; Yalom, 1975; Lieberman, 1976; and Shaffer and Galinsky, 1974.) It has already been mentioned that group-dynamics laboratories encourage settings that are similar in some ways to the settings for group psychotherapy. The group is usually small enough so that all members can interact easily with all other members. This usually means anywhere from about 5 to 15 people. The general structure of such groups is also similar, marked by minimal orientation and much ambiguity. And the designated leader in group-process laboratories takes a relatively passive role, as does the group therapist.

Important differences do, however, exist. First, the agreement (or informal contract) between patient and therapist is different from the agreement between the student of group dynamics and the laboratory instructor. The patient asks for alleviation of psychological symptoms of personal distress; the student asks for an opportunity to learn about interpersonal and group behavior. The patient may be suffering from a chronic disabling anxiety or psychotic condition; the student is essentially a normal, healthy individual who wants improved knowledge and skill in working with others.

Second, in the group-dynamics laboratory, ideas and feelings are explored because they have a bearing on the processes of the group. Heightened awareness of group processes is of crucial importance in group dynamics, and learning about one's own feelings and behavior, about one's impact on others, and about the pattern of one's relationships in the group is part of this growing awareness. It is relevant to consider attitudes of members in the group about the group; it is less relevant to trace the origins and early family sources of those attitudes. In group therapy, feelings of group members toward one another are explored as well as early family origins. In group therapy, dreams and other projective associations may be openly dealt with. In group dynamics, there is more attention to the here and now. Ordinarily, deep, unconscious conflicts are not analyzed or examined.

Third, group dynamics laboratories are of relatively short duration: a few days, weeks, or possibly a semester. Group therapy may go on for years and may be supplemented by individual psychotherapy.

Fourth, group-dynamics laboratories aim primarily toward cognitive change—learning of ideas, concepts, and theories—although in a more limited sense they are directed to behavioral or attitudinal change as well.

Alexander and French (1946), in their discussion of brief psychoanalytic psychotherapy, insist that a "corrective emotional experience" is essential for personality change and growth. They state that a corrective emotional experience may occur not only in psychotherapy but also in everyday life, as illustrated by the hero in Victor Hugo's *Les Misérables*. When Jean Valjean steals the silver candlesticks of the bishop who befriended him and is later caught by the police, the bishop refuses to see this as theft but rather as a gift to a man who needed the silver more than he did. Jean Valjean is stunned by this unexpected reaction, and he is forced to reevaluate his own worth. For him, it is the beginning of great change in both outlook and behavior.

A corrective emotional experience may occur in formal schooling, although it is certainly not a common event there. It may occur in the family, in business, or in contact with the arts. It may also occur in a group-dynamics laboratory where conditions are favorable for gaining new glimpses into one's relationships with others.

Group therapy may result in the acquisition of new knowledge, but this is not a primary goal (see Hartman, 1979). Students of group dynamics want to learn principles and generalizations so that they may better understand all kinds of groups, particularly the work group or social group back home. Consequently, group laboratories include lectures, theory sessions, and content seminars to broaden the base of learning. Books, journals, and articles are an integral part of many of the laboratories.

Transference and False Connections

Transference refers to feelings and attitudes that were originally directed toward significant persons, usually parents, early in life, and that are later directed toward another individual, the therapist. This transfer of emotional charge is done unconsciously. In psychoanalytic therapy, the analysis and working through of transference is considered to be the most important work of the therapist.

Countertransference is an emotional response by the therapist (or group leader) to a patient (or group member). The response is inappropriate because it is unconsciously derived from the earlier experience of the therapist and is triggered by the patient's behavior and identity. A therapist (or group leader), according to analytic theory, cannot be effective without an understanding of transference and the possibility of countertransference.

Both terms are drawn from Freud's earlier works (see especially Freud, 1955). Practitioners vary in their understanding of transference. Another definition places even greater power and significance on transference: "the patient transfers to the therapist all of his unconscious and unresolved needs and, to some degree, relives his old conflict within the therapeutic relationship — and, as in real life, consciously expects to be disappointed, rejected, humiliated, or otherwise frustrated" (Hutt, Isaacson, & Blum, 1966, p. 303; see also Lindner, 1974).

Because the therapist remains relatively obscure, the patient tends to perceive him or her in the image of earlier authority figures. Overreactions and distortions characterize transference attitudes (see Chapter 2). What one patient may see as strong and competent behavior by the therapist, another may see as weak and grossly incompetent. One may adulate; another persistently rebels. It is important to encourage the emergence of these attitudes and then later to help the patient work through and correct misperceptions.

In group therapy, the therapist may use various methods to deal with transference, and authorities in the field differ strongly about how much emphasis to place on transference in their practice. "I have seen some therapists hobbled by a conviction that they must at all times be totally 'honest' and transparent and others by the dictum that they must make only transference or only mass group interpretations or, even worse, make only mass-group transference interpretations" (Yalom, 1975, p. 194).

In this book, transference is viewed as part of a larger class of interpersonal perceptions (for a contemporary view, see Mischel, 1979). Sullivan's term *parataxic distortion* seems more appropriate; everyone, not just patients, may misplace feelings or distort perceptions of another person without awareness. A major objective in a group-process laboratory is to learn more about one's tendencies to misperceive others and to be seen inaccurately by others. And another purpose is to learn how the group setting and group development affect the various experiences of parataxic distortion.

The Zucchini Connection (Chapter 6) attempts to illustrate graphically the nature of interpersonal misperception and the component parts of the images we hold of one another. Within this framework, opportunities for correction and increased understanding may be identified and perhaps facilitated. Transference, with its special reference to authority relations, may thus be seen as a particular source of distortion, among many other kinds.

Prevention: On the Relationship Between Personal Problems and Group Processes

Many clinical psychologists, psychiatric social workers, and psychiatrists have long recognized the importance of community psychology in relation to clinical disorders. For example, as unemployment in a community increases, the number of mental health disturbances in individuals goes up. (See, for example, Liem & Rayman, 1982.) Other studies have identified clear relationships between tension and disturbances in community organizations such as schools, industries, interethnic and family groups and the increase in the clinical population. Working out group-based tensions and conflicts related to the job, schools, and communities may make a major contribution to improving mental health and preventing psychological disorders.

The Commons Problem: Group Failure on a Large Scale

The term *commons* originally referred to the shared open grazing area situated in the center of early towns and settlements. Too much grazing could destroy the commons, but it was left to each farmer to decide whether his cattle's grazing be curtailed. The *commons problem* is a term used to illustrate a shift in emphasis from clinical psychology to social psychology. Larger-scale group and intergroup processes are introduced briefly. This shift of focus to problems of communities calls attention to the impact of group processes on larger collectivities.

In small face-to-face groups, knowledge of personality theory is necessary but not sufficient for effective work with groups. An understanding of group behavior in terms of theory at the group level is also essential.

As the size and complexity of the collective problem increases, it is useful to keep in mind the different constructs at the different levels.

Level	*Relationship*
Intrapersonal	Individual's relationship to self
Interpersonal	Relationship between persons
Intragroup	Relationships within a group
Intergroup	Relationship between groups

In addition, relationships occur between levels, for example, the intrapersonal and the intergroup. Depending upon the nature of the problem under consideration, we may focus attention on the relevant connections among the levels of relationship.

Depletion of critical natural resources and pollution of air, oceans, and fresh water have generated sobering problems in practical, administrative, and political terms. Ecological deterioration, the disposal of solid, liquid, and gaseous wastes, and determining and maintaining effective natural balances are not being faced on a scale appropriate to the seriousness of the present situation. The immediate future looks bleak and threatening unless theories for the practice of collaborative action for mutual survival and benefit are created and advanced.

At the center is the conflict between individual and group needs and interests. A number of political and social scientists are pessimistic because, according to their theories, human beings are basically selfish, aggressive, competitive, and shortsighted. Further, the idea of teaching people to be cooperative, unselfish, or altruistic is unworkable because these people will quickly learn that others are indifferent, at best, and that the altruistic always lose. In short, some social scientists believe that mutuality is a myth and that democratic group practices will not stand the test of critical shortages of important resources.

Edney (1980) examines current sociobiological theories, political philosophy theories, economic theories, and relevant behavioral theories. He discusses the strengths and weaknesses of these proposals and goes on to explore possibilities as yet undeveloped. Edney suggests that certain administrative strategies are feasible. The idea is based on a partial division of commons to include individual resources and individual responsibility, while at the same time reserving common areas for the community as a whole.

Edney finally focuses on the centrality of group dynamics, especially the growth and development of trust. He feels that herein lies the greatest resource for enlightened social management without sacrificing dignity or autonomy. A soundly developing group can heighten cooperative work, responsibility through informed participation, and concern for emotional and social needs as well as rational and economic demands. At the same time he does not ignore the threat of free riding, that is, a cheating strategy based on a hypocritical, cynical relationship to society as a whole (p. 145). Perhaps we need a better understanding of the strategies of those who distrust as well as of how they failed to develop trust.

The present state of large-group theory and practice is limited, according to Edney. Sufficient progress has nevertheless been made to indicate that the community, and especially the small face-to-face group, holds the key to avoiding the tragedy of the commons that confronts us all.

CHAPTER 16

Theory and Practice:
The Jutenheim Discovery

The study of group behavior, as was mentioned earlier, tends to divide itself into two disciplines: group research and group practice. Researchers follow the canons of science; practitioners are identified as members of various professions who rely on naturalistic observations, including subjective data and experience-based approaches.

Many sophisticated observers are appalled at this split between theory and practice (Back, 1974; Bednar & Kaul, 1979; Zander, 1979). There was an exciting promise, immediately following World War II, that many social problems would be explored and unlocked and that the key was group dynamics. More specifically, it was hoped that, by combining scientific research with humanistic practice, many intractable problems of collective behavior would finally be alleviated or resolved. So much of society is made up of group activity in community, schools, churches, family, business and industrial organizations, and cultural, professional, and political associations that the ability to solve group problems seemed to indicate that a panacea was almost at hand.

Many practitioners held that the group approach was the best way to deal with individual problems and with individual growth. Resting on the assumption that an individual's personality consists of qualities derived from various group identities starting with one's role and position within the family (Freud, 1922; Hare, 1976; Sullivan, 1947), it made sense to provide a group experience for individual learning and enhancement.

A group offers more choices for the dramatis personae; the individual becomes the playwright as well as central character in his or her perennial story of interpersonal relations. The unstructured group is a bare stage. Self-casting proceeds. The staff member's job is to encourage participation, create a set toward learning, and let the play unfold.

The scientists disagreed on the basis that subjective methods yield bias. The practitioners granted that this was indeed true, but they claimed that bias was just what they were looking for, that is, individual bias in perception and behavior.

But what about validity, evidence, control, and predictability, asked the scientist, only to have the practitioner answer that truth is fine, but so are goodness and beauty. The scientist's evidence, they claimed, appears in isolated pieces and is gathered in unnatural, contrived settings, leading to the prediction of inconsequential events in an unreal world (Churchman, 1968; McGrath & Altman, 1966; Mills, 1979). The data are distorted because the experimenter influences the subject. In gathering information, he or she decides ahead of time what is to be looked for and what the criteria of proof consist of. Indeterminacy, my dear Watson—if true in the material world, how much more true it is in the self-reflective world of the person and of society.

With respect to evidence, many would agree that "there are conscious facts and events that can be shared through communication with others like ourselves, and there are physical events that can be observed or recorded on instruments, and the records then observed and reflected upon. Neither of these sets of facts produces infallible data, for data, if accurate, may be incomplete, and inferences, regardless of how the data are obtained, may be faulty" (Hilgard, 1980, p. 15).

And finally, when it comes to prediction, results are equivocal at best (see Hilgard, 1980; Koch, 1969; and especially Koch, 1981). "Some events are highly predictable. Some are not, and may never be" (Hilgard, 1980, p. 16). Hilgard goes on to say that there is new interest in the study of consciousness as a development in line with the new cognitive psychology (Mischel, 1978), new findings and theories have stimulated a reevaluation of the mind-body problem, in general, and a consideration of consciousness as an emergent in brain functioning, in particular (Sperry, 1964). The optimism of experimental psychologists has been somewhat tempered by these new developments. "My reaction is that psychologists and physiologists have to be modest in the face of this new problem [about consciousness] that has baffled the best philosophical minds for centuries. I do not see that our methods give us any advantage at the ultimate level of metaphysical analysis" (Hilgard, 1980, p. 15).

Campbell (1975) also calls for greater humility and relativism among behavioral and social scientists so that they may be more sympathetic to "social system truths when packaged in nonscientific or metaphorical language." On a plaintive, lyrical note, Campbell (p. 1120) asks: "Cousin to the amoeba that we are, how could we know for certain?" Then, referring to the views of philosophers of science on the nature of knowledge, he goes on to say: "Popper . . . Polanyi . . . Quine . . . Toulmin . . . Hanson . . . Kuhn . . . and others have convinced us of the message of Hume and Kant: All scientific knowing is indirect, presumptive, obliquely and incompletely corroborated at best. The language of science is subjective, provincial, approximative, and metaphorical, never the language of reality itself."

In short, the study of group processes is beset by the same kinds of problems that confound experimental psychology and other social sciences. It appears we can no longer afford the luxury of faith in a single methodology or world outlook.

One of the more promising directions in the study of group behavior is the possibility of increased communication between researchers and practitioners. That may not be easy because each speaks a somewhat different language, has different needs and ways of working, is guided by different fantasies, and appears to be heading in different directions without clear guidelines. But is not that the way most unstructured groups begin?

Practitioner and Researcher

A number of scholars have stated recently that "the scientist-professional model has been shattered" (Mills, 1979). People who work in the helping professions, such as counselors, training directors, clinical psychologists, and leaders in small-group process work, generally do very little empirical research and appear to have limited interest in social science investigations. On the other side, researchers seem to be working on problems that are more neatly researchable, but they appear to ignore the practitioner's need for usable knowledge. A number of authorities feel, as Zander (1979) does, that the two fields have little in common and that they rarely exchange problems and concerns.

Social psychologists speak of a crisis of paradigm (Mills, 1979) and claim that the field is in disarray (Ring, 1967; Schellenberg, 1978). Some even go so far as to proclaim that "psychology cannot be a coherent science" (Koch, 1969, p. 64; see also, Koch, 1981). Closer to our interests, Olmstead and Hare (1978, p. 4) observe: "The spate of small-group research which has occurred in the last three decades has introduced new data and new systems of analysis, but to the uaided eye at least, the impression is still of a bazaar rather than of orderly progress." Others referring to the small-group field speak of "conceptual malaise," "a tower of Babel," and "a pre-Galilean stage."

Some attempts to explain the dilemma (see especially Bednar & Kaul, 1979; Dies, 1979; Lieberman, 1976; Mills, 1979; and Zander, 1979) are based on the following observations: to study or experiment with a group alters the group (indeterminacy); expectations of change by participants affect outcome; unconscious collusion exists among experimenters, subjects, and observers; many experimental situations are not repeatable; autonomous groups appear to function differently from groups under investigation; group studies are affected in ways not well understood as the public becomes more sophisticated psychologically; leaders of groups may be prisoners rather than the controlling variables (Smith, 1975); and most group research turns out to be the study of individuals in a group setting.

In addition, practitioners and research scientists may differ with respect to the kinds of people they are, the way they see the world, how they function, and what they hope to achieve. The tender- and tough-minded categories of William James come to mind, as well as the hedgehogs and the foxes mentioned by Isaiah Berlin in his description of Tolstoy's characters. The hedgehogs tend to search for one large view of reality, while the foxes are busy with small bits and pieces.

In an informal survey by Bednar and Kaul (1979), stereotypes of practitioners and research scientists emerge. A condensed and modified list follows:

Practitioners	*Research scientists*
Interest in unique individual or group	Interest in general laws
Spontaneous	Planned
Experiential	Controlled
Intuitive	Rational
Emotional	Cognitive
Speculative	Deductive
Understanding	Analytical
Sensitive	Objective
Trusting	Skeptical
Accepting	Critical

Collaboration between two such groups is not very promising, according to Bednar and Kaul, unless one additional quality — efficiency — is added. Bednar and Kaul believe that capable practitioners and researchers actually share many of the same attitudes and values, which means there is hope for future progress provided the standards of each profession are sufficiently high.

Behavioral Science and Behavioral Arts

My own view is somewhat different, although I cannot disagree with the hopes for higher standards. Because of the nature of the enterprise, to study people in groups from a systems perspective requires, I believe, an awareness of both behavioral science and behavioral arts. The practitioner is closer to the artist, and the researcher to the scientist. Both, however, differ from their colleagues in the conventional arts and sciences. As

Churchman (1968, p. 25) states: "Aesthetics is the core of all action, that which makes action 'radiant' for us: beautiful, ugly, pleasurable, painful, comic, tragic, whatever. Since systems thinking is a kind of action, its significance lies in its aesthetics, and not in its 'validity.' Aesthetics is that which gives life to human action." We are slowly coming to recognize the overlapping fields of the teaching arts, the psychotherapeutic arts, and the healing arts, and closely allied are the aesthetic qualities in all human relationships, in family, work, and community. The artist operates primarily in the context of discovery, while the scientist spends more time explicitly in the context of verification. But both may at times act as artist or as scientist.

The methodologies of the scientist have been developed more explicitly with emphasis on objectivity and replicability. The practitioner has fewer technical tools because the person or the group cannot be manipulated or treated as an object. Ethical guidelines demand consideration of the other, as free as possible of dehumanizing or demeaning effect. Further, the skill of the practitioner must center on that person's own inner feelings and reactions. These promptings are guides for the practitioner as to what is going on and what to observe. The substance of these feelings, together with the cognitive structure of ideas and knowledge about people and change, is combined in an imaginative manner to fit the emerging picture of the group or the person in a particular context. Verbal and nonverbal language frequently bears the crucial responsibility for conveying what is being experienced. No formula exists to tell the practitioner what is going on; cues come from feelings, thoughts, and observations. The practitioner keeps searching, trying, practicing, correcting—reaching for new insights into self and others. But like any artist, the practitioner must step back metaphorically and check the perspective and then experiment with verbal brush strokes.

The practitioner and the scientist really need each other, but it is far too early to say precisely who leads the way or where we are heading. We are in a field closer to literature, poetry, and drama than to physiology or physics. Right now we must learn to sustain the dialogue, to be open to the unknown, the unexpected, the unimaginable.

The Jutenheim Discovery: A Viking Myth

A note of gloom pervades relatively recent publications in group psychology (*Journal of Applied Behavioral Science*, 1979; Zander, 1979). Reflections on a whole generation of research show that the amount of knowledge of group behavior is rather limited, methods and data are poorly conceived and difficult to collate, and practitioners and researchers have little to say to each other.

Enter the god Thor. He, too, was proud and powerful. He, too, was presented with a difficult challenge — to find out what was going on in the land of Jutenheim, an uncharted realm peopled by tough, troublesome giants.

Thor, disguised as an earthling, wanders into Jutenheim. He is treated with hospitality by the local king. Before taking leave, Thor is challenged to show his mettle, to see what kind of a man he is — compared to Jutenheimers. He is offered mead in a great drinking horn and is told that a real man could finish off the huge horn-cup in three swallows. Thor, who could hold his own even among the gods, takes a heroic swallow. The liquid hardly moves. Again he raises the horn and drinks. Again, small progress. Finally, on his last try, a mighty quaff! To Thor's dismay, the level barely goes down a little.

The king laughs and tells the disguised Thor not to be too disappointed. After all, he has performed well, considering he is not of Jutenheim. As Thor leaves, the king walks him to the gate and, in a serious tone, tells him what really happened. The horn from which Thor had drunk was a magic horn, and its long narrow end was connected to all the great oceans of the world. When Thor had drunk, he had actually frightened the king and his court aides. So mighty were his drinking efforts that he had lowered the level of all the seas. And, the king told Thor, the next time you approach an ocean, look at the shoreline and you will see how much the waters have been lowered. Thor turned to thank the king for his hospitality, but the king was gone, and the castle had disappeared.

Back to small groups, a large enough horn, to be sure, but it is also only the beginning, for groups are connected to all the great oceans of society (families, organizations, unions, communities, schools, prisons, presidiums, congresses, parliaments, neighborhoods), and groups are made up of individuals, each with a history, a culture, and a dimly lit psychological cellar whose very existence has only recently been rediscovered, leaving little time as yet for exploration.

Thor used two hats. The student of groups can be both practitioner and researcher. The practitioner at the moment is a bit happier. He knows groups work. He enjoys groups. He can get along without the hard drudge work of research. The researcher is beginning to concede that groups can help people. The better the research (Cooper, 1975; Lieberman et al., 1976; Smith, 1975), the more definite is the realization that groups are, in certain ways, uniquely effective. But the researcher-scientist remains dissatisfied because she still does not know what goes on in groups, why they work when they work, or why they fail. And she will not be happy until she begins to measure and explore groups in natural settings. Groups set up in laboratory experiments are bread and butter for the researcher—lots of quick and clean publications at the .01 level, but deadly dangerous to use in extrapolations.

Altogether, these are not very impressive results after three decades of hearty drafts—unless we realize that the small group is connected to all the oceans of the world. Skoal!

References

Alexander, F., & French, T. M. (1946). *Psychoanalytic therapies: Principles and applications*. New York: Ronald Press.

Anderson, L. R. (1978). Groups would do better without humans. *Personality and Social Psychology Bulletin, 4,* 557-558.

Anderson, R. E., & Carter, I.E. (1974). *Human behavior in the social environment: A social systems approach*. Hawthorne, NY: Aldine.

Annual Review of Psychology. (1982). (M. R. Rosenzweig & L. W. Porter, Eds.). *33,* entire volume, esp. pp. 343-370.

Argyris, C. (1975). Learning environment for increased effectiveness. In C. L. Cooper (Ed.), *Theories of group processes*. New York: Wiley.

Argyris, C., & Schon, D. (1976). *Theory in practice: Increasing professional effectiveness*. San Francisco: Jossey-Bass.

Asch, S. E. (1952). *Social psychology*. Englewood Cliffs, NJ: Prentice-Hall.

Babad, E. Y., Birnbaum, M., & Benne, K. D. (1982). *Inquiry into the social self*. Beverly Hills, CA: Sage Publications.

Back, K. W. (1951). Influence through social communication. *Journal of Abnormal and Social Psychology, 46,* 9-23.

Back, K. W. (1971). Varieties of sensitivity training. *Sociological Inquiry, 41,* 133-137.

Back, K. W. (1974). Intervention techniques in small groups. *Annual Review of Psychology, 25,* 367-387.

Back, K. W. (1979). What's happened to small group research. *Journal of Applied Behavioral Science, 15,* 265-432.

Bales, R. F. (1955). How people interact in conferences. *Scientific American, 3,* 31-35.

Bales, R. F. (1970). *Personality and interpersonal behavior*. New York: Holt, Rinehart & Winston.

Bales, R. F., & Borgatta, E. F. (1965). Size of group as a factor in the interaction profile. In A. P. Hare, E. F. Borgatta, & R. F. Bales, Eds., *Small groups: Studies in social interaction*. New York: Knopf.

Bales, R. F., & Slater, P. E. (1957). Notes on role differentiation in small decision making groups!: Reply to Dr. Wheeler. *Sociometry, 20,* 152-155.

Bandura, A. (1978). The self system in reciprocal determinism. *American Psychologist, 33,* 344-358.

Baritz, L. (1960). *The servants of power: A history of the use of social science in American industry*. Middletown, CT: Wesleyan University Press.

References

Barnlund, D. C. (1962). Toward a meaning centered philosophy of communication. *Journal of Communication*, *2*, 40.

Barnlund, D. C. (1968). *Interpersonal communication: Survey and studies*. Boston: Houghton Mifflin.

Bass, B. B., & Barett, G. V. (1981). *People, work, and organizations* (2nd ed.). Boston: Allyn and Bacon.

Bavelas, A. (1948). Some problems of organization change. *Journal of Social Issues*, *4*, 48-52.

Becker, W. C., & Krug, R. S. (1964). A circumplex model for social behavior in children. *Child Development*, *35*, 371-396.

Bednar, R. L., & Kaul, T. J. (1979). Experimental group research: What never happened! *Journal of Applied Behavioral Science*, *15*, 311-319.

Beier, E. G. (1966). *The silent language of psychotherapy*. Chicago: Aldine.

Békésy, G. von (1973). In G. A. Miller and R. Buchont, *Psychology: The science of mental life* (2nd ed.). New York: Harper & Row.

Benjamin, L. S. (1974). Structural analysis of social behavior. *Psychological Review*, *81*, 392-425.

Benjamin, L. S. (1979). Structural analysis of differentiation failure. *Psychiatry*, *42*, 1-23.

Benne, K. D., & Muntyan, B. (1951). *Human relations in curriculum change*. New York: Dryden Press.

Bennis, W. G. (1964). Patterns and vicissitudes in T-group development. In L. P. Bradford, J. R. Gibb, & K. D. Benne (Eds.), *T-group theory and laboratory method*. New York: Wiley.

Bennis, W. G., & Shepard, H. A. (1956). A theory of group development. *Human Relations*, *9*, 415-437. Reprinted in G. S. Gibbard, J. J. Hartman, & R. D. Mann (Eds.), *Analysis of groups*. San Francisco: Jossey-Bass.

Bennis, W. G. & Slater, P. E. (1968). *The temporary society*. New York: Harper & Row.

Bermant, G., Kelman, H. C., & Warwick, D. P. (1978). *The ethics of social intervention*. New York: Halsted Press.

Berne, Eric. (1961). *Transactional analysis in psychotherapy*. New York: Grove Press.

Bertalanffy, L. von (1968). *General systems theory*. New York: Braziller.

Bion, W. R. (1961). *Experiences in groups* (2nd ed.). New York: Basic Books.

Birnbaum, M. (1975). The clarification group. In K. Benne, L. P. Bradford, J. R. Gibbs, & R. O. Lippitt (Eds.), *The laboratory method of changing and learning*. Palo Alto, CA: Science and Behavior.

Bowlby, J. (1969, 1973). *Attachment and loss* (Vols. 1 and 2). New York: Basic Books.

Braaten, L. J. (1974). Developmental phases of encounter groups: A critical review of models and a new proposal. *Interpersonal Development*, *75*, 112-129.

Bridger, H. (1978). The increasing relevance of group processes and changing values for understanding and coping with stress at work. In C. L. Cooper & R. Payne (Eds.), *Stress at work*. New York: Wiley.

Bridger, H. (1980). On "interpretation at the group level." Personal communication.

Brown, C. T., & Keller, P. W. (1979). *Monologue to dialogue: An exploration of interpersonal communication*. Englewood Cliffs, NJ: Prentice-Hall.

Bruner, J. S. (1965). Structures in learning. In G. Hass & K. Wiks (Eds.), *Readings in elementary education*. Boston: Allyn and Bacon.

Buber, M. (1957). Elements of the inter-human contact. *Psychiatry, 20,* 95-139.

Buckley, W. (1967). *Sociology and modern systems theory*. Englewood Cliffs, NJ: Prentice-Hall.

Buys, C. J. (1978). Humans would do better without groups. *Personality and Social Psychology Bulletin, 4,* 123-125.

Campbell, D. T. (1975). On the conflicts between biological and social evolution and between psychology and moral tradition. *American Psychologist, 30,* 1103-1126.

Campbell, D. T., & Tyler, B. B. (1957). The construct validity of work-group morale measures. *Journal of Applied Psychology, 41,* 91-92.

Caplow, T. (1968). *Two against one: Coalitions in triads*. Englewood Cliffs, NJ: Prentice-Hall.

Carson, R. C. (1969). *Interaction concepts of personality*. Chicago: Aldine.

Cartwright, D. (1950). Emotional dimensions of group life. In M. L. Reymert (Ed.), *Feelings and emotions*. New York: McGraw-Hill.

Cartwright, D., & Zander, A. (Eds.) (1968). *Group dynamics: Research and theory*, (3rd ed.). New York: Harper & Row.

Cattell, R. B. (1956). *New concepts of measuring leadership in group dynamics* (D. Cartwright & A. Zander, Eds.). Evanston, IL: Row, Peterson.

Churchman, C. W. (1968). *The systems approach*. New York: Delacorte.

Churchman, C.W. (1979). *The systems approach and its enemies*. New York: Basic Books.

Coan, R. W. (1968). Dimensions of psychological theory. *American Psychologist, 23,* 715-722.

Coch, L., & French, J. R. P., Jr. (1948). Overcoming resistance to change. *Human Relations, 1,* 512-532.

Coffey, H. W. (1952). Socio and psyche group process, integrative concepts. *Journal of Social Issues, 8,* 65-74.

Coleman, J. S., & James, J. (1961). The equilibrium size distribution of freely forming groups. *Sociometry, 24,* 36-45.

Cooley, C. H. (1902). *Looking glass self: The way we feel about what we think the other sees is what we guess his reaction or judgment is or will be*. New York: Scribner's.

Cooper, C. L. (1975). *Theories of group processes*. New York: Wiley.

Cooper, C. L. (1977). How psychologically dangerous are T-groups and encounter groups? In R. T. Golembiewski & A. Blumberg (Eds.), *Sensitivity training and the laboratory approach* (3rd ed.). Itasca, IL: F. E. Peacock.

Cooper, C. L., & Mangham, I. L. (1971). *T-groups: A survey of research*. New York: Wiley.

Coser, L. (1956). *The functions of social conflict*. New York: Free Press.

Crutchfield, R. S. (1954). Social psychology and group processes. *Annual Review of Psychology, 5,* 171-202.

Crutchfield, R. S. (1955). Conformity and character. *American Psychologist, 10,* 191-198.

References

Csikszentmihalyi, M. (1971). An exploratory model of play. *American Anthropologist, 73,* 45.

Davis, K. (1981). *Organizational behavior.* New York: McGraw-Hill.

Davis, S., & Lawrence, P. (1977). *Matrix.* Reading, MA: Addison-Wesley.

Deming, W. E. (1980, Jan.). It does work. *Quality* (a journal on management and training, published by Hitchcock Publishing Co., Wheaton, IL), pp. 26-31.

Derlega, V. J., & Janda, L. H. (1981). *Personal adjustment: The psychology of everyday life* (2nd ed.). Glenview, IL: Scott, Foresman.

Deutsch, M. (1973). *The resolution of conflict: Constructive and destructive processes.* New Haven, CT: Yale University Press.

Dies, R. R. (1979). Group psychotherapy: Reflections on three decades of research. *Journal of Applied Behavioral Science, 15,* 361-373.

Dunnette, M. D. (Ed.) (1976). *Handbook of industrial and organizational psychology* (pp. 1309-1319). Skokie, IL: Rand McNally.

Dunphy, D. C. (1974). The function of fantasy in groups. In G. S. Gibbard, J. J. Hartman, & R. D. Mann (Eds.), *Analysis of groups.* San Francisco: Jossey-Bass.

Edney, J. J. (1980). The commons problem: Group failure on a large scale, alternative perspectives. *American Psychologist, 35,* 131-150.

Ehrlich, P. R. (1969). *The population bomb.* San Francisco: Sierra Club.

Emery, R. E., & Trist, E. L. (1965). The causal texture of organizational environments. *Human Relations, 18,* 21-32.

Eriksen, C. W. (Ed.) (1962). *Behavior and awareness.* Durham, NC: Duke University Press.

Erikson, E. H. (1964). *Insight and responsibility.* New York: Norton.

Esposito, R. P., McAdoo, H., & Scher, L. (1975). The Johari Window as an evaluative instrument for group processes. *Interpersonal Development, 6,* 25-37.

Esposito, R. P., McAdoo, H., & Scher, L. (1978). The Johari Window test. *Journal of Humanistic Psychology, 18,* 79-81.

Ezriel, H. (1950). A psychoanalytic approach to group treatment. *British Journal of Medical Psychology, 23,* 59-74.

Faucheux, C., Amado, G., & Laurent, A. (1982). Organizational development and change. *Annual Review of Psychology, 33,* 343-370.

Ferguson, C. K., & Kelley, H. H. (1964). Significant factors in overevaluation of own group's product. *Journal of Abnormal and Social Psychology, 69,* 223-228.

Festinger, L., Schacter, S., & Back, K. (1950). *Social pressures in informal groups.* New York: Harper & Row.

Fiedler, F. E. (1967). *A theory of leadership effectiveness.* New York: McGraw-Hill.

Fischer, P. H. (1953). An analysis of the primary group. *Sociometry, 16,* 272-276.

Ford, D. H., & Urban, H. B. (1967). Psychotherapy. *Annual Review of Psychology, 19,* 333-372.

Frank, J. D. (1961). *Persuasion and healing.* Baltimore: Johns Hopkins Press.

French. W. L., & Bell, C. H., Jr. (1978). *Organization development* (2nd Ed.). Englewood Cliffs, NJ: Prentice-Hall.

Freud, S. (1901). *The psychopathology of everyday life* (J. Strachey, Trans.). New York: Norton.

Freud, S. (1922). *Group psychology and the analysis of the ego.* London: Hogarth Press.

Freud, S. (1929). *Civilization and its discontents*. New York: J. Cape and H. Smith.

Freud, S. (1955). *Five lectures on psychoanalysis* (standard ed., Vol. 2). London: Hogarth Press.

Frost, R. (1962). *Robert Frost: Poetry and Prose* (E. C. Lathem & Lawrence Thompson, Eds.). New York: Holt, Rinehart & Winston.

Gadlin, H., & Ingle, G. (1975). Through the one way mirror: The limits of experimental self reflection. *American Psychologist, 30,* 1003-1009.

Garfield, S. (1981). Psychotherapy: A 40-year appraisal. Address to the American Psychological Association. *American Psychologist, 36,* 174-183.

Gibbard, G. S., Hartman, J. J., & Mann, R. D. (Eds.). (1974). *Analysis of groups.* San Francisco: Jossey-Bass.

Gibson, J. L., Ivancevich, J. M., & Donnelly, J. H., Jr. (1976). *Organizations: Behavior, structure, processes.* Homewood, IL: Irwin-Dorsey.

Goffman, E. (1967). *Interaction ritual.* Chicago: Aldine.

Goffman, E. (1969). *Strategic interaction.* Philadelphia: University of Pennsylvania Press.

Golembiewski, R. T., & Blumberg, A. (1977). *Sensitivity training and the laboratory approach* (3rd ed.). Itasca, IL: Peacock.

Good, L. R., & Nelson, D. A. (1973). Effects of person-group and intragroup attitude similarity on perceived group attractiveness and cohesiveness, II. *Psychological Reports, 33,* 551-560.

Green, C. H. (1975). The reciprocal nature of influence between leader and subordinate. *Journal of Applied Behavioral Science, 60,* 187-193.

Greenbaum, C. W. (1979). The small group under the gun: Uses of small groups in battle conditions. *Journal of Applied Behavioral Science, 15,* 392-405.

Grib, T. F., & Webb, N. J. (1968). The experimental use of small student-led discussion groups. Paper presented at the 8th annual meeting of the Wisconsin Research Association, Wisconsin Rapids.

Gross, N., McEachern, A. W., & Mason, W. S. (1958). Role conflict and its resolution. In E. E. Maccoby, T. M. Newcomb, & E. L. Hartly (Eds.), *Readings in social psychology* (3rd ed.). New York: Henry Holt.

Gross, N., Mason, W. S., & McEachern, A. W. (1958). *Explorations in role analysis: Studies of the school superintendency role.* New York: Wiley.

Hall, C. S., & Lindzey, G. (1978). *Theories of personality* (3rd ed.). New York: Wiley.

Hall, J. (1973). Communications revisited. *California Mangement Review, 15,* 58.

Halpern, H. M. (1965). An essential ingredient in successful psychotherapy. *Psychotherapy, 2,* 177-180.

Hare, A. P. (1976). *Handbook of small group research* (2nd ed.). New York: Free Press.

Hartman, J. J. (1979). Small group methods of personal change. *Annual Review of Psychology, 30,* 453-476.

Hearn, G. (1955, Dec. 7). The process of group development. Public lecture. Toronto: University of Toronto.

Hearn, G. (1967). Leadership and the spatial factor in small groups. *Journal of Abnormal and Social Psychology, 15,* 236-249.

Hebb, D. O. (1966). *A textbook of psychology*. Philadelphia: W. B. Saunders.

Herzberg, F. (1966). *Work and the nature of man*. Cleveland: World.

Highet, G. (1950). *The art of teaching*. New York: Knopf.

Hilfiker, L. R. (1969). *The relationship of school system innovativeness to selected dimensions of interpersonal behavior in eight school systems (Technical Report No. 70)*. Madison: Wisconsin Research and Development Center for Cognitive Learning, University of Wisconsin.

Hilgard, E. R. (1962). What becomes of the input from the stimulus? In C. W. Ericksen (Ed.), *Behavior and awareness*. Durham, NC: Duke University Press.

Hilgard, E. R. (1966, winter). The human dimension in teaching. *Delta News Journal* (Stanford University School of Education).

Hilgard, E. R. (1980). Consciousness in contemporary psychology. *Annual Review of Psychology, 31*, 1-26.

Hill, R. E., & Baron, L. S. (1976). Interpersonal openness to communication effectiveness. Personal communication.

Hill, W. F (1974). Systematic group supplement. In A. Jacobs & W. Spradlin (Eds.), *The group as agent of change*. New York: Human Sciences Press.

Hjelholt, G. (1972). Group training in understanding society: The mini society. *Interpersonal Development, 3*, 140-151.

Hogan, R. (1975). Theoretical egocentrism and the problem of compliance. *American Psychologist, 30*, 533-539.

Holzner, B. (1968). *Reality construction in society*. Cambridge, MA: Schenkman.

Horowitz, L. (1977). Group centered approach to therapy. *International Journal of Group Psychotherapy, 27*, 423-429.

Hsu, F. L. K. (1971). Psychosocial homeostasis and Jen: Conceptual tools for advancing psychological anthropology. *American Anthropologist, 73*, 23-44.

Hutt, M. L., Isaacson, R. L., & Blum, M. (1966). *Psychology: The science of interpersonal behavior*. New York: Harper & Row.

Icheiser, G. (1970). *Appearances and realities*. San Francisco: Jossey-Bass.

Jackson, D. D. (1962). *Interactional psychotherapy*. In M. I. Stein (Ed.), *Contemporary psychotherapies*. Glencoe, IL: Free Press.

Jacobs, R. C., & Campbell, D. T. (1961). The perpetuation of an arbitrary tradition through several generations of a laboratory microculture. *Journal of Abnormal and Social Psychology, 62*, 649-658.

Jacques, E. (1974). Social systems as a defense against persecutory and depressive anxiety. In G. S. Gibbard, J. J. Hartman, & R. D. Mann (Eds.), *Analysis of groups*. San Francisco: Jossey-Bass.

James, W. (1946). *Talks to teachers on psychology*. New York: Henry Holt. (Original work published 1899.)

Janis, I. L. (1972). *Victims of groupthink*. Boston: Houghton Mifflin.

Janis, I. L., & Mann, L. (1977). *Decision making*. New York: Free Press.

Janssens, L., & Nuttin, J.R. (1976). Frequency perception of individual and group success as a factor of competition, coaction, and isolation. *Journal of Personality and Social Psychology, 34*, 830-836.

Jones, M. (1968). *Beyond the therapeutic community*. New Haven, CT: Yale University Press.

Jones, M., & Pollack, P. (1968). Crisis and confrontation. *British Journal of Psychiatry, 114,* 169-174.

Journal of Applied Behavioral Science. (1979). *15* (3).

Kahn, R. L., et al. (1964). *Organizational stress.* New York: Wiley.

Kaplan, A. (1964). *The conduct of inquiry.* San Francisco: Chandler.

Kaplan, R. E. (1979). The conspicuous absence of evidence that process consultation enhances task performance. *Journal of Applied Behavioral Science, 15,* 346-360.

Katz, D., & Kahn, R. L. (1978). *The social psychology of organizations* (2nd ed.). New York: Wiley.

Kazdin, A. E., Bellak, A. S., & Hansen, M. (1980). *New perspectives in abnormal psychology.* New York: Oxford University Press.

Kelley, H. H., & Thibaut, J. W. (1954). Experimental studies of group problem solving and process. In G. Lindzey (Ed.), *Handbook of social psychology* (Vol. 2) (pp. 735-785). Cambridge, MA: Addison-Wesley.

Klein, M. (1948). The importance of symbol-formation in the development of the ego. In *Contributions to psychoanalysis.* London: Hogarth Press.

Koch, S. (1969). Psychology cannot be a coherent science. *Psychology Today, 24,* 64-68.

Koch, S. (1981). The nature and limits of psychological knowledge. *American Psychologist, 36,* 257-269.

Kolb, D. A., Rubin, I. M., & McIntyre, J. M. (1974). *Organizational psychology: An experimental approach.* Englewood Cliffs, NJ: Prentice-Hall.

Kowitz, A. C., & Knutson, T. J. (1980). *Decision making in small groups: The search for alternatives.* Boston: Allyn and Bacon.

Kuhn, T. S. (1970). *The structure of scientific revolutions.* Chicago: University of Chicago Press.

LaCoursiere, R. (1974). A group method to facilitate learning during the stages of a psychiatric affiliation. *International Journal of Group Psychotherapy, 24,* 342-351.

Laing, R. D. (1961). *The self and others: Further studies in sanity and madness.* London: Tavistock.

Laing, R. D., Phillipson, H., & Lee, A. R. (1966). *Interpersonal perception.* New York: Springer.

Lakin, M. (1979). Epilogue. *Journal of Applied Behavioral Science, 15,* 265-270, 424-427.

Lakin, M., & Costanzo, P. R. (1975). The leader and the experimental group. In C. L. Cooper (Ed.), *Theories of group processes.* New York: Wiley.

Landy, F. J., & Trumbo, D. A. (1980). *Psychology of work behavior* (rev. ed.). Homewood, IL: Dorsey.

Lawrence, P. R., & Lorsch, J. W. (1967). *Organization and environment.* Cambridge, MA: Harvard University Press.

Lazarus, R. S. (1979). Positive denial: The case for not facing reality. *Psychology Today, 13,* 44-51.

Leary, T. (1957). *Interpersonal diagnosis of personality.* New York: Ronald Press.

Leary, T., & Coffey, H. (1955). Interpersonal diagnosis: Some problems of methodology and validation. *Journal of Abnormal and Social Psychology, 50,* 110-124.

Leavitt, H. J. (1951). Some effects of certain communication patterns on group performance. *Journal of Abnormal and Social Psychology, 46*, 38-50.

Le Bon, G. (1960). *The crowd.* New York: Viking. (Original work published 1895.)

Lennung, S. A. (1974-1975). Implicit theories in experiential group practices. *Interpersonal Development, 5*, 37-49.

Levine, J., & Butler, J. (1952). Lecture vs. group decision in changing behavior. *Journal of Applied Psychology, 36*, 29-33.

Levinger, G., & Raush, H. (1977). *Close relationships.* Amherst: University of Massachusetts Press.

Levinson, D. J. (1959). Role, personality and social structure in the organizational setting. *Journal of Abnormal and Social Psychology, 58*, 170-180.

Lewin, K. (1935). *A dynamic theory of personality.* New York: McGraw-Hill.

Lewin, K. (1947). Frontiers in group dynamics. *Human Relations, 1*, 2-38.

Lewin, K. (1948). *Resolving social conflicts* (G. W. Lewin, Ed.). New York: Harper.

Lewin, K. (1951). *Field theory in social science* (D. Cartwright, Ed.). New York: Harper.

Lewin, K., Lippitt, R., & White, R. (1939). Patterns of aggressive behavior in experimentally created social climates. *Journal of Social Psychology, 10*, 271-299.

Libo, L. M. (1953). *Measuring group cohesiveness.* Ann Arbor: University of Michigan, Research Center for Group Dynamics, Institute for Social Research.

Lieberman, M. A. (1976). Change induction in small groups. *Annual Review of Psychology, 27*, 217-250.

Lieberman, M. A., Yalom, I. D., & Miles, M. B. (1973). *Encounter groups: First facts.* New York: Basic Books.

Liem, R., & Rayman, P. (1982). Health and social costs of unemployment. *American Psychologist, 37*, 1116-1123.

Likert, R., & Bowers, D. G. (1969). Organizational theory and human resource accounting. *American Psychologist, 24*, 585-592.

Likert, R., & Likert, J. G. (1976). *New ways of managing conflict.* New York: McGraw-Hill.

Lindner, T. A. (1974). Primary and secondary communications in the practice of group therapy. *Gruppendynamik, 5*, 259-265.

Lippitt, R., Polansky, N., & Rosen, S. (1952). The dynamics of power. *Human Relations, 5*, 37-64.

Lippitt, R., & White, R. K. (1952). An experimental study of leadership and group life. In G. E. Swanson et al. (Eds.), *Readings in social psychology.* New York: Henry Holt.

Littlejohn, S. W. (1978). *Theories of communication.* Columbus, OH: Merrill.

Lorr, M., & McNair, D. M. (1963). An interpersonal behavior circle. *Journal of Abnormal and Social Psychology, 17*, 68-75.

Lorsch, J. W. (1979, March/April). Making behavioral science more useful. *Harvard Business Review*, pp. 171-180.

Lubin, B., & Lubin, A. W. (1971). Laboratory training stress compared with college examination stress. *Journal of Applied Behavioral Science, 7*, 502-507.

Luce, G. G., & Segal, J. (1966). *Sleep.* New York: Coward-McCann.

Luft, J. (1969). *Of human interaction.* Palo Alto, CA: Mayfield.

Luft, J. (1970). *Group processes: An introduction to group dynamics* (2nd ed.). Palo Alto, CA: Mayfield.

Lundgren, D. C. (1979). Authority and group formation. *Journal of Applied Behavioral Science, 15,* 330-342.

Malcolm, J. (1981). *Psychoanalysis: The impossible profession.* New York: Knopf.

Manis, I. G., & Meltzer, B. N. (Eds.) (1967). *Symbolic interaction: A reader in social psychology.* Boston: Allyn and Bacon.

Mann, R. D. (1975). Winners, losers and the search for equality in groups. In C. L. Cooper (Ed.), *Theories of group processes.* New York: Wiley.

Manuel, F. E., & Manuel, F. P. (1979). *Utopian thought in the Western world.* Cambridge, MA: Belknap Press of Harvard University Press.

Margulies, N., & Raia, A. P. (1972). *Organizational development: Values, processes, and technology.* New York: McGraw-Hill.

Marrow, A. J. (1969). *The practical theories: The life and work of Kurt Lewin.* New York: Teachers College Press, Columbia University.

Maslow, A. H. (1966). *The psychology of science.* New York: Harper & Row.

Massarik, F., & Krueger, B. E. (1970). Through the labyrinth: An approach to reading in behavioral science. *California Management Review, 12,* 31-40.

Mayo, E. (1933). *The human problems of an industrial civilization.* New York: Macmillan.

Mayr, E. (1963). *Populations, species and evolution.* Cambridge, MA: Belknap Press of Harvard University Press.

McCall, G., & Simmons, J. (1977). *Identities and interaction.* New York: Free Press.

McGrath, J. E., & Altman, I. (1966). *Small group research: A synthesis and critique of the field.* New York: Holt, Rinehart & Winston.

McGregor, D. (1960). *The human side of enterprise.* New York: McGraw-Hill.

McKeachie, W. (1954). Individual conformity to attitudes of classroom groups. *Journal of Abnormal and Social Psychology, 49,* 282-289.

McLemore, C. W., & Benjamin, L. S. (1979). Whatever happened to interpersonal diagnosis: A psychosocial alternative to DSM-III. *American Psychologist, 34,* 17-34.

Merei, F. (1949). Group leadership and institutionalization. *Human Relations, 2,* 23-39.

Miles, M. B. (1963). *On temporary systems* (Subscription Service, No. 5). Washington, DC: National Training Laboratories.

Miller, S. M. (Ed.). (1970). *Max Weber: Selections from his work.* New York: Crowell.

Mills, T. M. (1967). *The sociology of small groups.* Englewood Cliffs, NJ: Prentice-Hall.

Mills, T. M. (1979). Changing paradigms for studying human groups. *Journal of Applied Behavioral Science, 15,* 407-423.

Mischel, W. (1979). On the interface of cognition and personality. *American Psychologist,. 34,* 740-754.

Moos, R. H. (1975). *The human context: Environmental determinants of behavior.* New York: Wiley.

Moreno, J. L. (1946). *Psychodrama.* New York: Beacon House.

Neumann, J. von, & Morgenstern, O. (1944). *Theory of games and economic behavior*. Princeton, NJ: Princeton University Press.

Nisbet, R. (1979, November 10). The Utopian mind. *New Republic*, pp. 30-34.

Nixon H. L., II (1979). *The small group*. Englewood Cliffs, NJ: Prentice-Hall.

Odiorne, G. (1963). The trouble with sensitivity training. *Journal of American Society of Training Directors, 17*, 9-20.

Olmstead, M. S., & Hare, A. P. (1978). *The small group* (2nd ed.). New York: Random House.

Ouchi, W. G. (1981). *Theory Z*. Reading, MA: Addison-Wesley.

Pascale, R. T., & Athos, A. G. (1981). *The art of Japanese management*. New York: Simon & Schuster.

Pepitone, A. (1981). Lessons from the history of social psychology. *American Psychologist, 36*, 972-985.

Peters, T. J., & Waterman, R. H., Jr. (1982). *In search of excellence: Lessons from America's best-run companies*. New York: Harper & Row.

Piaget, J. (1979). Relations between psychology and other sciences. *Annual Review of Psychology, 33*, 1-8.

Porras, J. I. (1979). Comparative impact of OD techniques. *Journal of Applied Behavioral Science, 15*, 156-178.

Porras, J. I., & Berg, P. O. (1978). The impact of organization development. *Academy of Management Review, 3*, 2.

Porter, L. W., Lawler, E. E., III, & Hackman, J. R. (1975). *Behavior in organizations*. New York: McGraw-Hill.

Portmann, A. (1965, November). The special problem of man in the realm of the living. *Commentary*, p. 40.

Read, W. H. (1962). Upward communication in industrial organizations. *Human Relations, 15*, 3-15.

Rice, A. K. (1958). *Productivity and social organization*. London: Tavistock.

Rice, A. K. (1963). *The enterprise and its environment*. London: Tavistock.

Rice, A. K. (1969). Individual grouping and intergroup processes. *Human Relations, 22*, 565-584.

Ring, K. (1967). Experimental-social psychology: Some questions about some frivolous values. *Journal of Experimental Social Psychology, 3*, 118-123.

Rodgers, D. (n.d.). The necessary and sufficient criteria of leadership. Unpublished manuscript.

Roethlisberger, F. J., & Dickson, W. J. (1939). *Management and the worker*. Cambridge, MA: Harvard University Press.

Rogers, C. R. (1970). *Carl Rogers on encounter groups*. New York: Harper & Row.

Rohrbaugh, M., & Bartels, B. D. (1975). Participants' perception of "curative factors" in therapy and growth groups. *Small group behavior, 6*, 430-456.

Rosenthal, R. (1968). Self-fulfilling prophecy. *Psychology Today, 2*, 46-51.

Rosenthal, R., & Jacobson, L. (1968). *Pygmalion in the classroom: Teacher expectation and pupils' intellectual development*. New York: Holt, Rinehart & Winston.

Ross, L. (1977). The intuitive psychologist and his shortcomings: Distortions in the attribution process. In L. Berkowitz (Ed.), *Advances in experimental social psychology* (Vol. 10). New York: Academic Press.

Rossi, I. (1973). The unconscious in the anthropology of Claude Levi-Strauss. *American Anthropologist, 75,* 20-48.

Rosten, L. (1968). *The joys of Yiddish.* New York: McGraw-Hill.

Rotter, J. B. (1980). Interpersonal trust, trustworthiness and gullibility. *American Psychologist, 35,* 1-7.

Rutter, M., et al. (1979). *Fifteen thousand hours: Secondary schools and their effects on children.* Cambridge, MA: Harvard University Press.

Sanford, N., et al. (1971). *Sanctions for evil: Sources of social destructiveness.* San Francisco: Jossey-Bass.

Sapir, E. (1921). *Language: An introduction to the study of speech.* New York: Harcourt, Brace and World.

Sarason, S. B. (1981). *Psychology misdirected.* New York: Free Press.

Sarbin, T. R., & Jones, D. S. (1955). An experimental analysis of role behavior. *Journal of Abnormal and Social Psychology, 51,* 236-241.

Schacht, T., & Nathan, P. (1977). But is it good for the psychologists? Appraisal and status of DSM-III. *American Psychologist, 32,* 1017-1025.

Schaefer, E. S., & Bayley, N. (1963). Maternal behavior, child behavior, and their intercorrelations from infancy through adolescence. *Monographs of the Society for Research in Child Development, 28,* 1-127.

Schein, E. (1969). *Process consultation.* Reading, MA: Addison-Wesley.

Schellenberg, J. A. (1978). *Masters of social psychology.* New York: Oxford University Press.

Schmidt, W., & Tannenbaum, R. (1976). Dilemmas of leadership. In *National Training Laboratories reading book for human relations training.* Arlington, VA: National Training Laboratories.

Schmuck, R. A. (1968). Helping teachers improve classroom group processes. *Journal of Applied Behavioral Science, 4,* 401-435.

Schmuck, R. A., & Miles, M. B. (1971). *Organization development in school.* Palo Alto, CA: Mayfield.

Schmuck, R. A., Runkel, P. J., Saturen, S. L., Martell, R. T., & Derr, C. B. (1972). *Handbook of organization development in schools.* Palo Alto, CA: National Press Books.

Seashore, C. (1974). Time and tradition in the intensive group experience. In A. Jacobs & W. Spradlin (Eds.), *The group as agent of change.* New York: Behavioral Publications.

Seeman, M. (1950). *Leadership in American education.* Chicago: University of Chicago Press.

Seeman, M. (1953). Role conflict and ambivalence in leadership. *American Sociological Review, 18,* 373-380.

Shaffer, J. B., & Galinsky, M.D. (1974). *Models of group therapy and sensitivity training.* Englewood Cliffs, NJ: Prentice-Hall.

Shaw, M. E. (1981). *Group dynamics: The psychology of small group behavior* (3rd ed.). New York: McGraw-Hill.

Shepard, O. (1930). *Lore of the unicorn.* Boston: Houghton Mifflin.

Shepherd, C. R., & Weschler, I. R. (1955). The relation between three interpersonal variables and communication effectiveness: A pilot study. *Sociometry, 18,* 103-110.

References

Sherif, M. (1936). *The psychology of social norms*. New York: Harper.

Shibutani, T. (1961). *Society and personality*. Englewood Cliffs, NJ: Prentice-Hall.

Shrauger, J.S., & Schoeneman, T. J. (1979). Symbolic interactionist view of the self-concept: Through the looking glass darkly. *Psychology Bulletin, 86*, 549-573.

Simmel, G. (1955). *The web of group affiliations*. Glencoe, IL: Free Press.

Simon, H. A. (1969). *The sciences of the artificial*. Cambridge, MA: MIT Press.

Smith, P. B. (1975). Controlled studies of the outcome of sensitivity training. *Psychological Bulletin, 82*, 597-622.

Sperry, R. W. (1964, January). On split brain function. *Scientific American*, pp. 42-52.

Spitz, H., & Sadock, B. J. (1973). Small interactional groups in the psychiatric training of graduate nursing students. *Journal of Nursing Education, 12*, 6-13.

Stamps, J. (1980). Holonomy: A humanistic systems theory. Doctoral dissertation, Institute of Humanistic Psychology, San Francisco.

Steiner, I. D. (1972). *Group process and productivity*. New York: Academic Press.

Steiner, I. D. (1974). Whatever happened to the groups in social psychology? *Journal of Experimental Social Psychology, 10*, 93-108.

Stodgall, R. M. (1974). *Handbook of leadership*. Glencoe, IL: Free Press.

Stone, G. (1962). Appearance and the self. In A. Rose (Ed.), *Human behavior and social processes*. Boston: Houghton Mifflin.

Strauss, A. (1977). Sociological theories of personality. In R. J. Corsini (Ed.), *Current personality theories*. Itasca, IL: Peacock.

Sullivan, H. S. (1947). *Conceptions of modern psychiatry*. New York: Norton.

Sullivan, H. S. (1953). *The interpersonal theory of psychiatry*. New York: Norton.

Szasz, T. (1961). *The myth of mental illness*. New York: Harper.

Tannenbaum, A. S. (1962). Reactions of member of voluntary groups: A logarithmic function of size and group. *Psychological Reports, 10*, 113-114.

Tannenbaum, R., Weschler, I.R., & Massarik, F. (1961). *Leadership and organization: A behavioral science approach*. New York: McGraw-Hill.

Terkel, S. (1974). *Working*. New York: Pantheon Books.

Thomas, E. J., & Fink, C. F. (1961). Models of group problem solving. *Journal of Abnormal and Social Psychology, 63*, 1.

Toffler, A. (1970). *Future shock*. New York: Random House.

Trist, E. L., & Bamforth, K. W. (1951). Some social and psychological consequences of the Longwall method of coal-getting. *Human Relations, 4*, 3-38.

Trotter, W. (1916). *Instincts of the herd in peace and war*. London: Hogarth Press.

Tuccille, J. (1980). *Mind over money*. New York: Morrow.

Tuckman, B. W. (1965). Developmental sequence in small groups. *Psychological Bulletin, 63*, 384-399.

Tuckman, B. W. & Jensen, M. A. C. (1977). Stages in small group development revisited. *Group and Organizational Studies, 2*, 419-427.

Tversky, A., & Kahneman, D. (1974). Judgment under uncertainty. *Science, 185*, 1124-1131.

Van Kaam, A. L. (1959). Phenomenal analysis: Exemplified by a study of the experience of "really feeling understood." *Journal of Individual Psychology, 15*, 66-72.

Veblen, T. (1953). *The theory of the leisure class.* New York: Mentor Books.

Vogel, D. (1981, February 7). Why managers can't manage. *New Republic,* pp. 21-23.

Walter, G. A., & Miles, R. E. (1972). Essential elements for improving task group behavior. *Proceedings of the 80th Annual Convention of the American Psychology Association, 48,* 461-462.

Walton, R. E. (1975). The diffusion of new work structures: Explaining why success didn't take. *Organizational Dynamics, 3,* 3-22.

Washburn, S. L. (1962). *Social life of early man.* London: Methuen.

Waterman, A. S. (1981). Individualism and interdependence. *American Psychologist, 36,* 762-773.

Watzlawick, P. (Ed.) (1977). *The interactional view.* New York: Norton.

Watzlawick, P., Beavin, J. H., & Jackson, D. D. (1967). *Pragmatics of human communication.* New York: Norton.

Weber, M. (1970). *See* Miller, S. M.

Weinstein, M. S., & Pollack, H. B. (1972). The use of exercises in sensitivity training: A survey. *Comparative Group Studies, 3,* 497-512.

Weschler, I. R., Massarik, F., & Tannenbaum, R. (1962). The self in process: A sensitivity training emphasis. In I. R. Weschler (Ed.), *Issues in Human Relations Training* (Selected Reading Series, No. 5). Washington, DC: National Training Laboratories.

Whitaker, D. S., & Lieberman, M. A. (1964). *Psychotherapy through the group process.* New York: Atherton.

Wiener, N. (1954). *The human use of human beings: Cybernetics and society.* New York: Doubleday.

Wynne, L. C., et al. (1968). Pseudo-mutuality in the family relations of schizophrenics. In N. W. Bell & E. F. Vogel (Eds.), *The family.* New York: Free Press.

Yalom, I. D. (1975). *The theory and practice of group psychotherapy* (2nd ed.). New York: Basic Books.

Yalom, I. D., & Rand, K. (1966). Compatibility and cohesiveness in therapy groups. *Archives of General Psychiatry, 15,* 267-275.

Yankelovich, D. (1981a). *New rules.* New York: Random House.

Yankelovich, D. (1981b). New rules in American life. *Psychology Today, 15,* 35, 40, 60.

Zander, A. (1979). The psychology of group processes. *Annual Review of Psychology, 30,* 417-452.

Zurcher, L. A., Jr. (1969). Stages of development in poverty program neighborhood committees. *Journal of Applied Behavioral Science, 5,* 223-251.

Name Index

Adler, Alfred, 145, 146 (table)
Alexander, F., 199
Allport, Gordon, 146 (table)
Altman, I., 205
Amado, G., 124
Anderson, R. E., 94
Angyal, A., 145, 146 (table)
Argyris, Chris, 57, 119, 124
Asch, S. E., 11, 14–15
Athos, A. G., 162

Babad, E. Y., 110
Back, Kurt W., 11, 17, 18, 50, 139, 204
Bales, Robert F., 7, 17, 22, 23, 102, 106–7
Bamforth, K. W., 167
Bandura, A., 91, 92
Barrett, G. V., 116
Bartels, B. D., 47
Bass, B. B., 116
Bavelas, A., 15, 114
Bayley, N., 106
Beavin, J. H., 76, 81, 128, 130, 132, 133
Becker, Marion, 85n
Becker, W. C., 106
Bednar, R. L., 204, 206, 207
Beier, E. G., 76
Békésy, Georg von, 127
Bell, C. H., Jr., 165
Benedict, Ruth, 143
Benjamin, L. S., 103, 106, 196
Benne, K. D., 110, 187
Bennis, Warren G., 15, 34–35, 36, 152, 166
Berg, P. O., 163

Berlin, Isaiah, 207
Berne, Eric, 76
Bertalanffy, Ludwig von, 128, 163 (table)
Binswanger, L., 145, 146 (table)
Bion, W. R., 11, 12, 14, 19, 29, 34–35
Birnbaum, M., 110
Blake, R. R., 83
Blum, M., 88, 200
Blumberg, A., 51
Borgatta, E. F., 23
Bowers, D. G., 166
Bowlby, J., 138
Braaten, L. J., 33
Bridger, H., 12, 167
Brown, C. T., 24, 30, 131
Bruner, J. S., 188–89
Buber, Martin, 89, 132
Buckley, W., 128, 176

Campbell, Donald T., 18, 25, 135–36, 205
Caplow, Theodore, 23
Carson, R. C., 104
Carter, I. E., 94
Cartwright, D., 1, 11
Cassirer, Ernst, 9
Cattell, R. B., 11, 69, 146 (table)
Churchman, C. W., 90, 205, 208
Coan, R. W., 59, 133
Coffey, H. S., 103, 125
Coleman, J. S., 23
Cooley, Charles Horton, 90
Cooper, C. L., 35, 50–51, 124, 209
Coser, L., 24
Crutchfield, R. S., 10, 11, 15

225

Subject Index

ACS4381